Covert Warrior

Covert Warrior

Fighting the CIA's Secret War in Southeast Asia and China, 1965–1967

The Vietnam War Memoir of
Warner Smith

PRESIDIO

Published by Presidio Press
505 B San Marin Drive, Suite 300
Novato, CA 94945-1340

Library of Congress-in-Publication Data

Smith, Warner.
    Covert warrior : fighting the CIA's secret war in Southeast Asia and China, 1965–1967 : The Vietnam War memoir / of Warner Smith
        p.   cm.
    ISBN 0-89141-597-1 (hardcover)
    1. Vietnamese Conflict, 1961–1975—Secret service—United States. 2. United States. Central Intelligence Agency. 3. Espionage, American—China. 4. Vietnamese Conflict, 1961–1975—Personal narratives, American. 5. Smith, Warner. I. Title.
DS559.8.M44S677   1996
959.704'38—dc20   96-26107
                                                              CIP

Printed in the United States of America

To my teammates from FRAM 16 who have passed ad astra *and into the arms of God.*

Think where man's glory most begins and ends.
And say my glory was I had such friends.

—*William Butler Yeats*

Contents

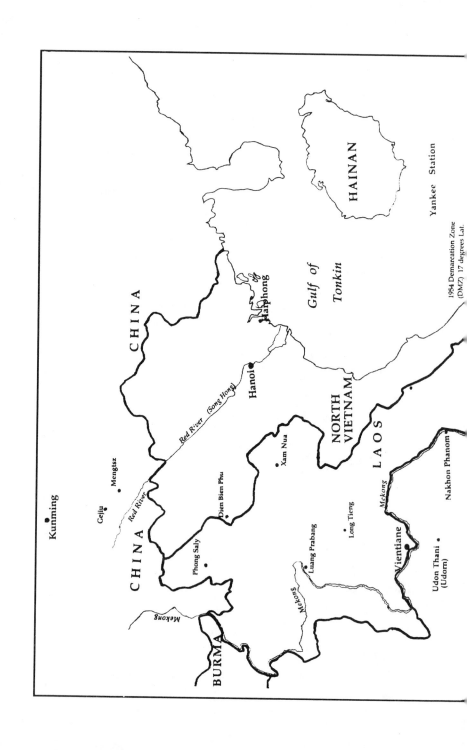

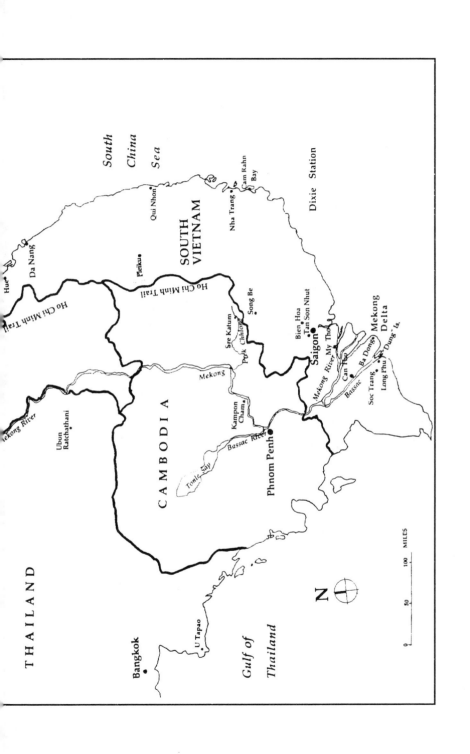

Acknowledgments

There are several people to thank for their valuable assistance to me. To Col. William R. "Spider" Reed, USAF (Ret.), for his friendship, wise counsel, constant encouragement, and multiple critiques; to Lynn Smith, Marv Bruce, Debbie Pettit, Scott Suhr, and John Steen for their serious critiques, suggestions, and questions; to Chad Ervin, Steve Smith, Harry Foster III, and W. L. Lowrey for their research and counsel; and to Bob Kane and E. J. McCarthy for performing a very difficult and valuable job.

Preface

The United States military commitment in Vietnam began in February 1955 and lasted until the evacuation of all Americans in April 1975. The involvement began with the establishment of the U.S. Military Assistance Advisory Group (MAAG), which provided training for military forces from South Vietnam in their defense against the Communist aggressors of North Vietnam. The North Vietnamese Army (NVA) was supported largely by the Communist governments of Russia (USSR) and China. The support from these two nations consisted of military equipment, as well as medical, economic, and training aid of all kinds. They also supplied manpower to the North Vietnamese in the form of military advisors and some fighter aircraft pilots.

Early intelligence data-gathering in Vietnam was conducted by various U.S. special operations groups, or "study and observation groups," (SOG) attached to MAAG, and related groups attached to the U.S. Central Intelligence Agency (CIA). The intelligence data was given to South Vietnamese military and political leaders with recommendations for its use in planning tactics and strategy. Both the MAAG and the CIA operatives were quite active with covert military actions in Laos and Cambodia from 1963 until the final U.S.

withdrawal in 1975. The first large American combat units from elements of the 3d Marine Division arrived in Da Nang in early March 1965. Prior to that event the United States involvement was relatively limited, in recognition of the truce between Vietnam and France, which finally ended when the French were defeated at Dien Bien Phu on 7 May 1954.

Through the years of fighting against the French and South Vietnamese, the NVA had developed excellent tactical and strategic fighting experience. They were fortunate enough to have the time and manpower to develop an amazing system of military storage reserves throughout western and south central South Vietnam, eastern Laos, and eastern Cambodia. These reserves were sometimes grand networks of tunnels beneath the jungle canopies. The most common evidence of tunnel works was the discovery of small air vents protruding from the jungle floor; but even these were skillfully camouflaged, and construction of tunnels went on under a great shroud of secrecy. Access paths through the jungles to tunnel entrances were amply guarded by NVA point guards, who could ring out the alarm in advance of discovery of the tunnels by U.S. or ARVN (Army of the Republic of Vietnam) soldiers.

The tunnels were built, expanded, and replenished over twenty years, and frequently contained vast inventories of food, water, ammunition, weapons, fuel, medical supplies and facilities, and troop resting places. U.S. and ARVN aerial and foot reconnaissance rarely identified the locations of these reserves. Enemy NVA troops, maneuvering either offensively or defensively, were able to magically disappear, rest, recuperate, rearm, reinforce, and reappear to fight. The immense reserves gave the NVA an enormous tactical advantage over the defenders of South Vietnam. It is most difficult to fight and defeat an enemy that you cannot find. Many of the NVA hid out in Laos and Cambodia, jumping over into North and South Vietnam at will. Laos and Cambodia were out-of-bounds for U.S. forces after the Geneva Accords were signed in 1962.

With their many years of fighting experience, using Russian- and Chinese-made weapons, and possessing a detailed knowledge of the often difficult terrain and weather, the NVA had substantial tactical advantage over many of the less experienced U.S. troops, who had been drafted, given a minimum amount of training, and shipped to the war zones of Vietnam. Americans had the might, but the NVA had the experience.

The mission statement verbally promulgated to most troops, including the members of FRAM 16, as justification for the United States military commitment to South Vietnam, is recalled as follows:

> The peaceful nation of South Vietnam is engaged in a civil war with neighboring North Vietnam, which is supported militarily and economically by the Communist Chinese and Russians. Should the North Vietnamese conquer the South Vietnamese, this will open up the "rice bowl" of the agriculturally fertile southern part of South Vietnam. It will further expose the nations of Laos and Cambodia to Communist incursion and potential Communist rule. The Chinese, in particular, are experiencing great population explosion and are having difficulty providing the population with its major food staple: rice. If the North Vietnamese troops prevail in this war, the door will then be opened to the hordes of Chinese to take over the rice paddies and other agricultural areas of southern Vietnam. They can be expected to leapfrog from these areas to Indonesia, Sarawak, Borneo, and eventually up into the intensely fertile Philippine Islands, our longtime ally, beginning with the southernmost island of Mindanao, on up into the capital city of Manila, on the island of Luzon. Our mission, therefore, is to prevent the exploitation of South Vietnam by Communist elements, thereby preserving the peace throughout Southeast Asia. Our mission is to support the South Vietnamese in the defense of their nation.

In the early to mid-1960s this mission statement was sufficient to gain support and commitment from the U.S. Congress, active-duty military personnel, and most of the American people.

Some U.S. military historians and other writers about the Vietnam conflict have claimed the United States *lost* the fight in Vietnam. For many U.S. military men and women who served in Vietnam, Laos, Cambodia, and Thailand, the statement that the U.S. *lost the war* is difficult to accept. In my own opinion, the U.S. did not lose the war in any sense of the word *lose*. The U.S. troops were ordered by our government to train and equip the South Vietnamese to defend themselves—ultimately to permit U.S. troops to withdraw. In reality, however, our troops frequently engaged the NVA without the presence of South Vietnamese military. In the end, after nearly twenty years of war, and the loss of thousands of South Vietnamese troops—and perhaps their loss of a keen will to fight and defend their nation—the South Vietnamese military was unable to defend South Vietnam, and the nation eventually fell to the Communist North Vietnamese (after antiwar sentiment in the U.S. demanded the withdrawal of U.S. forces).

Further, in my opinion, the U.S. troops were not allowed by our civilian government leaders to fight to win. Our gradual troop commitment and the unbelievable restrictions (called Rules of Engagement) largely precluded fighting to win. Some of our politicians and military leaders firmly believed that if U.S. military actions were construed by the Russian and Chinese governments as genuinely fighting to win, we might trigger World War III. (The appearance of fighting to win might have been a commitment by the U.S. of well over a million troops, together with unrestricted bombing of the city of Hanoi—capital of North Vietnam—and the entire North Vietnamese port of Haiphong, where Russian and Chinese supply ships filled every dock.) This was combined with the fact that beginning in the late 1960s, the Russians and Chinese could read and hear about the antiwar sentiment among certain politicians and nationally recognized Hollywood movie people, which began to have an effect on American liberals. In effect, the war was being won for the enemy in the United States, if the North Vietnamese could hold on long enough, which they did.

In the final analysis, I believe that U.S. leaders totally underestimated the will of the North Vietnamese to fight, endure, retreat, and fight again until they broke the will of the United States and the South Vietnamese to fight.

This concern about, or fear of (on the part of U.S. politicians and military leadership) committing a million troops perhaps avoided World War III; however, the Rules of Engagement lengthened the period of involvement of U.S. fighting forces resulting in a loss of over fifty-eight thousand American men and women in Southeast Asia. The question of whether the U.S. government ever should have committed troops to the defense of South Vietnam, beyond serving in a limited advisory and support role, will be debated for many decades to come.

There were few major battles fought in South Vietnam that involved several thousand troops fighting in a defined area. Rather, the fighting typically involved smaller groups of five to one hundred combatants. Usually the small teams were able to collect intelligence data and disrupt enemy communications and logistics more effectively than large numbers of troops could, and with fewer lives exposed.

This book recounts a handful of missions of a special operations group, directed by the CIA and the Military Assistance Command Vietnam (MACV)—as it was later called—as viewed by one man who was there. The time frame is May 1965 through January 1967. During this period, U.S. troops were in the field and in the air in increasing numbers, with and without ARVN involvement in combat missions. These troops experienced true guerilla warfare in the jungles, valleys, mountains, grassy plains, and in the marsh areas and rivers of the Mekong Delta region. The battleground was often similar to the military battles on the islands of the South Pacific in World War II. However, it was unlike the battles in Korea (early 1950s), in many instances. It was a different type of tactical and strategic action than many of our troops had been trained for in U.S. camps in the States. Certain military equipment in the U.S. inventory was ill suited to jungle fighting. Our troops experienced physical, psychological, and mechanical disadvantages during most of this military action. The carpet bombing by our Air Force and Navy aircraft never succeeded for long in dissuading the NVA from pursuing its fight, as U.S. leaders believed it would.

The U.S. war managers adopted a troop rotation plan whereby tours of duty in the Vietnam theater were typically limited to thirteen months, unless an extension was requested by the military person. For a military soldier directly involved in combat with the enemy, some four to five months were required for him to become experienced and effective as a fighter against the highly seasoned NVA troops—if he lived that long. Then, with about two months of time in country remaining, "short-timer" combat troops were typically held back from operations in which direct enemy contact was anticipated. Most unit commanders felt that combat troops with little time remaining in a combat zone might be less aggressive, take fewer chances, and therefore be less effective in combat conditions. Hence, there was a period of only about five to seven months during which the average, first tour U.S. soldier could be considered experienced and therefore effective against the NVA and the Vietcong.

All of the U.S. military branches trained small reconnaissance teams. The U.S. Navy had the UDT (Underwater Demolition Teams), formed in WWII, and in 1962 they created the SEALs (Sea, Air, Land teams). The Marines had their LRRPs (Long-Range Reconnaissance Patrol teams); the Army had its Rangers, and Green Berets or Special Forces. The Air Force created the Butterflies, the Steve Canyon program, and later the Ravens, serving as Forward Air Controllers (FACs) and operating out of airfields in Laos and Cambodia. The CIA had civilian Air America pilots, and Mike Force units operating with the mountain tribes (montagnards) in western South Vietnam. It also created and trained its own small teams and military operatives for reconnaissance and covert operations in areas important to their needs in Laos and Cambodia. FRAM 16, my team, was in my opinion one of best.

To the rest of the world FRAM 16 did not exist. I believe that what we accomplished was sometimes incredible, but is still largely unknown by the American public and military. I have never read or heard any mention of our team, its missions, or results.

But the North Vietnamese and Viet Cong knew who we were.

Introduction

The Wall: Fourteen Missing Names

It was mid-June in 1990. I was in the Washington, D.C., area on business. The meeting I had been attending at a law office in Crystal City, near Arlington, Virginia, ended shortly after lunch in a private dining room at the Marriott Hotel–Crystal City. Having thought the meeting would last longer, I had made plane reservations for around 7:30 P.M., and now had six hours to kill before my departure from Washington National Airport. I had enjoyed a visit to the National Air and Space Museum in 1977, so I decided to spend a few hours there before flying home. At the curb in front of the Marriott Hotel, I hailed a taxi and asked the driver to take me to the museum.

The taxi driver was a chatty fellow of Italian heritage, formerly from West Orange, New Jersey, but born in Queens, New York. Within the first ten minutes, and without any prompting from me, I learned more than I wanted to know about his background, family, hometown, prior businesses, political opinions, and lifestyle. During a brief pause in the delivery of his curriculum vitae, I casually asked the driver where the Vietnam War Memorial "The Wall" was located. He replied that we could drive by it on the way to the museum by going slightly out of our way. I consented, but had no conscious reason for wanting to drive by.

I had seen the Wall on television, and during those scenes I always felt twinges of anxiety, because of my experiences in Southeast Asia. I never dealt with those feelings when they occurred, and they usually passed without causing me any lingering emotion.

Several minutes later the cabdriver interrupted himself and pointed out our approach to the Wall. Motivated by some unknown stimulus, I asked him to pull over to the curb and let me out, explaining that I would forego the museum and visit the Wall instead.

As I walked away from the taxi, down a slightly inclined sidewalk toward the Wall, I experienced a sudden, strong, debilitating emotion that I could not recall feeling before. About twenty yards from the Wall my head and lungs abruptly became congested—similar to what has been described to me as an asthma attack. It became difficult for me to breathe deeply without coughing. My heart was pounding, but there was no associated pain. I began to feel weak in my legs, and dizzy, as though I might faint. My breath came in short gasps and I coughed frequently, attempting to relieve the congestion. Being rather frightened by all this, and wondering if I might be experiencing heart failure, I sat down on a bench beside the walkway that led to the memorial. Moments after sitting down I convulsed with choking cries. My nose began to run though I had not had a recent cold or flu. Coughing hard, I hung my head between my knees, choking up some clear mucus and sometimes gasping for breath between coughs.

Within moments, as if viewing an ill-focused movie, the faces of some of my teammates floated before me. It seemed like a living nightmare. Shortly, someone approached and sat down on the bench beside me. He placed his arm across my back and gripped my shoulder lightly. My nose was still running onto the pavement, my head was still between my knees, and my weeping was muffled but audible as I strived for self-control.

"It's okay, buddy, let it all out. It's gotta come out. You've held it inside too long. Let it all out now, son. It's okay. It's okay. Get it all out and you'll deal with it better from now on. That's it, that's it. I know it's tough, but you have to come to grips with it. Then it will all be better." The words were delivered in a soothing and confident baritone.

My sobbing and labored breathing subsided after several minutes. The man who had given me solace and encouragement finally gave me a couple more pats on my back, then got up and quietly walked away. I did not look up. I never saw his face. About ten more minutes passed before I could regain composure and become confident I was not experiencing something life-threatening.

I began to contemplate that if my current situation was not brought on by a medical cause, it must have been caused by my seeing the Wall for the first time. Emotionalism of this depth, however, was rare for me. I always had excellent self-control, and I hadn't reacted like this even when we had buried my father in 1978. That I had "lost it" both angered and mystified me. Seeking an understanding of my emotions and condition, I mentally retraced my steps from the point of leaving the taxi to sitting down on the bench, trying to discern what had overpowered me.

Finally I gazed down at the Wall, and the probable cause became clear. The setting, the polished black marble of the Wall and the great size of it was austere and awesome from my perspective. When I had first taken in the enormity of the Wall from the walkway, embracing almost 58,000 names of American military people killed in action (KIA) and missing in action (MIA), I realized I had been subconsciously deeply struck by the fact that none of the names of my fourteen teammates was etched in its black marble. None would ever have their names remembered along with the other American men and women who paid the ultimate sacrifice for the United States of America and the defense of the Republic of Vietnam. They were not listed as "military"; therefore, like the news correspondents and other American civilians killed in action, their names are not eligible to be etched on the Wall.

My teammates and I wore no identification in Southeast Asia. Our uniforms were unmarked, being sometimes black pajamas, sometimes blue jeans or a camouflaged material. We were operatives of the Central Intelligence Agency (CIA) and were engaged in a secret part of the war in Southeast Asia that, to my knowledge, has not been revealed to the public.

Sixteen of us, all volunteers, ages twenty-two to twenty-five, had been sent to Vietnam in 1965 after extensive training in a variety of skills. Only two of us returned alive. None of the others were believed to have been captured, and I had heard statements that only six of their bodies had been recovered. Of the two survivors, one came home on a stretcher, never to walk or have full use of his arms and hands again. He was the victim of a blast of a claymore mine that sent a piece of steel through his right lung, lodging in the cervical region of his spine. I was the sole survivor with the opportunity to go on to lead a full and normal life.

At my parents home, shortly after my return from Southeast Asia, I tracked down the family of my surviving teammate in south Florida. He had been wounded on the Laotian border near the Bassac River. Since I had not been a member of his mission team, all I could recall was that he was treated in Da Nang, South Vietnam, and transferred to Clark Air Force Base Hospital in the Philippines. Subsequently he was returned to the States for further rehabilitation.

When I telephoned Robert Gomez, his mother answered, and I explained who I was and that I believed her son and I had served together in the same unit in Southeast Asia. She listened without interrupting. I asked if I could speak with Robert. There was silence at the other end of the telephone. I thought I heard her sniffle, and seconds later detected that she was weeping. After several moments without a reply she was able to say in hushed tones that she did not feel it was a good idea for me to speak with her son. She explained, in a barely audible voice, that it would disturb him too much; that he was experiencing respiratory problems and remained mentally anguished, rarely speaking as a result of his wounds and his permanent paralysis. Sadly I concluded that to insist on talking to my teammate was inappropriate, and, respecting her wishes, I expressed my concern and apologized for the intrusion. I said good-bye after leaving my parents' telephone number in case events might occur that would change her mind.

I do not know if Robert is alive today. I hope he is not still lying there in bed like a wilted vegetable after being so vital. I believe he would make a good soldier for the Lord, as would each of my other fourteen comrades who have departed this life.

Twenty months and four days after I arrived in Vietnam with my team—code-named FRAM 16—I came home with several broken ribs and transverse processes of the lumbar vertebrae still mending; and a melancholy heart; but with a very private, personal pride of accomplishment intact. FRAM 16 was involved in covert and clandestine combat operations throughout Southeast Asia. A number of operations in which I took part are described in this book.

There were thousands of battles, skirmishes, and missions in Vietnam, Laos, and Cambodia. The ones included in this book are described here because I believe the information should be a part of the documentation of the Vietnam War.

For many years I have been successful in locking my experiences in Southeast Asia away in another compartment of my brain. That person in my image who served in the war in Southeast Asia and returned home alive, as best I can describe him, is somebody else. I can see him when I want to. I can watch him in action but I am quite detached from him, as though he is on a movie screen and I am in the audience. This psychological ploy, among other techniques, was recommended to me for my mental health by a U.S. Air Force physician in the Philippines. It has worked for me. The ploy has enabled me to survive lingering mental torment (also referred to as "posttraumatic stress syndrome") caused by my experiences in Vietnam.

Neither I nor my teammates were recognized as heroes. But our efforts made a difference and saved the lives of many Americans and other friendly troops. I am a very different person now, and fortunately my sanity remains preserved. My experience at the Wall was indeed the beginning of a catharsis, perhaps even a form of exorcism. It provided me the first impetus to write this book.

I confess that my memory is not capable of recalling the exact words people spoke, including my own conversations, while in Southeast Asia. Nor can every detail be recalled. I kept no journal because there was no time for that, and I was rarely in a place where I could record and store notes. We were an extremely mobile unit, with no permanent base of operation to which we returned after a mission, where I could accumulate notes. In fact, I never thought of keeping a journal while fighting in Southeast Asia. Therefore, the dialogues included in this book are reconstructed to the best of my recollection, serving mostly to illustrate.

The facts related to our missions are recorded as I remember

them. I have tried to avoid embellishment of any sort. I hope read-
ers will find this book of interest in revealing another side of the war
in Southeast Asia.

During my service in Southeast Asia, I took many enemy lives. I
cannot estimate how many, nor is the count relevant. In most cases
it came down to a choice: either my life or that of the enemy. I have
no regrets and make no apology for killing my enemies, because I
felt that I was protecting the lives of people on the American/South
Vietnamese side of the war. That was my job. From the beginning of
my writing, I have derived much mental therapy from the effort. If
they could dig deeply into my mind, psychiatrists might categorize
me as a complex personality.

When a person is taken out of a normal life for an extended period and directly confronted with killing, deaths of friends, lack of
sanitary facilities, festering sores, lack of water and proper nutrition,
a necessary shift must take place, when returning to the previous normal life, that is critical for physical and emotional survival.

My outlook on life has clearly changed as a result of the extremes
of my experiences. Material things and possessions are not particularly important to me anymore. I am well adjusted socially; however,
I am easily turned off by dishonesty, as well as social gossip about people and possessions, preferring to associate and socialize with those
who speak of concepts, ideas, and hopes.

I have always been proud to have served my country in the way
that I did. However, I deeply regret that my teammates will never enjoy the full life which was their due. They were part of the American
sacrifice for freedom in the world.

Chapter 1

The Beginning

It was 28 May 1965.

The four-engine jet transport and cargo aircraft, a U.S. Air Force C-135, taxied up to the parking apron 150 yards from the main terminal building at Tan Son Nhut Airport, a short distance northwest of Saigon, the capital of South Vietnam. Our team, known by its code name of FRAM 16, had arrived almost thirty-five hours after leaving Travis Air Force Base near San Francisco. We had made a fuel and repair stop at Barbers Point Naval Air Station north of Honolulu, then continued on to Anderson Air Force Base on the Pacific island of Guam. We picked up two members of a Navy Underwater Demolition Team (UDT) in Guam who had been on R&R (Rest and Recreation), then we flew to Clark Air Force Base in the Philippines, about forty-five miles north of Manila. Our plane, carrying American soldiers, airmen, and civilians, was only about half full.

The UDT guys were an engaging pair; not unlike ourselves in terms of training, attitude, age, and build, though they were definitely more cocky than we. During the flight they freely related their experiences with combat missions over the last three months in the Mekong Delta region of South Vietnam. I was impressed with the UDTs and was grateful to hear their various stories, about their luck, their losses, and particularly their personal views of the enemy. They made light of serious mission incidents, laughed often, and used the phrase *piece o' cake* with great frequency when describing the ease with which they handled difficult missions, tactics, and contacts with the Vietcong and North Vietnamese regulars. Everything was a "piece o' cake." I wondered if their lightheartedness, or their lack of serious concern on returning to combat duty, was their way of maintaining sanity during their frequently insane missions. Interestingly, I concluded from our various conversations that the UDT men fought chiefly for each other; for the care and safety of their teammates. This seemed their primary motivation. I wondered if this would be the case for the members of FRAM 16 as well.

One of the UDT men, with whom I spoke at great length, was particularly negative toward the new M16 rifles issued for combat in Vietnam. He told me the U.S. Marines had already rejected the gas-operated rifle because of frequent malfunctions, including jamming. The SEALs, which had not yet been deployed to Vietnam, had similar poor experiences with the M16 and its grenade-launcher attachment, especially in the wet and muddy combat practice conditions of Panama. When I asked him what rifle he used, he said he had been issued a Stoner, which was among the prototype designs for the mass-produced M16 by Colt and other manufacturers. He described it as an awesome, heavier rifle that fired a 5.56mm bullet, which is comparable to the .223-caliber cartridge. He said it was a far better weapon than the M16 in terms of reliability in humid and wet jungle conditions.

The Stoner was a sturdier weapon overall, compared with the M16, and it rarely malfunctioned even in the most raw conditions of the jungles and swamps. It was still important, however, to dismantle the Stoner from time to time to keep its moving parts free from fouling. The UDT fellow told me it was exceedingly difficult to requisition a Stoner, and that the cost to the military was ten thousand dollars each.

He said, "I'll tell you what, man, if you can get your hands on one, it will save your life. If they only have M16s around, use it to kill a VC (Vietcong) and then take his AK-47—the next best choice to a Stoner. The SEALs really liked the Stoner, I was told, and they are getting most of them back in the States for use during training maneuvers."

I took heed of these words and vowed to make a requisition for a Stoner as soon as possible. We had been told at one point during training that we would have our choice of weapons for our missions. We emerged from the C-135 at the Tan Son Nhut field at 4:30 P.M. local time. As we reached the forward door we were met with the piercing sounds of multiple sirens being emitted from fire engines and an ambulance racing past our parking pad. At the bottom of our aircraft's ladder we scanned the airfield, which was buzzing with aircraft of all types, but we saw no signs of a fire. I momentarily wondered if there was an air raid in progress.

"Man, look at that poor sucker!" shouted Tom Reed, one of our teammates. He stretched out his arm, pointing to a single-engine A-1 Skyraider on final approach for landing. The powerful, propeller-driven fighter-bomber appeared to yaw and wobble on its horizontal axis, as if hunting for a moving runway. The left landing gear was fully extended. The right landing gear was still retracted into the fuselage of the aircraft. There was black smoke pouring from the underside of the plane's engine cowling, etching a fuzzy dark trail several hundred yards behind the flight path. The propeller on the plane stopped turning just 100 yards from the end of the runway, and the Skyraider dove for the runway and flared at the last possible instant for a genuine full-stall landing.

The plane hit hard on its left main gear, bounced only once, and settled back to the runway. Immediately the plane pivoted around the tip of its right wing—the side on which the landing gear had not extended. With the Plexiglas cockpit canopy slid back, the pilot's head was leaning out of the cockpit for a clearer view through the black, billowing smoke. The left landing gear collapsed the moment the A-1 ran off the runway onto a grassed area between the active runway and a taxiway.

"It's going to hit us, guys," I screamed out as the momentum carried the fighter plane skidding across a taxiway and on to the parking apron. A few sparks flew from the underside of the plane, black smoke continued to pour out, and the sound of screeching metal on concrete froze our attention momentarily; then we all started to run for our lives. The plane stopped about twenty-five yards from where we had first stood to watch the saga unfold. Black smoke immediately enveloped the plane; however, we could see the pilot, partially obscured through the smoke, scrambling out of the cockpit, sliding down onto the wing, and springing off onto the concrete parking ramp. The exit route taken by the pilot brought him charging directly toward us, stopping next to us, completely out of breath. He wheeled around, panting, to see what remained of his aluminum-and-steel steed before it disappeared in a cloud of foam coming from a fire engine that had arrived on the scene.

"Welcome to Vietnam, fellas," shouted the youthful-looking American pilot to sixteen stunned new arrivals to the war scene. Obviously our gaping faces and clean green fatigues—and each of us clinging to our toilet kits—were a dead giveaway that we were "newbees." This was the beginning of a series of initiations to the war in Vietnam. But this event would forever be etched in our brains; especially the demeanor of that redheaded pilot, wearing no insignia of rank or unit, who appeared to take the incident as a "piece o' cake." It was likely he was issued a new "bird" within an hour or two so he could take the flight back to the North Vietnamese Army (NVA) or to the Vietcong (VC) (who resided in South Vietnam but sympathized and were allied with the North Vietnamese).

In July 1964, 227 candidates for training in various specialties within the spectrum of U.S. Navy intelligence met in an auditorium at the Pensacola Naval Air Station, Mainside, in the western panhandle of Florida. Most of the men present, like me, were newly commissioned U.S. Navy ensigns; there were a few lieutenant junior grades and maybe a half dozen full lieutenants. We were introduced by a Navy commander to Captain Smyth, of the Naval Intelligence staff, based at the Pentagon.

We learned that Captain Smyth had been a naval officer for twenty-two years, had graduated from the naval academy at Annapolis, and had worked for the Office of Naval Intelligence during several tours of his career. We were given the routine, affable greeting and welcome by the captain. He described the various areas of naval intelligence into which this assembled group would ultimately be assigned after training. There would be other schools for advanced training for everyone to attend. I was fascinated, sitting in the auditorium in my starched summer-white officer's uniform, hoping I would be assigned aboard a nice, big aircraft carrier—to ride around the oceans of the world interpreting data brought aboard by jet fighter pilots, preparing briefings, assessing complex situations, and preparing tactical plans. Toward the end of Captain Smyth's talk he asked for a show of hands for volunteers for a special operations team. He gave a brief list of the requirements for being selected. I volunteered out of curiosity, along with about fifty other men.

As I volunteered, I never foresaw muddy jungles in my military future.

My father was a career U.S. Navy officer who graduated from Harvard Medical School and did his internship at Massachusetts General Hospital. He had just begun his residency at the Massachusetts Eye and Ear Infirmary in Boston when the Japanese attacked Pearl Harbor on 7 December 1941. Because the U.S. government had subsidized most of my father's college and medical school tuition, he was obligated to serve in the war effort during WWII, and for several more years after the war was over, and chose to stay in the Navy Medical Corps for twenty-three years. He joined the U.S. Navy as the ship's doctor aboard a destroyer attached to the Third Fleet in the Pacific Theater. He won two military decorations for gallantry: bronze and silver stars for going ashore with the Marines' amphibious assaults to care for the wounded on island beachheads. On the beaches he performed emergency first aid on wounded Marines in spite of enemy bullets that occasionally hit the sand around him. There had been a dire shortage of medical doctors in the early part of the war and it was not uncommon to pull ship's doctors out of their floating operating rooms and send them ashore to care for wounded who required medical help beyond the expertise of the enlisted corpsmen.

It would not be correct to say that my father was a gung-ho military man. But I clearly remember him telling me over and over again, beginning when I was quite young: "When you graduate from college, you will do a tour with the military." Then he would always add the statement: "Every man has a basic obligation to this nation to serve in the U.S. military and you will put in the time." This declarative statement was accepted by me to the point that there was never a question of whether or not I would do some time in the military. For me it was just a part of going through this transitory life, and I never thought otherwise.

After WWII my father was frequently stationed at hospitals associated with Navy and Marine Corps airfields, where I developed a strong fascination for planes. As a youth I knew every name, model, capacity, and manufacturer of practically every U.S. military plane in existence. When we were stationed in Key West, Florida, I was fifteen years old, and I told my father that I wanted to learn to fly. He said I was too young and that the Navy would teach me how to fly. Being quite headstrong, I decided to find out for myself. One Saturday morning early in the summer of 1957, I boarded a local bus and rode out on Roosevelt Highway to the Key West Airport, where I had seen private planes landing and taking off. From the bus stop I walked over to a white wooden shack located two hundred yards south of the little Key West Airport terminal. The sign on the roof of the shack read FLIGHT TRAINING.

Shyly I entered the small shack and was greeted by a wiry little gray-haired man who appeared to be in his early sixties.

"Can I help you, young fellow?" bellowed Fred Johnson.

"Y-yes," I stammered in reply. "I am interested in learning how to fly."

Mr. Fred came out from behind the little counter and looked me up and down, paused, and asked, "How old are you, son?" I told him I was fifteen but quickly added that I would be sixteen in another month.

"Well, I don't think I have ever had a student pilot as young as you are. Do your parents approve of you taking flying lessons?"

I decided to tell the truth, and explained that my father thought I was too young. That response appeared to challenge Mr. Fred.

He said, "Look, I'll tell you what you do. You go home and bring your father out here. I will explain the process and the cost to both of you. Then you and your father can make the decision with all the information in hand. I think that when I get finished explaining what is involved, your father might agree to let you take lessons and earn your private pilot's license."

"How much will it cost for me to go through the training and get my license?" I asked.

Mr. Johnson said, "Well, that depends on how good you are and how well you learn from me in the air and in ground school. If you really apply yourself, and we use that yellow Cessna 140 out there, you should be ready to go through the Federal Aviation Administration [FAA] flight test for your private license after forty hours of flying time and twenty-five hours of ground school. It usually costs about $850 to get you ready for the FAA exam and flight test."

I thanked Mr. Fred, shook his hand, and said that I would try to be back soon with my father. In 1957, $850 was a lot of money! But my father was not as difficult as I expected him to be in giving me permission to take flying lessons. Perhaps I was a good salesman. However, my mother was horrified. It did not matter to her that I already had $375 saved up. Probably my mother's unspoken concern was over my growing independence and approaching manhood. Finally we all agreed. My father drove me out to the airfield the next weekend to meet Mr. Fred.

My father asked to see the type of aircraft in which I would take my training. Mr. Fred walked us down the flight line to a bright yellow two-seat Cessna 140, equipped with a tail wheel, and with the wings and fuselage covered in tightly stretched, painted cloth. The yellow paint applied to the cloth made it harden and the skin felt like light aluminum.

Stroking his chin, as he always did when very serious, my father said, "I'm not too excited about this plane. How old is it?"

"Well, it's about ten years old now. It's airworthy and easy to learn how to fly," replied Mr. Fred. "It went through its semiannual overhaul about seventy-five engine hours ago."

"What else have you got?" my father asked.

"Well, I have a newer Cessna 172. The plane has a nose wheel, and seats four people instead of just two."

We walked over to inspect the Cessna 172, and my father asked, "How much more would it cost to learn to fly in this plane than in the Cessna 140?"

"About $250 more for the forty hours preceding your son's FAA test," said Mr. Fred.

"Okay, I want my son to learn in the 172," my father said with finality in his voice. "That Cessna 140 looks a little . . . well, on the old and tired side to me." I was trembling with excitement.

So I began my lessons with Mr. Fred the next day, Sunday. I worked very hard at learning how to fly, mainly because I wanted to excel at flying, and also because it was partly my money paying for the lessons. My father paid for the balance of the cost of flight training, as he had promised. I progressed very rapidly, according to Mr. Fred's assessment. After thirty-five hours of flight training, plus ground school, he told my father, "Your son has a real natural instinct for flying. Hope you'll let him continue flight training after he gets his private license; maybe get his commercial and multiengine rating by the time he is eighteen. Might even get his instrument rating too."

During my solo practice time, I was very cautious and flew by the book, never doing any daredevil stuff. Occasionally, when practicing 720-degree turns around a point, I would really turn the plane hard into a 60-degree angle of bank and pull it through the turn so I could experience the thrill of two to three Gs of force on my body. I was always craving to do some acrobatics such as loops and barrel rolls; however, the Cessna 172 was not built to take the kind of stress that such maneuvers would generate. I had to limit my practice to chandelles, wingovers, and other simple acrobatic maneuvers, dreaming of the day when I could try inside loops and barrel rolls and flying upside down, like the Navy's Blue Angels Flight Demonstration Team.

I aced my FAA exam in the summer of 1957, and the examiner said he had never tested nor passed anyone as young as me. I was mighty proud. So was my father.

Pride in achievement was what motivated me from a very young age. I was always a good student in school. But the greatest pride and satisfaction always came from achieving something that very few other people could achieve. In 1960 I rowed on a New England championship high school eight-oar crew team. We went on to race at Henley-on-Thames, outside of London, for the Thames Challenge Cup. We were all seventeen to eighteen years old, and lost in the semifinals to the Harvard University Lightweight Varsity Crew. Most of the Harvard guys were in their early twenties. In the quarterfinals we defeated the United States National Prep School/High School champions. Our heads grew three hat-sizes with that win.

Later that same summer, while working as a busboy at the Wauwinet Hotel in Nantucket, Massachusetts, I was given permission by the hotel manager to replace an injured crew member of a speedy type of sailboat known as a Flying Dutchman. The six-race regatta was for the United States National Championship. My summer girlfriend had her own Flying Dutchman and she taught me to crew and ride the trapeze in a high wind using my weight to maintain the boat on a nearly flat keel. I was a crewman in the championship races for the last four of six races. We placed third in the United States.

I spent four years at an Ivy League college in New England. While in college I occasionally flew as a charter pilot for a local flight service, having obtained my multiengine aircraft and instrument ratings during the summer of 1963. I was able to fly charters on weekends and still maintain an acceptable grade point average during my college years.

As a college freshman I decided not to row on the college crew. I felt that I had achieved a very high level with the eight-oared crew. I wanted to try new things. Flying for the charter service enabled me to build up a sizable balance in my savings account. The summer between my sophomore and junior year, I saved enough money to purchase a two-year-old Corvette. I took the 'Vette to a mechanic who was experienced in souping up cars, and had him install a larger engine, new rear end, and beefed-up suspension. On weekends, when not out on a charter flight, I would drive up to northern New York, near Syracuse, and race on a track with other amateurs. That made plenty of money for me, as I won frequently. I loved winning.

In the fall of 1963, at the airport near college, a wealthy local private pilot brought in a homemade acrobatic plane that he called a "Mighty Mite." I soon met the owner/pilot, and eventually managed to talk him into letting me fly his plane. The small, red and white, low-wing plane had a 265-horsepower Lycoming engine: more power than necessary to satisfy my insatiable drive to achieve whatever it was that challenged me for the moment. I never really defined what achievement level I was attempting to reach in flying; however, I became quite proficient at flight acrobatics in the Mighty Mite, and even participated in a regional flight demonstration and air show.

Twice in acrobatic practice and once in the air show, I erred and nearly became an integral part of the real estate. That is, through miscalculation on my part I nearly crashed the Mighty Mite. These near-death experiences had an effect on me that was perhaps different from that of most people. Rather than being frightened and electing to give up flying, or taking caution to reduce the risk inherent in certain flight maneuvers, I grew more bold of spirit. My near-crashes carried me to the edge of life and, perhaps strangely, I loved it. I felt as though I had won something. Clearly, I had beaten the odds. The boldness created by the near crashes did not push me into more death-defying maneuvers; rather, my heart would momentarily hop into my throat, I would cuss for a few seconds as I set up for the next maneuver, and then I would resolve to learn from the errors of my calculation.

At my father's firm direction, I joined the Navy Reserve Officers' Training Corps (NROTC) in my first semester of college and received a commission in early June, four years later. On 7 July 1964, I reported to the Naval Air Station in Pensacola. Ten months later I arrived in South Vietnam.

Chapter 2

Training of the Team

After ten days of interviews, psychological testing, physical endurance tests, physical examinations, and interminable waits in line, the number of volunteers was whittled down from about fifty men to twenty-five. The intensity of this process allowed those of us involved no time for exchanges of dialogue on the purposes or end results of what we were doing. Our conversations during food breaks, while waiting in line, and prior to going to sleep at night were relatively superficial. We did not know each other when this process began, and as soon as a modicum of camaraderie developed between me and another volunteer, he did not appear on the roster for the next day's activities. Moreover, the evaluation process was extremely tiring for everyone. When there was an opportunity to sleep, we slept.

As one part of the physical examination, each of us was given an electroencephalograph (EEG) test, which evaluated brain waves for any indication of problems between our ears. The mechanics of this test seemed to be right out of Civil War medical books. The physician used about ten electrodes connected to ink pens that reacted to tiny electrical brain impulses by inscribing squiggly lines on a rolling sheet of paper, similar to the electrocardiograph (EKG) tests we'd all taken. The macabre part of the test was that the electrodes were forced through the skin of our scalps, seemingly right down to our skulls. No anesthesia was used. The electrodes were first dipped in alcohol to sterilize them, then forced into our scalps. Suffice it to say that we all endured this, cleaned up our slightly bloody scalps, and went on apprehensively with the next step in the program.

The psychiatric exams were the mental equivalent of the electroencephalogram. We took batteries of written tests and were subjected to the questioning of at least four psychiatrists—sometimes two psychiatrists at a time. I used every ounce of brainpower to summon consistent answers. I figured that inconsistent answers might lead the psychiatrists to conclude that I was unfit to continue. However, after a day and a half of oral testing I gave up trying to be consistent. I was nearly burned out, mentally. I answered the questions with whatever answer was dispensed by my brain to my lips. For me, this part of the testing was more grueling than the physical endurance tests out on the obstacle course.

None of us drew conclusions as to what this was all about. But the process of volunteer elimination, as the testing progressed, became somewhat of an ego-inflator for those of us whose names remained on the list. Those who were eliminated were given no reason for being dropped from the list. They were just told to report elsewhere on the naval base, and those of us who remained on the list reported to locations for more evaluations.

Eventually we reached a point where we assumed the list had been pared down to a final count of sixteen men. This assumption was based on the fact that about five days went by without anyone being cut from the list. Sure enough, one Monday morning we were instructed to meet in an office on the base. On entering the office at 8:00 A.M. we were met by three civilians dressed casually but conservatively in short-sleeved golf shirts, khaki pants, and brown loafers.

"Gentlemen, welcome to FRAM 16," said the older of the three men. "It's fairly certain you are wondering what this is all about, and we are going to explain it to you. You are a select group of young men of well above average intelligence; your country is going to be placing a lot of faith in your ability and success. We and a lot of others are going to train you fellows in a wide variety of skills over the next eight to nine months. Ultimately you will become a study and observation group (SOG), also referred to by some as a special operations group. You will be trained to observe the activities of the North Vietnamese and Vietcong forces in Southeast Asia, and to report your observations and conclusions. Our intent is that you not engage the enemy—merely observe him under a variety of conditions and in a variety of places. There are likely to be occasions when engagement with the enemy is inevitable and you will be well prepared to take him on if this occurs. However, your greatest value to the military action in Southeast Asia will be to supply information to the U.S. and South Vietnamese intelligence network.

"As you were told, this is a volunteer group. It will require your involvement in intense training, which we are confident each of you is capable of handling. However, we want no misunderstanding here. If you wish to drop out of this team, you may do so at the end of today and you will be reassigned. Obviously, we hope this will not happen. But because of our team training and unit integrity requirements, we stress the need for this group to remain together unless injury prevents it. The program is run by the CIA.

"You were selected as the brightest, the best conditioned, the most mentally stable, and the most likely to succeed in selected missions out of the original group of volunteers. This does not mean you are supermen. This country has hundreds of men in elite military units who are supermen. But in this group we have observed unique sets of qualities, abilities, backgrounds, and other factors that, when combined, cause us to believe you will be a first-class SOG team.

"We will work you to a peak of physical condition, and subject you to stresses that are as near as we can make them to the stresses of combat. We will train you in the disciplines of paramilitary specialties, weapons, parachute jumping, scuba diving, languages, small- and medium-size boat handling, demolitions, radios, climbing and repelling, and a host of other techniques. Your instructors will be among the best we have from practically every service branch as well as certain civilian specialists."

The one-sided dialogue went on for another thirty minutes or so without a pause. I was aware that we were being somewhat baited by three very smooth-talking men. The discussion certainly piqued my interest, and I assumed the others were equally inspired to hear more. The bait was in the form of positive reinforcement through affirmative statements, with the underlying assumption that we were all already "onboard." It was designed to have a galvanizing effect on us early on. The best way I can explain the initial effect of what I was hearing was that I wanted to hear more. I was not yet certain that I really wanted to be a part of this team, but my ego was being flattered and catered to, and I definitely would not have expressed any thought that I might possibly want to drop out. Obviously, though, the more I heard, the more questions I had:

"Why look for a SOG team among of bunch a guys who originally had been selected to train and become part of the usual information intelligence side of the U.S. Navy?"

"Why not take an existing team of Rangers, Special Forces, or Marine recon people and train them for intelligence data-gathering in the jungles of Southeast Asia?"

"What about the new SEAL teams we had heard about being trained up in Little Creek, Virginia? Why not use those guys?"

"Why no enlisted men on our team?"

"Why us? What kind of cannon fodder are we slated to be?"

"Are there other teams being trained here or elsewhere for the types of missions envisioned for FRAM 16?"

"What does FRAM mean or connote? Does the *16* mean sixteen guys on the team? Why not call us the Nighthawks, Nightcrawlers, or something more interesting than FRAM 16?"

"The CIA is a bunch of spooks and spies working their way into the Russian government and other sensitive positions around the world. Since when did the CIA get involved in military actions as a separate service from the standard Army, Navy, or Air Force?"

"Who authorized the establishment of FRAM 16? Are we serving at the 'pleasure of the president' or the pleasure of someone else?"

As time progressed we were able to ask many of these questions, but I cannot say we were given correct answers or answers that satisfied us. Yet the CIA guys were persuasive, pushing unit integrity, confidence in each other, the challenge and opportunity to make an important contribution to the world by thwarting the spread of Communism, and money. Yes, they spoke to our wallets. We would be earning more than twice the starting salary for U.S. military officers, and the salary jumps would be greater as well. We could not have made that kind of money even with dual Ph.D.s in biophysics and chemistry and going to work for Dow Chemical.

I was turned on by the money, the training, and the challenge. While this was far from what I had envisioned myself doing as a young Navy ensign, I admit to feeling rather elite at that point, and my ego was greatly inflated. So I overlooked the lack of direct answers to some of the questions we asked. For example, when we asked why a group of young Navy guys had been selected for this duty, the response was that every U.S. military service branch had its elite specialists, and that we would be working in areas where no U.S. military were allowed. Hence, the need for us to become affiliated with the CIA, where we would be considered civilians under certain international agreements. I accepted this without question. Being rather excited over the challenge, I admit to ignoring any cognitive dissidence within myself with respect to the lack of answers to our questions.

The training process over the next nine and a half months was physically arduous and unremitting. In fact we had so little free time—and we moved from training site to training site with often less than eight hours' notice of departure—that keeping track of where we were and what we were taught at each military base is difficult to recall. However, with the volunteer group finally pared down to sixteen, we found more free time to speculate among ourselves on exactly what our mission was all about. We learned to be stoic about our physical condition. If our instructors (there were many) became aware of our individual physical ailments, they seemed to play on those injuries, forcing us to perform more in spite of the afflictions and/or deprivations.

We quickly learned that we could exceed what we previously had believed were our physical and mental limits. The medical community tells us that we use only about ten percent of our mental capacities. I would swear that each team member learned to use twenty percent of his mental capacity and could do so during extremely stressful physical activities. Judgment and the ability to use one's physical senses frequently break down under stress brought about by long marches, miles of swimming, and varying extremes of danger to one's physical well-being. Over time we each learned to tune out these stresses and to become imperturbable. The particular stresses of pain, hunger, and thirst are often debilitating with respect to decision making, tactical thinking, and using heightened senses of sight, hearing, and smell. In short, stress can become all consuming in our thoughts. The indispensable part of much of the physical side of our training was that we learned to endure, to persevere, and to know we could keep on going because we could will ourselves to overcome the "walls" against which most human beings give up. Working as a close-knit team, we found we could always do more than we thought we could, and we learned to constantly encourage each other as an important aid to accomplishing the goal. It is called developing mental toughness and team cohesiveness.

For example, when all your muscles howl for oxygen, when your mouth is totally parched from dehydration, when the poisonous snakes have you surrounded, and when you still have three miles of thick underbrush to navigate in order to elude the aggressors, you have to think constantly, and be able to do so clearly without making mental mistakes. This capability only comes the hard way, through practice, and it often spells the difference between success and failure. Your life and the lives of your teammates depend on it.

After the medical testing and five days of classroom training, we were bused two hours from Pensacola Naval Air Station to Eglin Air Force Base in the south-central Florida panhandle. This eighty-square-mile reservation provided the backdrop for our first encounter with our overinflated, egotistical beliefs in our physical and mental prowess. Our egotism emanated in large part from our being finalists in the tough selection process.

Eglin is characterized by mild topography, miles and miles of scrub pine forest, sandy soil, desertlike heat, and palmetto bushes housing families of rattlesnakes. It was early August. With four Army Rangers as instructors, we were required to complete daily (or nightly) objectives, usually seven to ten miles from the previous objective. To make it interesting, the mission included about one hundred elite U.S. Army Rangers whose function was to find and "destroy" the sixteen of us. To add to the realism of the exercise, the rifles of the "enemy" Rangers were loaded with blank cartridges. So the sound effects were real. If one of us was "shot," the Ranger squad or platoon leader used a small hole puncher to punch a hole in a thin, laminated card that each of us carried in our breast pockets. We were not told how many lives we had, but I recall I was shot twice and Richard Shell was shot six times, as evidenced by a comparison of the round holes punched in our cards. Everyone on the team was shot at least twice.

This was a combination exercise—escape and evasion as well as survival. Each team member was equipped with an empty parachute pack, several yards of nylon parachute cord, a canteen, a K-bar knife mounted on a webbed belt, mosquito repellent, camouflage paste, and a poncho. Personal items such as toilet paper, toothbrush, shaving razor, and fork were not permitted. We were divided into two teams of five and one team of six. Each team was given one compass, one first aid kit, and one machete. We were not allowed to carry guns. Our clothing was standard camouflage, plus boots and soft boonie hats. The purpose of the exercise was to survive and evade the "enemy" Rangers for twelve days.

I lost fourteen pounds during this period and my forearms and face bubbled with blisters from sunburn. I was consumed with hunger by the middle of the third day and could think of hardly anything else but how and when I would get my next meal. There were plenty of streams around for our water consumption, but the taste of the water was ruined because of the requirement to add iodine tablets to all water for purification before drinking. We snared rabbits, flying squirrels, and one nasty-smelling skunk, which we devoured after cooking over fires built in hand-dug pits to avoid "enemy" detection. We ate only in the late afternoon. The most sought-after delicacy were the large snakes, which were abundant at Eglin. Normally we would have run at the scary warning sound of a rattlesnake. By the fourth day we had overcome our fear of rattlesnakes in the palmetto bushes. We frequently prayed silently that there would be several rattlesnakes in a clump of the small palmlike bushes. The sound of the rattle became our dinner bell. Ben White and John "Turkey" Schneider captured the largest rattlesnake—seven feet long by our estimate. While eight team members ate squirrel meat, the snake was food for the remaining eight hungry men that night, as we cut it into sections, boiled it, and sucked the meat off the thousands of tiny rib bones. It tasted like boiled chicken. We ground up our salt tablets and sprinkled the grains on the snake meat. We took the roots of small cacti, removed the thin bark from the roots, cut them into thin slices, and affixed these to long green sticks. Toasted over the pit fire, we convinced ourselves that the sliced cactus root tasted like potato chips.

Halfway through this exercise, we came upon a beautiful stream in the pine forest. It was late afternoon as we reconned the area and deemed it to be safe from the lurking Rangers. Setting our lookouts in place, the rest of us shed our clothes and took sitz baths in an area where the stream widened into a stony shoal. The water was cooler than the air, which was a godsend to our parched and foul-smelling bodies. We scrubbed ourselves and our clothing with sand in the absence of soap.

Thirty yards downstream from this lovely resort amenity, the stream split around a small island about twenty feet wide by forty feet long. One of our lookouts happened to spot a large wild pig standing among the saplings on the island, and he passed the word to us nudists bathing upstream. What followed would be the envy of any Hollywood comedy film director. Calmly the bathers worked their way over to their respective piles of clothing and picked up the K-bar knives and machetes.

The Ranger instructors had told us that we could eat anything we captured and killed. So we visualized having a pork barbecue with thin-sliced broiled cactus roots that night, and to hell with the "enemy." If we were attacked during the barbecue dinner, we would make peace offerings to the Rangers of cooked pork in lieu of having our cards punched. This was my first experience with the negative effects of real hunger on my decision-making processes.

With great stealth and cunning, eleven nude men formed a loose ring around the wild pig on the island. It was 6:00 P.M. and still quite light out. The large pig observed us, grunting occasionally. We kept a vigilant eye on the beast as we closed our ring around its position, each of us holding a K-bar knife or machete at the ready. At some point, when our tactical ring was about fifty feet in diameter, it occurred to the pig that it was in jeopardy. It made short sprints of ten to fifteen feet, stopped, contemplated the odds of escape, turned about, and sprinted again. We froze in position, standing in the stream during this part of the episode, knives poised to stab at any moment. Shortly, the animal deduced it was time to make a break for the safety of the other million-odd acres of Eglin Air Force Base. She bolted between two of my teammates who, standing shin deep on cannonball-size rocks in the stream, lunged at either side of the escaping pig. Tommy's knife pierced the 150-pound pig's left hindquarter, causing it to issue a shrill squeal that I can still hear nearly thirty years later. Driven by hunger, frustration, and greed, and with total disregard for our safety from the "enemy" or lounging snakes, eleven naked men raced after the wounded pig hoping to pick up on a trail of blood, finish the deed of killing it, and return triumphantly to camp to feed our hungry brethren.

After running nearly a hundred yards through the scrubby pine forest, we sadly abandoned the chase, ultimately having been outsmarted by a fleet-footed female swine. Instead, that night we sucked the salted meat from the fine bones of more boiled snake.

There were many firsts on this first exercise. We encountered two deadly coral snakes, ate skunk (which we skinned underwater to reduce the smell), delighted in catching rabbits and flying squirrels (which we snared), and developed the seeds of team camaraderie that would endure for the future. Learning to work as a team in all exercises was essential to surviving what we would ultimately experience in Southeast Asia.

In the succeeding months we were trained in making and setting all types of explosive charges and weapons; survival; first aid; land and sea navigation; topographical map reading; power boat handling; scuba diving and long distance swimming; demolitions; escape and evasion; parachuting; repelling and climbing; radio communications; hand-to-hand combat; the Vietnamese language; heavy weapons (tanks and artillery) identification; small unit tactics; and camouflage techniques. Extra physical conditioning began and ended each day. Our training bases included Parris Island, Fort Bragg, Little Creek, Panama Canal Zone, Key West, Monterey, Coronado, and Fort Benning. We also picked up some training at a little-known base in northern Virginia; however, its name is long forgotten.

Beside being cruel, inhuman, mean-spirited, and completely unreasonable, our instructors saw to it that we developed into a tight-knit, smart team that could outthink and outfight any enemy. The instructors were the best of the best, members of the most elite fighting units then existing in the United States, from Navy Underwater Demolition Teams (UDT), Army Rangers, Marines, Special Forces, and U.S. Navy river patrollers (later dubbed Riverines).

In retrospect, and having since read a few books about the training of UDT people and Sea, Air, Land, (SEAL) teams and the Army's Rangers and Special Forces units, I have tried to recall the details of our training for comparison. At the time of our training I believed nothing could be more difficult or arduous. However, after reading details of what these other units were subjected to in their training, I have wondered if we got off a little easier in terms of physical punishment. In many situations, when we believed we had endured and accomplished the assigned tasks and could not physically do more, our instructors seemed to have a reserve of stamina. When we collapsed, our instructors remained standing and yelling at us in spite of their having endured the same physical requirements that we had suffered. Now, when I read of our Delta Forces, Long Range Reconnaissance Patrols, SEALs, Special Forces, Rangers, and other military special ops teams who have been at the point of more recent actions in Panama, Grenada, and the Persian Gulf War ("Desert Storm"), I know what those people are made of, and frankly, I stand in awe of them. I know from my own experiences that these men are superhuman in combined mental and physical prowess.

Our training regimen left no time for family, vacations, or time off (none of us was married). Once a month we had a Sunday off, which we used mostly for sleeping and tending to our wounds. We were fortunate that none of us was injured during training exercises to the extent that we had to lay out for more than three or four days. Some of us broke bones in our hands or feet; we had some dislocated shoulders, bad sprains, a few deep cuts that required multiple stitches, at least four cases of hypothermia, a snake bite, one near drowning, and assorted cranial contusions. More important, we learned to cope with and function reasonably well with our injuries and not to complain, even to each other, about our physical woes.

Ed Brown and I became dangerously dehydrated in Panama from some form of dysentery. The dehydration, caused by incessant diarrhea and vomiting, caused us to be evacuated by helicopter to an Army infirmary in the Canal Zone. We were delirious on arrival but the doctors immediately diagnosed our conditions. We were both reconstituted by an intravenous drip with huge hypodermic needles inserted into the top of each thigh. The needles looked to be the size of those used by veterinarians on elephants and horses. Within forty-eight hours we were back with our teammates.

Robert Gomez was bitten by a snake of unidentified species in the swamps of Parris Island, South Carolina. One of the Marine instructors immediately administered first aid to Robert by cutting a + over the two fang entry points in his calf, then sucked the wound to remove as much venom as he could. We carried Robert to dry land where a truck transported him to the base hospital. Later, Robert admitted to us that he had been extremely frightened that he would die from the snake bite. One of our teammates reminded him that if he wasn't dead in the first ten seconds from the venom attacking his central nervous system (such as results from the bite of a coral snake), he was probably only in minor danger. I felt that the Marine who administered first aid was the unheralded hero of the event. If the snake bite had contained the kind of venom that attacked the nervous system, he might have died too, having sucked the venom into his mouth. But the Marine obviously observed that Robert had not quickly become comatose from the bite, and therefore he didn't seem to care that the snake that bit Robert had escaped before it was identified. In this case, the instructor had a man down from a snake bite and immediately assumed the responsibility for that man's care and survival. This was one of several thousand crucial lessons learned by my teammates and me.

Captain Scott O'Grady, a U.S. Air Force F-16 fighter pilot, was shot down by a Bosnian Serb antiaircraft missile in late May 1995. He was able to eject from his burning aircraft and, using his training and knowledge, was able to escape from and evade the enemy for six days, until being rescued by our Marines and their helicopters from the USS *Kearsage*. The young pilot related to the world some of the techniques he employed to avoid capture and death. He told interviewers of eating ants and grass for sustenance, and of ringing out his socks for a few drops of moisture to lessen his dehydration. Most people are likely disgusted at the thought of eating ants (or any other form of insect). Eating grass and leaves is an acceptable source of human sustenance for short periods; however, bugs are not thought of in the same way by most Americans. It is practically an axiom that when you are starving, your body weakening from lack of food and your thought processes becoming impaired, you will eat anything to survive. Modern-day people have reported eating human flesh to survive plane crashes and sea disasters. In the jungles of central Panama, our Ranger instructors forced us to eat handfuls of live grubs gathered from rotting trees. The first swallow of live, wiggling bugs is the worst. The second swallow becomes a little easier. When you find that the bugs have not commenced eating your stomach lining, the third and subsequent swallows of a handful of mustard-colored, one-inch grubs become only slightly worse than eating slimy, boiled okra. Captain O'Grady ate the ants, and he lived to escape and survive. That's all that counts. Admittedly, bugs (particularly roaches) are not a food source that you ever crave or hope to see again on a hotel buffet line, not even in a stir-fry.

On a training exercise at Fort Benning we were encamped in a forested area. We were sleeping on ponchos with no tents, and certainly no mosquito netting. Sometime just before dawn I had been sleeping on my back, my head resting on a roll of toilet tissue (which I had smuggled along among my sparse toilet articles), when I awoke, involuntarily choking. Quickly sitting up, I spit out what seemed to be hard feathers that had become lodged in the back of my throat. Shortly, a large mass attached to wings escaped from my mouth as a result of my coughing and the prying of my right index finger. I switched on my flashlight. The sight caused me great mental discomfort and near nausea. As I slept, a large cockroachlike bug had found my open mouth a desirable, moist location in which to bivouac for the night. My four-letter profanities awoke my entire team and two instructors. When I was finally able to explain what had happened, I received a round of verbal reproaches, which would have made even a salty sailor blush, for having disturbed the sleep of my comrades over such a minor matter. I silently vowed to find a way to get even with them for their insensitivity. Later, in Southeast Asia, we all ate mosquitoes and flies because hordes of these winged creatures sometimes invaded our food as it made its way from the container to our mouths. Such was life in the woods and jungles.

We trained for parachute jumping at Fort Bragg. After four days of ground school, including parachute packing, we were ready for our first static-line jumps. By the time we reached Fort Bragg, the worries over jumping out of an airplane and floating to the ground under a canopy of silk seemed to sixteen tough guys to be more like an opportunity to take a short nap in between jumping from the aircraft and smashing into the ground. We jokingly concluded during ground school that only the jolt of the parachute opening might awaken us momentarily.

But the first jump was not a cakewalk for me and several of our team. Richard and Robert were first and second out the door, each shouting "Geronimo-o-o-o" as they disappeared, caught by the slipstream of the aircraft. I was third in position to leap. I balked at the hatchway. There was about forty-five hundred feet of clear air between the aircraft in which I was standing and the ground below. The wind was blowing past the door at about ninety mph. Overcoming the obstacle of fear was momentarily difficult for me; however, my hesitation at the hatchway was short-lived—about 1.8 seconds in duration—because the sole of a large boot was placed on my butt, and I was unceremoniously booted into the free airspace. The static line opened my chute automatically, and I drifted down and out of the slipstream. I shouted a vile name over to Richard and he shouted back at me. Carrying on a conversation at that altitude was a new experience. Pulling alternately on the parachute risers gave me practice in steering the parachute to the extent steering was possible. I landed about three hundred yards from the target area and none of our team got closer to it than about a hundred yards. With practice at static-line jumping we became more proficient, although I never came close to hitting the target circle.

Free-fall jumping was exhilarating; however, for me, looking down at about eight thousand feet of clear air was daunting, particularly for the first several jumps. The fact that I had packed my own chute, and a professional parachute rigger had packed my reserve chute, was little comfort at first. Once again I had to be booted out the door. "Big Guy" (my nickname), was launched again. I watched the altimeter, which rested on top of my reserve chute on my chest. Spreading my arms and legs, I flew down like a giant eagle just as the instructors had told us to do and as the training films had depicted. The four teammates who had gone out the hatchway before me blended into the landscape below, and I could pick them out only occasionally. I felt for the D-ring at least half a dozen times just to make sure I could find it when I reached the altitude at which I had been instructed to pull it to release the chute.

I watched the ground rising to meet me at a speed of about ninety-five to one hundred mph, and the farther I fell the more I mistrusted my altimeter. The instructors had told us to pull the D-ring at four thousand feet, and if the main chute failed to open properly we were to release it, as instructed, and pull the D-ring to open the reserve chute. When my altimeter indicated five thousand feet the distance to the ground looked more like three thousand feet to me. The four jumpers ahead of me had already opened their parachutes. In simple terms, I panicked. I pulled the D-ring just after passing the five-thousand-foot mark on the altimeter. The drogue chute deployed, pulling out the main canopy, and with a mighty yank on my thigh straps it filled with air and slowed me to a crawl.

It was only when Ben zoomed past me still in free fall that I felt very foolish. He correctly opened his chute at four thousand feet while I was still floating around forty-six hundred feet.

The jump instructors on the ground took me to task for not following instructions, and I did not grope about for a response, since I had long before learned that excuses of any kind were unacceptable in this business. I did resent being labeled a "gutless wonder" and a "douche bag."

At Coronado we experienced still another escape and evasion school, during which I very nearly failed a claustrophobia test . . . my Achilles' heel. As a phase of interrogation training, as a mock-prisoner, I was placed into a metal box in a sitting position. The metal top of the box was closed on me, forcing my head nearly down to my outstretched legs. I was able to move only my arms. I was forced to remain locked in the box under direct sunlight for thirty minutes.

When finally released, I was a screaming nut-case for several minutes. It was a terrible experience for me.

On an island off the coast of Coronado we were taught by UDT instructors to use C-4 demolition charges as well as construct and detonate claymore mines. I was extremely impressed with how little C-4 explosive was required to create an enormous explosion and devastation. Our primary instructor in demolitions was a thin U.S. Navy chief petty officer nicknamed "Bomber Bob." Being curious as to how Bomber lost the top joint of three of his fingers on his left hand, one of our team asked him how that happened. We fully expected him to tell us his fingers were blown off by an explosive charge that went awry.

"Well," said Bomber, "it happened when I was about fifteen. I was in shop class in high school and ran them through a saw. No big deal. I didn't need those joints anyway."

We chuckled at this response and went on with the class.

In the morning classes at the Monterey School of Languages we were taught Vietnamese; however, after about ten days it was determined by someone in authority that the FRAM 16 team either did not need to learn Vietnamese or there was something more pressing with respect to our training.

The language classes were terminated and we flew up to Travis Air Force Base, outside San Francisco. At Travis we checked into the BOQ (Bachelor Officers Quarters) and were met by a man, whom we presumed was a CIA case officer, who directed us to be back in the lobby in 15 minutes. We were told we would be picking up our equipment bags, getting a few final inoculations, and having a briefing that would last most of the afternoon.

We received word at the briefing that we would be leaving for Vietnam at noon the following day. At that particular point, the reality of it all hit each of us with a large bang. This was what we had been training for.

Chapter 3

First Practice Mission

Having experienced the excitement of observing the Marine pilot exit safely from the smoking A-1 Skyraider at Tan Son Nhut Airport, we went into the Operations ("Ops") Building and stood inside looking for someone who fit the description of Paul Seward, a CIA case officer. We had been given his description and local telephone by a case officer on our departure from Travis AFB, and we assumed he would be dressed in the classic CIA uniform of light blue shirt and khaki pants. We drew some minor attention from military types and others who were milling around in the building, because we were dressed in camouflage clothing that bore no markings as to rank, nor did we have our names on patches sewn on our jacket breast pockets.

"Gentlemen, let me welcome you to South Vietnam. How was your trip from CONUS [continental United States]?" asked a six-foot-five fellow wearing "the uniform."

He went on, not waiting for a response from us. "I'm Paul Seward. Your assigned case officer, Bill Dunn, couldn't be here to meet you and I will act in his place. We're going to put you fellows up here for the night and will have a briefing for you around 4:00 P.M. this afternoon concerning your first mission. Right now I want you to exit with me through that door over there and load yourselves and your gear on the bus. The rest of the gear that was on your flight will be taken to your temporary billet. Feel free to grab some food from the mess hall adjacent to your barracks. I'll be there to see that you don't have any hassles getting fed at the little mess hall operation. Any questions?"

None of us had any questions, and we followed Seward out of the building. With our duffel bags on our shoulders we walked about seventy-five yards, through light rain, to a ramshackle old Vietnamese school bus. The bus took us about a mile to a cinder-block two-story barracks where we took a few minutes to rest on our bunks before loading up with some chow.

Following a mid-afternoon spaghetti lunch, we were led by Seward to an adjacent building used for meetings and briefs. The meeting room was drab with a concrete slab floor, unpainted cinder-block walls, three ceiling fans, and about forty metal folding chairs set up in five rows. Fluorescent light fixtures lined the ceiling from front to back. At the front of the room was a wooden lectern on a table, several maps mounted on easels, and a chalkboard.

Seward entered the room and began the briefing with a nod in welcome. He explained that most of our missions would be staged out of Cambodia and Laos, which we had already been told back in the States. The headquarters people wanted FRAM 16 to go through two missions with experienced combat personnel before beginning missions on our own. Seward explained in careful detail that our primary function would be to gather information by "observing" the enemy—the North Vietnamese and the Vietcong—and report it back for processing by the intelligence networks in South Vietnam. We had already heard this too.

"In the course of your work it is certain you will engage the enemy in spite of your efforts to avoid getting into firefights. In the first two missions we have planned for you, you are probably going to get into firefights. Count on it. And you can count on it changing you forever. We know you have received outstanding combat training; however, there is nothing like the real thing. We want you to go through this guided by experienced men who know how to fight and win because they've been there before.

"Your first mission will involve an attempt to capture a North

Vietnamese officer. We are aware of the constant infiltration of the demilitarized zone (DMZ) by North Vietnamese regulars heading into South Vietnam, and we are anxious to interrogate an enemy officer who can be invited to devulge information concerning numbers, equipment, supply dumps, and other valuable information. We'll handle the interrogation."

We were told in the briefing by Seward that we would be flown in two C-47s (carrying cargo in addition to FRAM 16) to a small tactical airfield in Quang Tri, located in the northeast corner of South Vietnam, just below the DMZ. We were to be met there by five U.S. Army Special Forces soldiers who would lead the mission. Seward went on with the mission outline, covering the helicopter incursion into the North Vietnamese–occupied land near the DMZ. He described the terrain we could expect, pointed out on a map the known enemy concentration areas, and concluded by saying that the Special Forces men would cover the tactical details of the mission when we arrived in Quang Tri.

Seward closed by saying that by the next morning he wanted each of us to tell him the type of weapons we preferred for the mission. This request, I thought, was odd. After a discussion among the team members there was a consensus that we did not know enough about the tactical mission to know the type of weapons we might need. Would we have helicopter gunship cover if needed? There were too many unknowns for us to communicate our weapons needs to Seward. We appointed Richard to get back to Seward and discuss the matter with him before we stated our weapons preferences. Richard returned from meeting with Seward just before we went to dinner.

"He said that a normal complement of M16s, M2 carbines, M3 grease guns, semiautomatic pistols, and fragmentary grenades would be the best choices. No need for shotguns, grenade launchers, or light machine guns. The Special Forces guys will be loaded for bear. There should be helicopter gunship support for insertion and extraction; however, we could not depend fully on gunship support if we got into a firefight between the time of insertion and the time of extraction. As he said in the briefing, Seward thinks this will be a two-day mission at most."

We had trained with many types of weapons; however I was still hoping for the chance to requisition a Stoner as soon as our regular case officer showed up. For this mission I chose the M2, being wary of the M16 based on what I had heard from the UDT fellow.

Before the flight up to Quang Tri two days later, we were free to catch a bus into Saigon to tour around the old city. I was still stressed over my arrival in South Vietnam and had slept very little on the flight over. We were finally here, and the combat zone was nearby. This was it. This is what we were trained for, and it was coming down fast. Four of my teammates and I decided to grab dinner at Tan Son Nhut and take in a movie. The rest of the team went into Saigon.

The mission appeared to be a fiasco of miscommunication and mishaps from the beginning. One of the C-47s going to Quang Tri, carrying nine members of FRAM 16, had to divert to a friendly airfield due to mechanical problems in flight. The remaining seven of us went on to land at Quang Tri. When we arrived we were met at the foot of the plane's ladder by three Special Forces men who drove us to our tent. The airfield compound was completely cleared, flat, and surrounded by a berm of dirt. It was bleak in appearance. The sky was a dull gray, with clouds at about twenty-five hundred feet, and the humidity must have been ninety-eight percent.

In the briefing tent the senior Special Forces officer greeted us without a hint of a smile. He was a major, and from his appearance it was obvious he had seen plenty of combat. His head was covered with only a stubble of hair; he looked tired and dirty.

"We expected only five of you to be coming in to operate with us," he said. "We received a communication early this morning that they were sending sixteen of your types up here. Don't know what we would have done with sixteen on this mission. But then we heard that the other aircraft bringing your team was diverted due to a mechanical problem. By the way, their plane landed safely. The word we got was to prepare to receive and mission-train five of you guys. Now we have seven of you, and we haven't decided if we will take all of you on the hunting trip or leave two of you behind. This mission calls for a rapid insertion, grab an NVA officer, and get the hell out as fast as possible. It makes it tough for us to get you seven and one of our five-man teams in and out fast. We may have to use two helicopters, which increases the odds that we may attract NVA attention and lose one or both of the helos in the process of insertion and extraction."

The Special Forces major definitely did not appear to be a happy fellow. As he proceeded with the briefing, he changed the insertion point from the one Seward had described to us in the early briefing at Ton Son Nhut. We would now be inserted just below the DMZ, near a small village. Apparently there was some new intelligence that there was a platoon of NVA camped on the DMZ near the village, and the NVA troops loitered around the village in the early evening. The intelligence source had reported seeing two, possibly three, NVA officers in the group of approximately thirty-five soldiers. We would insert two miles from the encampment and the village, and patrol in from there.

It seemed odd to me that twelve U.S. fighters would move in on an estimated thirty-five enemy soldiers. But I decided not to raise the question. Instead, I was willing to follow along with the experienced Special Forces soldiers. I felt that the element of surprise would be in our favor and perhaps we could prevail as a result. But my subconscious held doubt and concern. Our mission departure time would depend on further confirming intelligence reports and the weather.

The briefing, which was attended by five of the toughest-looking Special Forces soldiers I had ever seen, lasted about forty-five minutes, at which point all of us opened cans of rations and engaged in a light lunch. Suddenly the clouds, brimming with moisture, opened up and we experienced a downpour. I swore we got five inches of rain in the next hour, before it stopped. The bare ground turned to mud.

We remained in the briefing tent during the downpour and introduced ourselves to the five Special Forces men. Over the next hour we listened intently as the Special Forces guys told us what we could expect, taught us their hand signal system, and gave us plenty of warnings about what to do and not do under certain circumstances. Our brains were like sponges. Each tip we could pick up from these experienced soldiers could be the tip that saved our lives. Most of the tips had already been taught to us during Stateside training; however, now these tips were a reminder or refresher, and we made sure we understood and remembered. We asked many questions that afternoon before finally feeling we could work well with our combat trainers.

I slept very fitfully that night, having dreams of combat situations that woke me from my light sleep. I was aware of the need to sleep in order to be fit and alert when we received the call to board the helicopters. But such awareness was of no use; I still had difficulty remaining asleep for more than fifteen minutes at a time.

In the late afternoon of the next day, though the cloud cover remained low and ominous, we got the call to load up in one hour. All seven of the FRAM 16 team members present would be in on the mission. We had already packed up the gear into light backpacks, checked and range-fired our weapons—which had been delivered to us along with ammunition—drank water, and filled our bellies with rations. The time of our next drink of water and meal was unknown. That depended on what lay ahead of us. I was bothered because, while we had been through a detailed briefing and conversation with the Special Forces team that would lead the mission, there were always unknown factors. It was the way it would always be for us. We could just hope we were properly trained to react to the unknown factors and escape unscathed. Hope accompanied by positive thinking was always a part of our mission preparation and endured throughout the mission itself. This was our first mission into what was a situation where we would potentially encounter the enemy as we sought to capture and extract an NVA officer for interrogation. I wondered why this mission had been selected for us. The chances of getting into a firefight were, in my opinion, very high. Hence, it was probable that we would have casualties.

I rationalized my own concerns by cavalierly saying to myself, "If your time is up, your time is up. It may happen on this mission or one in the future. You never know when your number is going to be called. All you can do is your best. If that is not good enough, then it ain't good enough."

The helicopter ride took about twenty-five minutes. We were accompanied by three helicopter gunships. The helicopters made two false insertions to confuse and trick enemy soldiers who might be in the area. The idea was to make the enemy think there had been insertions elsewhere, masking the real insertion. The landing zone (LZ) was in a large, cleared field, and the helicopters landed only twenty-five yards from a heavily wooded area. We unloaded from the helicopters and ran fifteen yards before taking up prone firing positions in an arc facing the treeline. There being no firing coming at us from the woods, we ran and covered each other until reaching the treeline, and paused again to determine whether our insertion had been detected or whether there was a company of NVA soldiers bivouacked in our path. Our helicopters had taken off and were quickly flying away to the south.

We patrolled slowly in the direction of our objective, east-southeast of our LZ. Staying ten to fifteen yards apart, we moved single file behind the point man, a Special Forces corporal. Intelligence on enemy presence in this area was nonexistent, so we patrolled with great caution.

After just under an hour of patrolling we received a hand signal to crouch low and spread out. Moving apart, then getting into a squatting position, we waited about two minutes. Then we patrolled forward another thirty yards or so before being signaled again. This time, the point man's hand signal indicated he had spotted enemy soldiers. Seconds later I heard my first shots fired in combat. Our squad had been spotted, and it was the sound of an AK-47 firing on full automatic. The first burst was short, followed by a longer burst, and this was followed by several other AK-47s firing at once. From my position I could not see any source of the firing, and I was cognizant that none of our team was returning fire. Everyone had taken cover in whatever cover was available.

A hand signal was passed back that we were to move in a flank to our left. I crawled on my belly, elbows, and knees a distance of thirty yards. Reaching a natural berm line that rose variably from three to five feet above our previous position, I stopped to observe. On my left side was a Special Forces soldier, and on my right was Larry Jacques. We worked our way up the berm on our bellies. The underbrush in this wooded area grew low, and the trees were about ten to fifteen inches in diameter. My first view of the woods beyond the berm was of three NVA soldiers moving directly toward me from about twenty-five yards away. Before I could click off my safety, the three enemy soldiers were dropped in a hail of automatic fire from the Special Forces soldier on my left. I glanced at Larry to see his reaction. Larry was aiming his rifle ahead of him but not yet firing. I rolled over on my back to check out the area from which we had crawled, wanting to make sure the enemy was not sneaking in from behind us. I saw nothing and rolled back to the action. Instantly I saw several enemy soldiers running from my right to my left at a distance of about thirty yards. Larry fired a burst of three shots and two seconds later I did the same. None of the running NVA was hit, and they disappeared quickly into a more dense area of the woods. Almost everyone on our side seemed to be shooting. The crescendo of rifle fire became a roar beyond Larry's position. The enemy was shooting hard at us, and we were returning fire. My ears blocked up from the loud rifle fire, and I worked to equalize the pressure in them by alternately opening wide and closing my mouth. I had no saliva in my mouth to swallow.

My field of fire was somewhat limited by my being between two substantial tree trunks growing from the top of the berm. Abruptly two NVA came dashing toward me in virtually the same path as the first three NVA had come. I was ready this time and opened fire with three quick bursts of three rounds per burst. Both NVA were caught in the chest by my shots and were instantly blown over on their backs. Once on the ground they did not move, which did not mean they were dead, but I believed they were. I had no time to think about having just killed someone, because I was too busy trying to be prepared to defend against the next assault.

Several minutes later I was firing at a running NVA soldier some distance away when out of the corner of my eye I saw Larry flip violently onto his back, landing below the berm. From his body's position on the ground, I was certain he had been hit. Rather than looking at him immediately, or rushing to his aid, I first checked to see if I could determine where the enemy was who had fired the shot. I rolled over several yards to my right and observed again. Seeing no movement of enemy soldiers, I glanced down and saw the entry wound, which was nearly in the center of Larry's forehead. He looked very dead, and I felt that going to his aid at that moment would jeopardize my life and those of my comrades, because I could not chance vacating my field of fire. My field of fire now included Larry's.

I had seen a few dead people in my lifetime; mostly at funerals and when passing a few vehicular accidents. But I was unprepared for the death of a friend occurring right next to me. No matter how one steels himself to be prepared under combat circumstances, it is always a shock when someone gets killed, especially when it is a close comrade.

The small red hole in Larry's forehead looked to be less than half an inch in diameter. A small pool of blood and brains was visible on the bare ground to the side of his head. His eyes were open, but it was obvious he was dead. He probably never felt any pain. He was firing his rifle at the enemy, and in a split second it was over. His young life was taken in battle. I kept firing, fearing the next bullet aimed at me would take me out, and glancing over at Larry's body . . . and scared out of my wits, and changing clips and firing. Listening to the shouts of my teammates and orders being shouted by the Special Forces men, I was filled with anger, fear, and sorrow, none of which was stronger than the others. With the air often thick with lead from weapons being fired at us on full automatic, I would sometimes wonder how the hell we would get Larry's body out of there. I could not envision us leaving him there; but getting him extracted by helicopter could get more of us killed, assuming we could even get out of the firefight, board the helicopters, and extract. My mouth remained dry and sour-tasting. I was consumed by the desire to survive!

There were occasional lulls in the firing, but never for more than thirty seconds. I began to think about our ammunition supplies, whether or not helicopter gunships had been called in, and most of all whether or not we were going to get extracted. Firing intermittently as I saw the NVA moving about, I continued to be concerned about extracting Larry's body and how the rest of us would return to Quang Tri safely.

Larry was a good buddy. He and I had teamed on a number of occasions during training. We had drained several bottles of beer together over the preceding months, and had often laughed at each other's foul jokes. He was the youngest of four children, all born in Gaithersburg, Maryland. In fact, his older siblings were all girls. His father was an electrical engineer, and Larry had studied to be an engineer in a New England college. Like me, he held a commercial and multiengine aircraft license, was a scuba diver, and was an avid outdoorsman. He was a pitcher on the varsity baseball team. Early on we chided him that he should be very accurate on the hand grenade range. His last name was of French origin, and we had first taken to calling him Jacques; then later "Jocko." He never had the chance to test his baseball pitcher's talents in combat by throwing a hand grenade.

Hand signals were passed along indicating we should begin a retreat, back in the direction from which we had inserted. I was troubled at having to abandon a position on the berm, because it was better cover than anything I had observed previously. Yet I did not pause when I saw the hand signal; rather I slung my rifle over my shoulder and immediately moved off the berm to pick up Larry's body.

"Leave him!" shouted a Special Forces sergeant to my left. "If he's dead or dying, you leave him there or someone else will get hit! I said *leave him!*" the sergeant shouted again. I disobeyed his order and lifted Larry's limp form over my shoulder. He weighed only about 160 pounds, and I felt I could make it out to the helicopter without difficulty. I assumed that someone would cover my back as I retreated. The rifle fire had stopped for a time, and I jogged through the woods carrying Larry's body for a distance of about 150 yards before Ben caught up with me. He urged me to let him carry Larry, and I slid the body off my shoulders gently. As I released his body, I could see the back of his head. The bullet exit hole was large and sickening to look at. I was revolted but mostly saddened.

Ben took over the portage of Larry, and the rest of our team came to our aid from time to time. Again the point man was a Special Forces soldier, and the rest of the Special Forces men formed our rear guard.

It was tough going through the underbrush, and all of us were panting from the stress and exhaustion. I took several swigs of water from my canteen as I moved along. Finally, after nearly half an hour of retreat, I heard the wonderful sound of several helicopters responding to our radio call for extraction.

Our point man had guided us back to virtually the same place where we had first entered the woods from the LZ. On reaching this location I noted that a smoke grenade, belching red smoke, had already been tossed out into the field, marking our position for the helicopters. Three gunships swooped in and took positions about a hundred yards out and about a hundred feet in the air. The extraction helicopters came in under the gunships, and in groups of four we raced out and jumped on the waiting chariots.

Robert was carrying Larry's body at that point. When he arrived at the helicopter, Tom and I were already aboard and helped lift Larry from Robert's shoulders. Having not even had time to see if all were accounted for, especially from FRAM 16, I was only satisfied that we were about to reach safety. Ben, Tom, Robert, Larry's body, and I, together with three Special Forces men, were aboard the helicopter when a Special Forces sergeant gave the helicopter crewman the thumbs-up signal. The crewman signaled the pilot, and we rose about ten feet above the ground, whirled 180 degrees, and flew out under the gunships. Then the helicopter climbed rapidly to around forty-five hundred feet, heading for Quang Tri. The others followed in the second helicopter.

Larry's body was lying faceup at my feet in the helicopter. I found it difficult to hold back the tears as I thought about his family and their sorrow when they received the news of his having been killed in action, less than five days after he arrived in South Vietnam. I stared out the open door, not looking at anything in particular, but not looking down at Larry's face, which by then had turned a bluish gray. I was nauseous and upset by all this; and I did not have enough experience or insight to comprehend why we had been put in this situation.

On landing at Quang Tri, a jeep with a stretcher mounted across the back seating area rolled up to the helicopter before the rotors had stopped turning. Two Special Forces men lifted Larry's body from the deck of the helicopter, placed it on the stretcher, covered his body with a poncho, and strapped it down on the stretcher. When they had pulled away, we unloaded from our side of the helicopter. It was drizzling as I saw the jeep drive off with Larry, and I stood there on the helipad watching with my teammates in deep sorrow.

We gathered in the briefing tent with the Special Forces major who began the mission debriefing without even acknowledging the death of Larry. I thought it excessively hard-nosed of him. One of the sergeants explained to the major the lack of positive results from the mission, explaining the details from the point of insertion through the extraction. He described Larry's head wound and the fact that he must have died instantly from the single gunshot through his brain. Then he explained that I had been told to leave the body behind due to the continued rifle fire from the NVA soldiers, and that I had disobeyed the order. There was silence in the room.

The major stared at me and said, "Mister, disobeying a direct order under the circumstances you were all under could have caused your death and the death of others. When you are under fire and in retreat, you do not stop to recover bodies. What do you have to say for yourself, mister?

"I have no experience in combat, sir," I replied. "There was never a moment in our training when the subject of recovering a dead or wounded person under fire was covered. When we received the signal to retreat, there was a significant lull in the incoming fire. I believed at that point that the NVA were regrouping or retreating. Therefore I saw no reason to abandon the body of my comrade."

Glaring at me with icy eyes, the major sneeringly said, "You're a dumb shit, mister. The lull in firing could also have been the result of the NVA moving into your position from a flank. You were eleven men, strung out in a line on a berm in the woods. Your flanks and rear were completely exposed. All of you had been firing your weapons at the NVA, and they knew exactly what your position and strengths were. The NVA soldier is a smart soldier, mister. He is an experienced fighter. Don't ever forget that. You were damn lucky you were able to extract with the body without getting somebody else killed or wounded. If you had been wounded in retreat you would have created an additional burden on the rest of the squad. I'll tell you this, mister, if you were one of my men, I would have you court-martialed and thrown in the brig for a few years. What you did was disobey a direct order from one of my men, and you did so without concern for the possible jeopardy of the other men. That's all, men. Dismissed."

As we left the tent, my teammates walked with me toward our tent. Once in the tent, Ben admonished me, saying that he hoped nothing like that would happen on any future mission in which he was a part. The rest of my teammates verbally jumped all over Ben, defending me and indicating that the major was wrong. A loud argument ensued, while I remained sitting on a cot in the corner, trying to think about what had happened. The argument went on for several minutes before I stood up and told my teammates to calm down. I explained that I would do the same thing again if one of them went down under fire. I explained to them that I wanted their bodies returned to their families for interrment back in CONUS so there would be a finality to the death of their son. An unrecovered body of a loved one can cause the family to hold out hope that the person will be found and returned alive someday. Being able to ceremoniously dispose of a body after death brings closure to the loss, though the sadness lingers for years to come.

There was silence in the tent for several seconds. Then Ben stood up and walked out of the tent without saying anything further. I felt confident that I had made a good impression on the remaining members of my team, though that was not very important to me then. I just wanted to put an end to the discord.

Our first mission had ended in the death of a teammate and failure to accomplish the objective. It was an unfortunate beginning.

Chapter 4

River Patrol

The FRAM-16 team was flown to Soc Trang, thirty-five miles south of Can Tho in the Mekong Delta region, for our next assignments. We were flown in a C-47 from Quang Tri to Da Nang, changed planes, and flew to Soc Trang in two groups aboard helicopters, with a fuel stop at Tan Son Nhut.

The roar of the helicopter engine and the constant vibration we felt during the flight made me wonder, as I always had, why anyone would ever want to be a helicopter pilot. The helicopters, flown by CIA-paid Air America pilots, were old H-19s, sometimes referred to as HS-1s (or "Hiss Ones") in U.S. Navy circles. They were first used toward the end of the Korean War and were gradually being replaced in South Vietnam by the famous Huey helicopters.

We flew at an altitude of about 4,500 feet, beyond the accuracy range of most enemy small-arms fire, with the cabin doors open allowing a view of the terrain en route and observing the tremendous amount of military air traffic of every description traversing the area. A few miles south of Saigon we could see the beginnings of the wetlands constituting the Mekong Delta region. It looked like the Florida Everglades except that there were clumps of tropical rain forest where the trees seemed larger and the foliage more dense than in Florida. It was obvious there were plenty of places to hide in the forests. Estuaries, ponds, and stagnant standing water were everywhere, and the agricultural development was less widespread. On flying over a wide river, and without the benefit of having tour guides onboard, we assumed it was the Mekong River. It was swollen with water and stained gray-brown with mud. Hundreds of boats could be seen moving on the river, which flowed southward from its beginnings in the mountains of northern Laos (some say the river has its beginnings in the Himalayas), passing Vientiane (capital of Laos), forming the border between Laos and Thailand, bisecting Cambodia, turning southeast at Phnom Penh (capital of Cambodia), and heading into southern South Vietnam, where it flowed east-south-eastward to its terminus in the South China Sea. Parts of the Mekong River and its many estuaries were among the water highways used as an adjunct to the Ho Chi Minh Trail by North Vietnam.

We flew over five or six wide "rivers" and were bewildered as to which might be the fabled Mekong. In fact the rivers were all part of the Mekong, which had divided into several smaller rivers beginning south of Sa Dec.

On arrival in Soc Trang, we were escorted to a small metal building where we were met by Bill Dunn, the CIA case officer who would be in charge of our missions and other activities for the time being. Bill was an interesting study. He was about thirty-five years old, blond hair, ice-blue eyes, athletic; about 5'10" tall, 165 lbs., trim and muscular. In appearance, but absent the black military uniform, he epitomized that Nordic ideal which was prerequisite to service in Germany's Nazi SS of World War II. But, in fact, he had graduated from a Midwestern university, dropped out of law school at the end of one year, and went to work for the CIA. His "uniform" consisted of khaki pants, blue long-sleeved shirt with cuffs rolled to the elbows, and brown penny loafers.

As we grew to respect Bill over the next several months, we found him to be an exceedingly organized, conscientious, and detail-oriented man who went by the book. He was cordial, somewhat collegial in style of management, and capable of quickly getting things done for us when we needed something. Three of us had put in requests to be issued Stoner rifles, and through Bill's connections we got two of them in less than a week.

Bill divided us into three teams for the next mission.

The five-man A-team was assigned to join a UDT Team in Long Phu for a search-and-destroy mission on "Dung" Island, at the mouth of the Mekong, leading into the South China Sea. Their objective was to destroy a small 70 mm recoilless rifle assembly facility and ammunition bunker, hidden deep in the island's jungle. The facility was reported to have been partially damaged in a previous raid by the UDTs. The As were going in to make sure nothing was left that could be used against friendly forces. I was a bit jealous after I heard details of their briefing, because I greatly admired the talents of the UDTs and wanted an opportunity to work with them in the hope that some of their techniques, gained from much experience, would rub off on me.

The B-team of five men was briefed on a mission with some Army Special Forces in southeastern Cambodia, near the Svay River. Their mission was to destroy a radio tower in that area. The radio, operated by the Vietcong, directed small boat traffic in the various rivers of the area. The boats were carrying supplies and weapons believed to be for both the Vietcong and North Vietnamese regulars.

Finally, the C-team, of which I was a member (now down to five men since we lost Larry), was assigned to a U.S. Navy river patrol operation near the South Vietnam–Cambodia border on the Bassac River, fifteen miles north of Long Xuyen, where the Bassac River has a brief connection to the Mekong River. The main stream of the Bassac flows from the huge Tonle Sap Lake, located about forty miles northwest of Phnom Penh, Cambodia.

After the three teams received their briefings, we all gathered in a Quonset hut around 1:00 P.M. and had several rounds of cold beer. We kidded one another about which mission would likely generate the most "hot lead" in the air, discussed the advantages of working with the Navy UDTs, and compared other details of the missions. After a few beers we were all pretty loose, and the competitive banter and laughter grew more raucous. In our own way we were preparing ourselves for our second live-fire training mission. As we drank beer, the perception of the danger involved with these missions made us all comedians (at least in our own slightly inebriated estimation), perhaps in an ephemeral attempt to sublimate fear in our subconscious minds. After all, we were a bunch of young studs, all fairly tough to the core, and we had just lost one of our favorites, Larry. For our mental health each of us probably needed to deal more directly with the loss of our teammate, but there was no time to be concerned about our psychological well-being. The deaths of Larry and subsequent other team members would haunt us unmercifully, especially when we were all so interdependent as trustees of each other's lives.

Being one of the quieter souls present at the beer fest, I silently looked over the laughing group and wondered if we would all be back together again the next week. Or would our ranks be smaller? It was a horrid thought to deal with. My gaze circled the room, taking in all the faces of the merrymakers. Maybe I was a little different from most of my teammates. I drank more beer and did my utmost to enjoy the time we had remaining. After seven cans of beer, consumed in ninety minutes or less, I weaved drunkenly out the door of the Quonset hut and threw it up, bubbles and all. We drank a lot of beer that afternoon and evening. I had not had that much to drink at one time in the previous eight or nine months.

Most of us awoke the next morning with varying degrees of upset stomachs from all the beer consumed. The A-team had already departed on their mission with the UDTs. The ten of us remaining gathered at the mess hut hoping that a little solid food would help cure us of the previous night's binge. Robert said he felt great, and that we were all a bunch of pansies for not being able to have a few beers without getting hungover. I was chided by everyone when one of the guys pointed out that I was the first in the group to throw up.

Two helicopters arrived just before noon to pick up the B- and C-teams and take us to our respective mission staging areas. As my C-team mates and I flew northwest, I tried to mentally prepare myself for what might come. In the firefight near the DMZ I thought I had wounded or killed at least three NVA soldiers, but I wasn't sure it was my bullets that hit those men. There had been a tremendous amount of lead in the air. I psyched myself up for my next "kill." I wanted to put some Vietcong (VC) in my sights, squeeze the trigger, and kill them to avenge Larry's death. I was angry and wanted revenge in the worst way.

After enduring the psychological testing and evaluation in Pensacola, some of my teammates felt that part of the evaluations were, in small part, to evaluate whether we were capable of pulling the trigger without hesitation or remorse. I had no idea how one could be tested for that with any degree of confidence in the results. I knew I had never been asked any direct questions in this regard. Possibly we were selected as likely to be unhesitating killers of enemy soldiers based on comparisons with psychological profiles of battle-experienced soldiers. I confidently felt that I had no problem killing the enemy if given the opportunity. I never dealt with the fact that in God's view this might be murder. It seemed we were always being swept along by the tide of training or action, so I never took time or felt compelled to grapple with those thoughts.

The objective of this mission was "search and destroy," which simply meant we were to find the enemy and destroy him. This was not what FRAM 16 had been trained for. In fact, we were supposed to avoid enemy detection and contact, if possible, in our efforts to gather intelligence about the enemy. Our case officer explained that this mission was still part of our training, and each team could expect to engage the enemy. The mission was supposed to give us first-hand experience in tactical combat in case we were drawn into firefights in future missions. We joked with one another because this training involved real bullets fired by a real enemy, usually referred to as baptism of fire. This was to be our second baptism.

The area of our river patrol mission, the Bassac River, was the waterway for a massive number of riverboats used by Vietnamese, both North and South Vietnamese. The riverboats carried cargo of every possible classification. We would be looking for boats with soldiers infiltrating the South, and any type of war material. I was troubled by the mission, because it clearly put us in harm's way, and again I didn't think we needed to be in the position of being used for fire support. If we lost team members, future intelligence data-gathering missions for which we had been trained would be jeopardized. This was the beginning of the seed of doubt that grew within me and has remained with me ever since: Why were we—CIA military operatives—performing in live-fire military missions for practice? It seemed foolish.

A helicopter delivered us to a small outpost, a mini-firebase, on an estuary feeding the Bassac River. South Vietnamese soldiers guarded the perimeters of the outpost with machine gun emplacements and M16 and M1 carbines. Navy boatswain's mates and some Vietnamese were working on gunboat repairs as we disembarked under the rotor wash of the helicopter.

Moments later we were approached by an American of thin build, sporting a neatly groomed handlebar mustache. His "uniform" consisted of filthy, oil-stained blue jeans and an equally filthy, long-sleeve camouflage shirt. He saluted us casually (which was unusual, since we wore no insignia of rank), and said, "Greetings, men. I'm Chief Boatswain's mate Kelly. We'll be taking off in a PBR [patrol boat river] as soon as we can finish a few repairs and gas up. While you're waiting, grab some soft drinks over there in the hooch, help yourself to the bananas we cut down yesterday, check your weapons and ammunition carefully, and don't take any target practice around here or you'll draw fire on yourself. Our guys don't think twice about firing in the direction of any gunshots they hear. Each of you needs at least three hundred rounds of ammo in clips. We're sure glad you guys are here right now. We're short on firepower, and we may need all the help we can get." The chief casually waved to us as he turned to walk back toward the docks, neither asking for questions nor giving us a chance to ask any.

I wondered what we were going to be up against that would require such heavy ammunition capability. I carried only five thirty-round clips, including one in my Stoner and four in my vest. Not thinking I would need my 150-round drum magazine, I had left it behind. I followed the chief and informed him of this. He told me to grab a steel ammo box of 5.56mm shells in the ammunition bunker, which I did. I found it curious that the bunker was unlocked and there was no one guarding its access. At U.S. military bases, each round of ammunition is carefully guarded and accounted for. Not here in the woods.

C-team lounged around in the shade, observing the repair activities on the three out of four PBRs until it was time to cast off. All of us were curious about the hybrid boats we saw docked at the shoreline. They are difficult to describe in terms of any other vessels afloat. Two were about forty feet long, and the two others looked to be about twenty-five to thirty feet long. The hull of each PBR was of three-quarter-inch plywood clad in fiberglass, painted medium gray. The beam of the larger vessels was about thirteen feet at most. Forward of the cockpit was a single .50-caliber machine gun. The .50 was covered with what looked like a tennis net, partially camouflaged with leafy tree branches, but from our vantage point there was no mistaking what was beneath the net. The stern mount was a twin .30-caliber machine gun. Neither machine gun was protected by any type of armor for the operator except for small, half-inch steel shields, each about twenty inches wide by three feet high, positioned on either side of the gun barrels. To us it appeared that the gunners would be sitting ducks in a firefight.

The cockpit was far better shielded in steel. The boatswain's mate, or coxswain, responsible for steering the PBR, was required to stand in the cockpit and peer through two-inch by thirty-six-inch rectangular cuts in each of the four armored sides of the cockpit. Immediately aft of the cockpit was a makeshift cabin area constructed of six-inch by six-inch posts at the four corners, connected by bamboo joists lashed to the posts, and thin bamboo curtains that could be raised or lowered like window blinds. The light-brown, split-bamboo blinds were hung on each of the four sides of the cabin. This boat was truly customized, except for the hull.

The chief hailed us aboard one of the boats after about two hours of waiting. We had already discussed with each other what kind of armor protection we hoped to have in the cabin area, since it was obvious that that was where our battle station would be for the mission. It was of some relief when we observed the three-quarter-inch-thick steel plates surrounding the inside of the cabin from the top of the gunwales to somewhere below the floorboards covering the bilge. At least we would have some protection from small-arms fire and .30-caliber machine-gun fire. The floor area of the cabin was about ten feet by fifteen feet. It was obvious from the gear boxes stacked in the middle of the cabin that the crew ate and slept in this area. There were no visible comforts such as benches, lounge chairs, card tables, or suntan oil lying around. The roof was more of the tennis net material, stuffed with a variety of vegetation. Except for the machine guns mounted ominously on the bow and stern, the boat reminded me of a slightly updated version of the Humphrey Bogart vessel in the *African Queen*.

At 1:45 P.M. the chief ordered the crew to start engines, cast off, and maneuver out of the sheltered backwater cove of the gunboat base. As the twin engines coughed and growled to a start, I suddenly wondered to myself, "Hey, do we just ride to battle in this garbage scow, or are we going to get a briefing on what to expect and how to handle various conditions?" Surely we were not going to be thrown to the wolves without getting some tactical advice.

As the coxswain revved up the engines, one thing was certain based on the big engine sounds: This was one fast boat. My confidence improved. As we traversed the small inlet, the chief came out of a small hatch in the cockpit and sat on the floorboards, motioning for us to get off the gunwales.

The chief introduced himself again, this time as Bobby Kelly, and suggested that everyone call him "Boats." He identified the other crewmen aboard, including the two Gunner's mates, the engineman, and the coxswain. Boats said we would be moving northwest, up the Bassac River toward Cambodia, attempting to locate and destroy riverboats carrying enemy soldiers (both North Vietnamese regulars and Vietcong) and weapons into the Mekong Delta region of South Vietnam. Boats warned us that there was a twenty-five percent chance we would get ourselves into a firefight attempting to interdict a riverboat carrying enemy soldiers. If we did, we were to follow his orders or the orders of the next in command, the coxswain. He explained that to conserve ammunition, we should allow the two machine gunners to lead the firefight and then we would be brought into the fray. In any contact with the enemy, we were to keep our heads below the gunwales until ordered to return fire. When returning fire, we should set our weapons for single or three-shot auto-bursts, briefly exposing our heads only when firing.

"We don't want any heroes here, men. Our job is to knock out the enemy, destroy his weapons and boats, and return safely to base," said Boats.

I looked at the Navy crewmen on the PBR and wondered how long they had been engaged in this hazardous contribution to the war effort. With the exception of Boats, all looked to be between the ages of twenty and twenty-five. They wore green camouflage clothing and steel pot helmets. The serious expressions on their faces made it apparent they had experienced several of these missions. I wondered again what the attrition rate was, particularly for the gunner's mates, as we motored upriver at about twenty knots. Our large wake created problems for the smaller Vietnamese riverboats that we passed. Some of them shipped water over their gunwales from the rolling wake, and they were forced to stop and bail the water out before continuing.

We cruised for about half an hour, passing more than a hundred riverboats varying in length from twelve-foot open dugouts to forty-foot inboard-motor crafts that were hauling a variety of cargo to unknown destinations. To our untrained eyes, it was impossible to tell if any of those boats carried enemy soldiers and/or weapons. The gunner's mates kept their machine guns trained on each boat as we passed by, fully prepared to fire on them if only slightly provoked. Almost without exception, the riverboats carried women and children, fully visible, along with their roosters and piglets. Sometimes the children would wave happily to us, but most just paused from their play and watched us with serious dark eyes filled with youthful curiosity. I wondered if the women and children were there solely to mask the real cargo out of sight below the gunwales. Boats stood with the coxswain in the steel cockpit area as we steered among the boats, never slowing down to inspect one.

At about 2:45 P.M., the engines of the PBR slowed, and the coxswain steered the boat toward the heavily forested southern shoreline. When the forward gunner pointed out something, the engines were brought to an idle, the transmission was shifted into reverse, and we began to back in toward the shore, where tree limbs hung over and touched the water. We backed directly through the limbs into a small cut in the bank at the mouth of a little hidden estuary. As in a tunnel, the light beneath the trees was quite dim, and we were protected from being seen from the river as the branches closed behind our bow. The hide was excellent.

The crewmen tied ropes off the bow and stern to low, sturdy tree branches and the engines were shut down. I felt like we were in a green womb. Boats ordered the five of us out to patrol the area along the bank. He gave us whistle signals to use to indicate when we were returning through the deep underbrush to avoid being shot by friendly fire. John Schneider and I moved upriver, while our three other teammates patrolled downstream. We found nothing of concern, and about forty minutes later, after signaling our return with the proper whistles, we reboarded the PBR.

Boats said we were going to sit and wait for a strike, which meant we were going to watch the river traffic until he felt that one of the boats on the river looked suspicious and might be carrying men or weapons. The forward gunner's mate and the coxswain, carrying M1 carbines, disembarked and moved over to the riverbank for a clear view of the traffic. Boats sat on a stool by the steering wheel and engine controls, while the rest of us lounged on the deck in the small cabin.

The mosquitoes were ferocious, and apparently fearless, extracting blood from our faces, hands, and necks. We spread Avon cream all over our exposed surfaces, which helped a little. It was hot and humid, and all of us were sweating profusely. I wished I were a youngster again back at Camp Robinhood in Maine, enjoying sixty-five-degree breezes while sailing with fellow campers on Penobscot Bay out of the Bucks Harbor Yacht Club. But in Vietnam, sheltered in the womb of trees and shrubs, there was no breeze, and so we continuously dripped sweat onto the floorboards.

I never grew used to the heat and humidity in Southeast Asia. I could lose up to five pounds of water a day from sweating, without exerting myself at all. Along the rivers, if you clapped two slices of bread together, enough mosquitoes could be trapped between the slices to make a meaty meal. Of course, there was always the threat of malaria from the mosquitoes. You did not have to eat them to catch that disease, which could put you out of commission for three to twelve weeks. We took quinine tablets regularly to combat catching the disease.

Just before 4:15 P.M., the coxswain and gunner's mate came scrambling back along the bank of the estuary toward the PBR. Boats spotted them and lit off both engines. The coxswain told Boats what they had seen, and I overheard him say over the hum of the idling engines, ". . . and all clear upstream." The other gunner's mate and the engineman quickly untied the mooring ropes from the over-hanging tree branches as the lookouts jumped aboard. Just as we had all settled at our stations, Boats advanced the throttles and the twin engines roared, launching us out through the tree branches and into the river. Fifteen yards out from the riverbank the coxswain, who had taken over the controls from Boats, pushed the throttles full forward and within a few seconds we were accelerating down-river at thirty knots. Suddenly I heard the sound of distant automatic gunfire and our bow machine gun opened up full with a barrage of .50-caliber bullets. Once you hear it, you never ever forget the sound of a .50-caliber machine gun firing on automatic with its awesome power. The coxswain swung the bow to the right in a hard turn at full speed, which then brought our stern machine gun into a clearer field of fire, and the .30s opened up. With both machine guns fir-ing, the sound was so loud that we had to protect our hearing by sticking our fingers in our ears. As we pressed ourselves against the steel armor below the gunwales, we felt enemy bullets, which had penetrated the wooden hull, slamming against the interior armor plating less than an inch from our prone bodies. That will put real fear into any human being! Several bullets also hit the armor around the cockpit of the PBR and ricocheted as we made a full-cir-cle turn away from the riverboat we were chasing and again came up from behind the vessel.

For at least four minutes the firing went on and we kept waiting for Boats to order our team to return fire. I silently prayed that that order would not come anytime soon, because there was so much lead flying through the air in our direction. I wondered with some fear if I would catch the "golden B-B" when I raised my head above the gun-wales to return fire. Above the sound of the machine-gun fire from the enemy riverboat I could hear the automatic fire of small arms, and the branches and leaves of the makeshift roof above us began to disintegrate from enemy bullets. Pieces of the bamboo curtains and leaves rained down on us. I was concerned that if we took some hits at or below the waterline we could flood and sink. Our machine gunners poured out lead until Boats suddenly gave the order to cease fire. The coxswain throttled the engine back to near idle.

"Okay, men, you can take a look now, but don't stand up. We'll hang around for a few minutes and then sink 'em," said Boats through the slit in the aft cockpit armor.

I raised up slowly, nose first, and peaked over the port rail at the object of our attack. The enemy riverboat was about thirty-five feet long, painted white. Part of the bow had been blown off, and the homemade superstructure was nearly all blown away. There were at least twenty dead bodies hanging over the gunwales or lying on the small deck, their blood draining over the white painted freeboard of their boat. I noted a few bodies floating in the water were being carried downstream, along with the riverboat, whose engines were stopped. I guessed that more bodies had already sunk into the river's depths. No human moved on that boat—it appeared all were dead. We slowed, made a wide 360-degree turn, and again approached the riverboat from its stern. Boats told us to free-fire if we observed any movement. We didn't. The bow gunner's mate kept the .50 trained on the boat as we approached. Once alongside, the rest of the carnage came into view. There must have been fifteen more men lying dead on the floorboards of the boat, some shredded into pieces by our machine guns. I noted the muddy water around the riverboat was becoming reddish in color. Covered by our weapons, our engineman hopped aboard the riverboat with two hand grenades, which he armed and dropped below the floorboards into the bilge. Scrambling back aboard our PBR, the gunner immediately lay prone on our foredeck as the coxswain gunned the engines to get us out of the way of anticipated flying debris when the grenades exploded. But no significant debris was thrown as the grenades went off simultaneously. With two large holes blown in its hull below the waterline, the river boat quickly sank in about fifteen to twenty feet of water, leaving a few bodies briefly floating on the surface as final evidence that we had won the skirmish.

As we headed back to the river base, we joked bravely among ourselves about how nice it was to win a firefight without having fired a shot ourselves. Boats came out of the cockpit and sat on the floorboards with us and told some stories of the PBR crew's exploits. One story in particular illustrated an important lesson for us. A PBR commanded by Boats had backed into an estuary along the Mekong River, looking for a strike. They had been in that position for almost two days when the lookouts came scrambling back. The PBR roared out into the river to attack a boat, aboard which the lookouts had spotted several uniformed North Vietnamese regulars casually standing up or leaning on the gunwales. What the lookouts had failed to observe were three other similar riverboats trailing the one being attacked by about a quarter of a mile. As soon as the PBR opened fire on the lead riverboat, the trailing enemy boats sped up and opened fire, immediately killing the unprepared stern machine gunner on the PBR. Hundreds of machine gun rounds had hit the PBR, which, being defenseless from the rear, fled downstream at full throttle. When it came abreast of the first enemy craft, the enemy troops onboard opened fire with machine guns, AK-47s, and every other gun available. The PBR's hull was effectively "air-conditioned" with bullet holes and it returned to the fire base for repairs. Fortunately, it's powerful engines enabled it to easily outrun the enemy boats. But it sank while moored at the dock before crewmen could seal bullet holes at the waterline. When the PBR had been on a plane at full speed, the bullet holes below the armor plating had been above the waterline; however, when the boat slowed to enter the dock area and it came off-plane, the bullet holes at the waterline began to flood. The PBR sank in ten minutes.

Boats was about forty-seven years old, and in my opinion was too old for this kind of service. He said he had been married four times, had four children, and thought he might marry again when he returned to the United States from this tour. He had less than five months left in Southeast Asia, and said that he would probably be assigned to teach river patrol tactics at Little Creek, on his next tour of duty back in the States. Casually he told us that his "hit" rate was about once every fourth mission; and he figured they had "knocked off" about five hundred enemy troops in the last eight months. He had lost two sailors to enemy gunfire and two others had been wounded. We found it amazing that his PBR team had killed five hundred enemy soldiers in eight months, but did not question Boats for fear of offending him. We had just killed between thirty-five and forty enemy soldiers. Most startling to us was Boats's estimate that 1,500 to 2,000 North Vietnamese soldiers were carried into South Vietnam every month along this waterway.

"We kill off about fifty to seventy-five enemy gooks a month and send many tons of their weapons to the bottom of the river as well. But that's just a drop in the bucket. If we could get some air support on the river when we needed it, we'd take out a lot more. The enemy is getting wise to our patrols on the river. They keep their men below the gunwales most of the time, put their women and children up on the foredeck as decoys, so it is getting much tougher to spot boats carrying men and war materials downstream. They already know most of the areas where we hide our PBRs and are prepared for us when they approach those areas. We keep going at this because we figure we save a few American and ARVN lives every time we kill one of the enemy. It is toughest for me when we lose one of our PBR guys on patrol. I ain't much of a writer, but it is my job to write a letter to the family if one of our guys gets killed in action. That's the worst part of this damn job, writing the letter of condolence about a sailor who gets shot up and dies. Wish we'd just bring in some low-yield nuclear weapons and end this war quick."

For an hour we listened to the stories Boats shared with us. He was a fine storyteller with many chilling stories to relate. We listened intently, trying to learn lessons from this seasoned sailor. As we pulled into the docks at the firebase, I stood up and leaned over the gunwale to inspect the hull damage. The port-side hull looked like a piece of Swiss cheese. The fiberglass had more than a hundred holes in it. Boats said it would take two or three days to patch it up and make the PBR like new again. As we disembarked at the dock, I looked at the steel bullet shields attached to the forward machine gun. They had several pockmarks from bullet strikes, and it was difficult to understand why none had passed between the two shields, where the barrels protrude, and hit the gunner.

We ate some canned rations and went to sleep on the floor of a hooch that night. Shortly after 11:00 A.M. the next morning an old H-19 helicopter picked us up and flew us back to Soc Trang. Boats said he was sorry to see us leave the PBR base, because he could always use more firepower. Then he somberly thanked us for allowing him and his men to show off for us. We all agreed Boats was a tough guy, a battle-seasoned professional. Those shredded NVA bodies floating in the water and those hanging over the gunwales were a harbingers of what we had come to pass and what lay ahead.

As we landed on the helipad at our base in Soc Trang, it was noted that no one came out to greet us. Perhaps they were all in the mess hut having supper. We shed our gear, took lukewarm showers, toweled off, put on clean fatigues, and walked over to the mess hut. Only three teammates from the A-team and Bill Dunn were there, and they barely glanced at us as we walked in offering our cheerful greetings. It was immediately apparent that something had gone wrong while we were away.

Bill was sitting at the long table; the food on his plate had not been touched.

"Sit down, fellows, we have some real bad news," he said. We sat down, fully anticipating that Bill would report casualties to our team.

"Ed Brown and Richard Shell, on A-team, went out with the UDTs before dawn this morning to finish off the 70mm recoilless rifle facility on that downstream island. The facility was too heavily guarded, so they decided to abort the mission. During the extraction, they were clobbered by Vietcong gunfire as they followed the UDTs up the bow boarding net. As the medium boat backed out of its mooring Ed and Richard were hit by several rounds, and killed, according to the coxswain. We have not been able to recover their bodies and probably won't attempt to do so, because of the unexpected enemy concentration in that area. We figured the Vietcong knew we were coming."

The silence in the room was broken only by the fan buzzing overhead in the hut. I had an overwhelming desire to walk outside and scream and shout to release my emotions. Ed and Richard were the two teammates of FRAM 16 who were my closest friends at that point. And they were gone. There would be no bodies for their families to bury. There would be no finality to their deaths for months or years to come. I could not hold back the tears. I cried quietly, my face buried in my hands, not caring if my teammates found this a sign of my weakness. Two great buddies were dead. Gone.

I became angry; ready to avenge their deaths by killing as many VC as I could find. If the VC had been tipped off as to the arrival of the UDTs and our A-team, I wanted to find out which of the South Vietnamese who worked on our base was the culprit. I silently vowed that if this spy was found, I would pull him up the flagpole by his heels and slowly, very slowly, skin him like a deer; except that I would skin him alive. I wanted to make it hurt. I was ready to torture in animal-like revenge.

The deaths of these friends brought about my first true realization that though we were well trained, we were not immortal, as perhaps I had originally felt. For some reason, the death of Larry had not affected me in this way. I cannot explain why.

Bill ordered in helicopters to take us to Saigon for a three-day R&R. I needed the rest, but the loss of my teammates was like a hard punch in the stomach every morning when I woke up. I did not enjoy the R&R. None of the team did. We went to a few girlie bars; John played tennis; the rest of us window-shopped, drank beer, and slept. I wrote letters to Ed and Richard's parents. They were long letters, which I later threw away and rewrote in a shorter form, because I felt the first letters were too emotional in explaining our team's sorrow over their deaths; and too much detail was offered attempting to explain why we had not recovered their bodies.

I remembered the comments expressed by Boats on how difficult it was for him to write those letters to the families of "riverines" who had been killed. There is no book that explains how to write these letters. How do you find the right words to explain to proud parents that their son was killed by enemy bullets halfway around the world, and we couldn't even send them a body to bury? Three years earlier, most Americans had never even heard of Vietnam. Yet here we were, fighting a tough, experienced enemy, while we were just now beginning to question why we were really fighting.

Following the loss of Ed and Richard, I became aware that none of us was as close to each other in brotherhood or camaraderie as we were before. The mutual trust was still there, but everything seemed more serious. It was a state of mind and being in which you are so devastated by the unexpected, violent death of someone very close to you that you protect yourself from having that hurt occur again. Hence, you put some distance between yourself and your teammates in an effort to circumvent the impact of the hurt if you lose them. Many months later, after returning to the States and my home, I debated whether to call Ed's and Richard's parents. I decided not to, using the rationale that they had been through enough tragedy, and my call would only awaken their bereavement. Nearly thirty years later now I regret not having made those telephone calls when I returned from Southeast Asia. They may have wanted very much to talk with me about their sons, and I never gave them the chance.

Chapter 5

Chance Discovery of a POW Camp

In a military ground action, some soldiers prefer to operate as part of a platoon or larger group of combatants supported by air and artillery units. They take comfort in numbers and firepower. FRAM 16 team members strongly preferred to operate alone, or with no more than a five-man team. In spite of my 6'2", 175-lbs. frame, I could hide from the enemy; surprise and kill him, then evade his support elements and escape from harms way. All of us believed we could outthink and outsmart the enemy—if alone or in a small-unit of competent fighters. Our training in small unit tactics had been excellent. Admittedly, I never experienced, nor received training in, patrols or maneuvers with a large number of soldiers; however, it was our belief that a large group draws attention, because it cannot move with the stealth of a smaller group. Furthermore, a small team can usually stay together and not get strung out in an area of operations. Hence, we did not run into the constant problem of having to account for one another and also run the risk of having to rescue a squad that had become separated from the main body. As we patrolled, we always knew where each team member was at any moment.

However, if the objective is to take on a large number of the enemy in order to clear a particular piece of real estate of enemy presence, you usually need to engage with larger numbers of combat troops on your side, with air and artillery support to get the job done effectively.

In a firefight with the enemy, it is human nature to protect yourself by concentrating with the rest of your team and confronting the enemy with a withering rate of firepower, trying to intimidate and kill. The members of FRAM 16 were taught to operate differently, using small-team tactics and logic. Because we were operating in unfriendly territory, miles from any support and resupply source, ammunition was limited to what we could efficiently carry in our vests and backpacks.

We endeavored to accomplish our intelligence-gathering missions by stealth and cunning without engaging the enemy. However, firefights could not always be avoided. Ambushes, though thankfully infrequent for us, happened on occasion. The strategy was to secure the best information we could and to extract ourselves as soon as possible, using our ammunition only if necessary.

Another of our many apprehensions was discovering, during an insertion by helicopter into an area, that we were inserted into the wrong area of operations (AO)—perhaps in the midst of an enemy concentration. This never happened to us (except in our first practice mission), although on one occasion we had been working an area of Laos and suddenly observed what appeared to be well over 250 NVA moving into the area, setting up a large encampment within three hundred yards of our position. We headed to an extraction point with great speed and then reported our observations.

C-team of FRAM 16, my squad at the time, was assigned a mission in September 1966 in which we were to observe riverboats that diverted from the main stream of the Mekong River in eastern Cambodia into an estuary called the Prek Chhlong. Our objective was to locate suspected enemy supply dumps in the area. Aerial photography had recorded a significant number of suspected enemy boats, of twenty-five to thirty feet in length, departing the Mekong and navigating east, up the Prek Chhlong; however, the riverboats quickly disappeared in the estuary beneath a canopy of trees. Hence, it was impossible to establish how far the riverboats traversed the estuary, and where they unloaded cargo. Old maps of this area led intelligence analysts to believe the estuary was sufficiently navigable to permit riverboats to travel within five miles of the Cambodian border with South Vietnam. While some of the riverboats traversing the Prek Chhlong were engaged in legitimate commerce, an unknown number were suspected of carrying soldiers and supplies for the North Vietnamese and Vietcong war effort.

At this point in the Vietnam conflict, the U.S. command would not authorize our fighter pilots to strafe or bomb in Cambodia. We knew it was against the 1962 Geneva Accords for American soldiers to be in areas west of the Vietnam border. But the North Vietnamese never respected the Geneva Accords. They constantly used Cambodia and Laos as havens for resupply, escape and evasion, and battle preparations. We heard it was estimated there were more than ninety thousand North Vietnamese troops in Laos and Cambodia during the latter part of 1966. From time to time South Vietnamese pilots were brought in to do the bombing and strafing where needed west of the South Vietnamese border.

Based on a compilation of intelligence reports, U.S. military leaders at MACV headquarters in Saigon believed there was a huge stockpile of weapons, munitions, and food somewhere near the head waters of the Prek Chhlong. The stockpile was believed to be proximate to the Ho Chi Minh Trail in this area of Cambodia. C-team was selected to pull the recon to confirm this belief and to prepare a plan to chart the location in order to improve the odds of a successful air strike. As operatives of the CIA we were not American soldiers, and somehow this exempted us from the Geneva Accords. This was just a part of the many aberrant games played in this conflict.

Ben White, John Schneider, George Townsend, Tom Reed, and I climbed aboard a new, unmarked, Air America Huey helicopter early on a Sunday morning. From a firebase near Song Be, South Vietnam, we flew northeast at 4,500 feet, shortly crossing into Cambodia to an LZ about eight miles west of Sre Khtum. The Ho Chi Minh Trail was about twenty-five miles or so farther east of our LZ.

The helicopter once again made two false insertions before we jumped out at 6:15 A.M., and then it made another false insertion after leaving us. These tactics were to confuse the enemy if they had been attracted to the sound of the helo. As the helo hovered three feet above the tall grass and marshland, we exited and dashed twenty yards toward the trees to our north. Spacing ourselves fifteen yards apart, each within sight of the next man down the line, we threw our bodies to the ground beneath the canopy of trees with our weapons ready to fire. We could faintly hear our helo departing in the distance. Then it was quiet. Very quiet.

As I hit the ground I inhaled deeply, and a mosquito or some other winged varmint was sucked up my nose. Involuntarily, I sneezed before I was able to grab my nose to stifle the sound. It was not a loud sneeze, but John and Tom scowled toward my direction. I grabbed my nose and pinched it tightly, alternately sliding my thumb up and down the outside of my nostril, attempting to squash the unsuspecting critter in my nasal passage. I was not going to attempt to daintily blow the bug out of my nose and risk sneezing again. Plus, a gentleman's handkerchief was not on my checklist of equipment for this patrol.

We lay in position for fifteen minutes, not moving as we listened for any sign that the enemy might have heard the sound of the helicopter and were maneuvering in our direction. It was John's turn in the rotation to be our pointman. I was to operate from the rear of our short column as we maneuvered toward the Prek. Ben was designated squad leader for this mission. As we set off toward the river, I walked backward and sideways to watch for an attack from the rear of our squad. All five of us moved from cover tree to cover tree in short sprints; never were all of us moving between trees in the open at the same time. This was a measure to prevent a major loss of life if we were ambushed.

We patrolled toward the river for a distance of about three and a half miles through moderately dense forest and underbrush. For most of the patrol it was impossible to see more than twenty-five yards in any direction because of the dense vegetation. We avoided the few trails we found because of the possibility of ambush or booby-trap. It was difficult to patrol silently in the underbrush.

About 9:30 A.M. we could smell the Prek Chhlong River mud, and by 9:45 A.M. we could hear the distant drone of a riverboat's engine as it cruised along the river. Just before 10:30 A.M. we reached the banks of the Prek. After ninety minutes of patient observation, we had seen three riverboats go by. Only two boats were of sufficient size to be carrying supplies or soldiers. From our vantage point we could not see what they were carrying belowdecks. Shortly, a hand signal was passed by Ben, and we retreated about forty yards back into the underbrush for a strategy meeting.

"There's nothing we can see on those boats. We need to patrol farther east along the river until we can find the location of the supply dumps, if there are any out here," said Ben.

I interrupted, suggesting we first attempt to observe the cargo being hauled by these boats before patrolling upstream. It appeared obvious to me that if we saw no troops or war materials aboard these boats, there would be less chance of the existence of a stockpile upriver. The others agreed, except Ben.

Of all my teammates in FRAM 16, I respected Ben's judgment the least. He was the oldest, shortest in stature, the most aggressive, and in my opinion had the least common sense of the group. In the team leader rotation, it was Ben's turn to lead the patrol. He frequently issued orders as though he were a Marine platoon leader and we were a bunch of green troops right out of basic training. Moreover, he sometimes made snap decisions—not thinking through the details, influences, options, and derivatives that should have been part of his decision-making processes. The rest of the team members had a more collegial style of leadership.

Because the intelligence data we had on this area was limited to aerial photographs, there was no certainty of our finding an enemy supply cache; it was only a suspicion of someone in a command position who was willing to expend a few lives to prove or disprove the suspicion. If we found the supply dump or a massing area for enemy troops, then the person who ordered the reconnaissance would take credit for generating a successful mission. There sometimes appeared to be no command consideration of the level of risk in ordering a recon. But if the recon was ordered and the team was wiped out, there would probably be no reprisal directed at the officer who conceived of or ordered the mission. I was beginning to realize how truly expendable we were as human participants in an irrational war—as all wars are. It was a serious game being played, with human lives on the line. Loss of life in combat is expected, and people issuing orders often appear to be callous to this. For these reasons and many others, the FRAM 16 team members fought for each other—total unit integrity—not for anyone else, not even for the glory of the United States of America.

I was successful in prevailing over Ben's plan by arguing that there was no logical reason for trying to locate the supply dumps if the boats were just carrying foodstuffs to be sold or traded to noncombatants. Ben was a team member and a good fighter, and I hesitated to undermine him when he was in the lead capacity. Two months later he was killed during a helicopter extraction from a recon mission with Paul Johnston and John Schneider in east-central Laos. I regretted my negative feelings toward Ben when I learned he had died as he climbed onto the helicopter landing skid.

John and I climbed trees above the riverbank and set up an observation post from which we could look down into the boats. When I was approximately forty feet above the forest floor I realized I still could not get an adequate view of the riverboats because other tree limbs blocked the scene. I climbed back down, quickly found another more suitable tree, climbed up and waited, watching everything that moved on or beside the river. The remaining team members lay in the undergrowth, covering approaches to our positions. We remained in position for nearly two hours but observed no type of cargo in the larger riverboats that would lead us to believe there would be a stockpile of war materials farther east on the river. Two boats had tarpaulins or bamboo screens covering parts of the lower deck, and we could not see what lay beneath. Neither type of screen seemed to cover a large enough area of either riverboat to be suspicious.

At 3:10 P.M. I climbed down from the tree and joined the rest of the team for a second meeting. John and I reported what we had seen. Ben strongly suggested we should extract early the next morning and have the helicopter insert us again farther east, if we could find a decent LZ. The rest of us argued against the need for a reinsertion, since we had not seen any riverboats carrying war materials or troops aboard. Finally, it was agreed that our observation sample of boats over a two-hour period was insufficient to judge whether there was a cache of weapons or massing of soldiers farther upriver. We all agreed to work a second insertion after we went over the maps and aerials again. Based on the number of boats that were exiting from the Mekong and traversing to some point on the Prek Chhlong River, we believed something significant was going on and we decided to find out what.

George Townsend transmitted to an orbiting unmarked helicopter the extraction coordinates for a 6:15 A.M. pickup and reinsertion the next morning. We retreated to the edge of the forest near our selected extraction point and broke out rations—our first food since we had departed from Song Be that morning.

About 5:25 that afternoon, as we were relaxing in the underbrush, I heard a gentle hissing sound. I looked up the line to George's prone position. He had his left arm stretched toward my position and his hand showed four fingers. As we had been taught, in situations where we were in a general perimeter setup, with each person looking in a different direction, twelve o'clock was always north. So three o'clock was east, six was south, and nine o'clock was west. Obviously, when patrolling we were ever cognizant of which direction was north in relation to our immediate position. On seeing the signal from George, I instantly rolled from my sitting position into a prone position, signaled four fingers to John, and prepared to fire my Stoner. I looked out into the direction of four o'clock, into a marshy field beyond the edge of the tree line, slightly south of east.

With his neck outstretched and nose held a few inches from the ground, sniffing, a mongrel dog observed us. We moved not a hair. Neither did the dog. He obviously had picked up our scent (our body odors were nearly rancid by now) and I was convinced he had seen me move to a prone position. All that was needed to expose our position was for the dog to start barking at the five green-painted monsters in the forest. Seconds later a young Cambodian boy wearing only tan shorts, came running along the edge of the forest. He passed the pointing dog, calling to it as he sprinted by. The dog promptly broke his point and ran to catch up with the boy, leaving us much relieved that we would not have to deal further with the situation. If the boy had discovered us, we would have tried to catch him, taped his mouth, and tied him to a tree. We would have had to monitor him all night, carry him out to the helicopter, and release our little detainee just prior to boarding the helo. At Ben's signal we moved farther back into the forest for better cover.

Each of us looked forward to darkness, when we could relax slightly. Meanwhile, I lay back and played my usual game of visualizing my family, women, past sporting events, my fraternity days, and anything else that would help pass the time. We did not get together in small groups to talk, preferring to maintain distance between us in case we were accidentally discovered and a firefight ensued. I fought to prevent more thoughts about what we were doing there, what we were being used for, or anything relating to the fighting in Southeast Asia. Those stressful thoughts continued to creep into my head, and I valiantly tried to sublimate them.

It rained on us that night. The rain exploded on us so quickly, we were soaked to the skin before we could break out ponchos. When you wear a poncho, the air does not circulate well, and we would sweat, soaking ourselves further. We endured the rain, ate some more rations, and waited for the helicopter to arrive in the morning. At least the rain drowned the damned mosquitoes.

Two minutes before the scheduled extraction I could hear George talking on the radio to the helo pilots. He had moved to the edge of the tree line. Seconds later I could hear the distant *whomp-whomp-whomp* of the rotors as the helo honed in on George's signal. George threw a canister of red smoke into the field, and the helicopter pilot acknowledged visual contact. As the helo arrived and hovered a few feet off the ground, we raced out in a line, hopping onto the landing skid and settling into the seats on the helicopter deck.

Each of us dreaded that brief period of time during extraction—between the moment of rushing out to jump aboard the helicopter and the time when the helo reached a safe altitude, beyond the reach of most small-arms fire. The skin of a helicopter is made of a magnesium-and-aluminum alloy, offering no protection from enemy small-arms fire. Enemy bullets could penetrate the skin as though it were papier-mâché. Furthermore, a single 7.62mm bullet from an AK-47 rifle hitting a rotor blade of the helicopter could easily unbalance or break the blade. Even if only a small piece of the rotor is knocked off by a bullet, the centrifugal balance of the rotor system could be lost, especially if the piece is blown off near the tip of a rotor blade. The extreme vibration generated by the loss of centrifugal balance would usually cause the complex rotor cam system to simply break apart. The usual result of such an incident was the loss of everyone onboard, unless the pilot had time to autorotate and crash land. Whatever the case, when bullets flew at such a large target, someone aboard was bound to get killed. All it might take to bring a helicopter down was one bullet (one "golden B-B").

Ben was onboard first, and he scrambled up between the pilots, handing them the map marked to indicate our next point of insertion. I was the last to climb onboard, and instantly the helicopter lifted about ten feet, turned ninety degrees, and began its full-power ascent. As we gained altitude we headed north directly, away from the direction in which we would reinsert. We circled in a five-mile arc before coming back toward the new LZ, and did two false insertions before we landed around 6:40 A.M. in a position some six miles east of our landing zone of the previous day, and on the south side of the river. We were then three miles south of the Prek Chhlong River, four miles west of the Cambodian village of Sre Khtum. Most of the ground underfoot at our landing zone was a watery bog. We sank into the bog just above our high-top black basketball shoes, then slogged along trying to quickly reach firm ground from which we could maneuver and find cover. Within thirty seconds we were out of the clearing and into the cover of the trees. We spread out and waited for ten minutes, but neither heard nor saw anything.

Dark cumulonimbus clouds were gathering to the north, and we were in for what appeared to be another drenching rain. Actually, rain would aid in masking our patrol, deadening sounds we might inadvertently generate in the forest and washing away our footprints. We had a love-hate relationship with the rain. This time it worked in our favor.

The four of us crouched around Ben and his map to orient ourselves before heading out in a northeasterly direction to find the river. Several times we had to circumnavigate huge stands of impenetrable bamboo, which grew so thick and unyielding that no human could pass through them. With all the shunting around the bamboo barriers, elephant grass fields, and other natural barriers, problems obviously arose. One was orientation, and another was time. The process of dead reckoning, using map and compass, is complicated when the line between the landing zone and the objective is spoiled by having to dodge those natural barriers, departing from the straight line. Accurately establishing how far you have traveled off the desired line often becomes quite difficult, especially when you have no topographic maps or aerial photographs. The calculation of time, rate, and distance (d=rt) is further exacerbated by the time taken to rest, to assess the terrain, and to recon for possible enemy entrapments or booby traps, each adding enormous amounts of guesswork in dead-reckoning navigation. We knew we would intercept the Prek if we simply moved in a general northernly direction. But it was important in this patrol to move in a direction that was about fifteen degrees west of north, because of the possibility of running into Cambodian "residential" development on the southern banks of the Prek Chhlong.

John had the point this time. We had patrolled about two miles when I saw him crouch quickly, his right hand raised, signaling the rest of us to crouch. We froze in position and waited beside a large stand of bamboo, which we had been working around in knee-high grass. Minutes later John indicated by hand signals that he was moving ahead alone and wanted the rest of us to conceal ourselves in the bamboo. We took advantage of the break to rest and to drink some water from our canteens. Shortly after I heard a double hiss from George, who was next in line ahead of me, and we left the bamboo, remaining in a crouch. John came back in a crouching jog, and we each fell into line behind him as we retreated about thirty yards to assess whatever it was that he had seen.

"*Bingo!* I think we've hit on an incredible find," said John in a hushed voice. "We have a POW [prisoner of war] camp in the clearing ahead—about two hundred yards from here. There are armed North Vietnamese all over the place, maybe ten to fifteen that I could see. I saw three bamboo cages with what I estimated to be from four to five people in each cage. About thirty yards east of the cages is a long hooch that is probably used as the command center, living quarters, and supply storage area. More NVA could have been inside the hooch. I could not see the faces of the men in the cages, but two of them were wearing olive drab, one-piece flight suits. I am sure of that. They looked tall enough to be American pilots, but I could not be certain. Again, I couldn't see faces clearly. I think we should recon this place for the next couple of days and plan a way to free the prisoners. I don't know if they have any perimeter defense, but I got within ten yards of the clearing and saw no perimeter guards."

We were all quite excited at that point, hoping we might be able to rescue some Americans and get them home. That would give us all tremendous satisfaction. There was no question that if we could keep the element of surprise, our team of five men could easily take out ten to fifteen NVA. The first tasks, however, were to determine how many guards there really were, and what the surrounding area held in terms of reinforcements for the prison guards. If we discovered reinforcements, we would have to call for support, and there was no telling how long that might take.

Chapter 6

Extraction from Ring of Fire

In the first stage of our plan to rescue the POWs, we moved to observation positions around the camp, to watch and make notes of the times of everything that happened within our view. Our recon had to be a *total assessment*. We not only had to know everything we were up against in terms of the enemy's defenses, but we had to do several things flawlessly. We had to check distances from one point to another; determine whether there were any potential areas holding minefields by observing the routes walked by the guards; determine the number and physical condition of the prisoners; know the location of each prisoner; plan the location of landing zones for extraction helicopters; know the distance to the nearest enemy reinforcement camp; determine the types and number of enemy guns; and more. We had to determine all of this information in order to organize a safe, rapid extraction of every prisoner and get ourselves out of there. It was unlikely any of our soldiers would be authorized to come to our rescue or support. American soldiers were not supposed to be where we were and we preferred not to request help from the South Vietnamese. We had never patrolled in situations like this with the South Vietnamese. Our training in small-unit tactics made us all comfortable working as a team, knowing what each one of us would do in any given circumstance. There could be no language barrier when communicating the tactics of this mission. We used our own unique set of hand signals and field of fire procedures, and employed other techniques using our own SOP (standard operating procedure). These techniques, though not particularly complex, could not be quickly taught to others, especially the South Vietnamese. There was no margin for error in the game of guerrilla warfare.

At 1:20 P.M. we moved into our planned observation positions. It was raining again.

Using my binoculars, I concentrated on the prisoners in the cages. They were shaded by the bamboo tops of their cages and by overhanging tree limbs. The NVA had hidden the cages well from the cameras used in aerial photography. Three small huts, each manned by two or three guards, were out in the open area. The guards on duty sat in these huts on rough-hewn stools, chain-smoking cigarettes, chatting, and laughing among themselves. Every hour or so, another guard would come out to the hut, say a few words, bring water or food, and move on to the next hut.

Very slowly, I scanned every inch of the tree line around the open area of the camp. Suddenly I saw movement. It was an NVA guard who walked out of what I realized was a camouflaged fourth guard hut containing two other NVA guards, that I had not seen before. The hut was partially hidden from my view by one of the prisoner cages and by a tree trunk. I rolled several turns to my left to gain a better view of the hut, which did not appear to be oriented toward any prisoner cage; rather, it was oriented toward the open field area to my left, away from the cages and the enemy operations hooch. Observing the actions of the guards, I could see they were watching over the open field area, which looked to be a rectangle of about seventy-five feet by one hundred feet. It quickly became clear to me that there might be prisoner cages below the surface of the ground, out in the field. I had heard about these methods of imprisonment in casual conversations with Air America pilots in Udorn. The grass in the field, on closer binocular inspection, had been bent or cut down in a wide area.

At 4:00 P.M., my suspicions were confirmed. A prisoner, whom I observed through my binoculars to be an American in a mud-covered flight suit, was dragged out of a subsurface cage by his flight suit collar. The prisoner struggled to stand up. It was obvious that he had been in a cramped position for a long time. His legs simply would not work when he tried to stand up, and the North Vietnamese guard cruelly kicked and jabbed the prisoner in the ribs with his rifle muzzle, and shouted at him as he struggled. The prisoner could only crawl. It was a pathetic sight. Each time he tried to stand, his left leg would crumble and he fell to the ground. The guard would kick and jab him, and the prisoner would try again. He was just too weak to do anything, and I was becoming violently angry at the cruelty of the scene. One of our own was being brutalized, and I was totally frustrated that I couldn't do anything about it for the time being. I vowed to personally execute that SOB guard when the time came. I can still picture that NVA guard's facial features in my mind's eye today.

After about five minutes with the prisoner who was unable to walk, a second guard appeared in the field carrying a ten-foot-long bamboo pole, which was about four inches in diameter. The two guards lashed the prisoner's wrists and ankles to the pole with thin pieces of hemp or vine, then they picked up the ends of the pole and carried the screaming and groaning prisoner like a live hog being carried to slaughter. From the prisoner's screaming, I guessed that he must have a broken limb or something equally painful, and the way he was being carried caused him great pain. I was certain my teammates had seen the same thing from their scattered positions around the complex. It was all I could do to hold my fire. Part of me also wanted to put the poor prisoner out of his misery, but I quelled those thoughts and watched the guards carry the hog-tied pilot into the operations hooch.

From my position, I had counted twenty-seven guards or soldiers in all. I might have counted a few twice; however, it was better to err on the high side than underestimate enemy strength. They moved in and out of the operations hooch, and at about 5:00 P.M. I saw a soldier walk out on the porch. He appeared older than the others I had observed, perhaps thirty-five to forty years old. He had red patches on the epaulets of his tan shirt, and some metal insignia was affixed to the epaulets. It occurred to me that this soldier might be the commanding officer of the POW camp. Minutes later, the

American prisoner who had been carried into the hooch was carried out again on the bamboo pole. No longer was he screaming. His head hung back, and it was obvious he was unconscious. I wondered if he was dead as a result of an interrogation by the NVA. The soldiers dragged him to one of the aboveground bamboo cages. Opening the cage door, the NVA soldiers stood back and pointed their weapons at the other prisoners in the cage and motioned to them to take the injured American prisoner back into the cage. I got a clear view of the three prisoners who came out to pick up the prisoner. They were Caucasian, most certainly Americans, wearing olive drab flight suits. They carried their fellow captive into the cage and a guard again locked the door.

My feelings after observing this deplorable treatment of a fellow American were anger, deep frustration, and a strong desire to retaliate. It did not matter that I did not know that American victim. My feelings were far stronger than those felt when a fellow football teammate received a cheap shot from an opposing player. It was more like the feelings I would expect to have if I observed some big fellow hitting my little sister. I wanted to kill, and I had the power in my hands to do so. But I would have to wait for that opportunity.

At 5:20 P.M. the sun had dropped below the trees that surrounded the camp, and I decided to move out to our predetermined gathering place. I moved in a crouched run from tree to tree, approximately twenty yards from the clearing into the jungle. Patrolling the clearing took about thirty-five minutes. Linking up with my teammates was achieved with hand signals—no more would we use Indian warbles or other sounds from Hollywood movies. We melted back about 150 yards from the clearing and crouched in a small circle to report our individual observations.

From different vantage points, each team member had observed the handling of the American prisoner, and the collective anger was nearly sufficient reason for us to attack that night. Ben, however, exercised his leadership privilege and cautioned us to cool down and get a plan together. The consensus was that we should hold back and observe the activities around the POW camp for one more day, just to be sure we were totally familiar with the daily schedule, the number of NVA soldiers, and their locations. I suggested that we contact our operations control officer that night, advise him of the situation, and make certain we would have at least seven helicopters scheduled to evacuate the prisoners and ourselves. We did not have to ask for gunships to protect the extraction process. That was a given. It would not have surprised us if there were a few fighter aircraft assigned to a nearby holding pattern in the event NVA reinforcements appeared to interfere with our new mission.

From the day's reconnaissance, it was apparent that we could get five helicopters into the open area at one time. The other two helicopters would hold to the north of the POW camp until called in.

John and I lit up the upper sideband high-frequency radio. and spoke cryptically to an operations officer. The ops officer sounded extremely excited at the news of our discovery of a POW camp. We could hear it in his voice as he read back the map coordinates, date, time, and smoke color. The news would probably reach Saigon headquarters within the next five minutes. We passed on the map coordinates and smoke color for the seven helicopters that would be required.

The first five helos would extract the POWs. We overestimated these helos, because we did not know the exact number of POWs who were in the aboveground and belowground cages. The sixth and seventh helos would be directed to land as soon as the field cleared of the other helicopters, and the FRAM 16 team would be extracted in one of these. The one remaining helicopter would be used to evacuate in the event any of the other helicopters had mechanical problems. We were certain the operations and tactical people would be planning the mission for the next several hours.

After eating rations, we spread out for the night. Under the canopy of trees the rain fell in a light patter on our ponchos, and I got a fairly good night's sleep for once.

I awoke at 5:30 A.M. and looked around for a teammate. I saw John still snoozing fifteen yards to my right. Ben was sitting up, having obviously just awakened too, and I crawled over to him. He told me he had thrown up twice and had diarrhea during the night. He did not seem particularly concerned about this. We whispered a few minutes about the plan for the day for and shortly thereafter observed the rest of the team awakening. It was amusing to realize that we were all so programmed for a group wake-up time.

We ate rations, drank water, discussed the positions we would man for the day's operations, and reapplied camouflage paste to our faces, necks, arms, and hands. The sun was just coming up and beginning to filter through the jungle canopy. Suddenly a rooster crowed. We all simultaneously snapped our heads in the direction of the sound, rifles at the ready. It was a programmed reaction to any unexpected sound. Seconds later we were all smirking at each other, realizing that every camp and village in Southeast Asia had its chickens.

Chickens were not only a food staple in Southeast Asia; but they were used in cockfights where men would bet money on the cocks. The rear toe, or spur, of a male was fitted with a three-inch-long, thin steel spike. The steel spike was sharpened to a needlelike point, then affixed to the chicken's spur using string, hide, or thin vines. Bets were taken, and the handlers would carry the cocks into a ring formed by the cockfight fans. To arouse the males into a fighting frenzy, one handler would bend the cock's neck to the side and the other handler would hold the opposing cock in a position where it could peck hard, several times, on the exposed neck of the other cock. Then the positions were reversed. This was supposed to make the cocks angry. At this point the handlers would back up a couple of yards, place the cocks on the ground facing each other, and release them. The natural instinct of cocks in battle is to try to dig their natural spurs into their opponent. Obviously, with the sharpened sliver of steel attached, the effect was far more mortally devastating than a cock's natural spur. The last one left standing was declared the winner, and the prize money was distributed. Fights lasted anywhere from thirty seconds to five minutes and were a frequent source of amusement and entertainment for Asians. It was not unusual for a cock to keel over dead moments after being declared the winner. Though illegal, this vile "sport" still goes on in various parts in the United States today.

We knew the sound of the rooster would cause other roosters in the area to start crowing as well, and this would awaken sleeping guards in the main hooch. We moved out silently to our observation positions. Perhaps because the POW camp was so hidden, and because it was in Cambodia, where the NVA certainly did not expect to be discovered by Americans or South Vietnamese soldiers, there were no booby traps such as trip wires or pungy-stick pits around the perimeter of the complex. Clearly, each team member was on careful watch for this type of enemy weapon; thankfully however, there appeared to be none in place.

I moved off about a hundred yards west to a preplanned position. The main hooch was forty yards in front of me, and about thirty degrees to my right. I hid behind a leafy shrub, laid down on the still damp ground, and waited for something to happen. I could observe the yard in front of the hooch, one of the three partially hidden POW cages, and the field where the day before the NVA soldiers had dragged the American pilot out from a belowground cage. From time to time I could hear low tones being spoken inside the hooch. About fifteen minutes after I had taken up my position, an NVA guard walked out on the porch of the thatched-roof hooch and blew two short blasts on a whistle. NVA soldiers came jogging out of the hooch. I counted sixteen of them. The were joined by six others who had been occupying the two small guard shacks near the cages and the shack overlooking the field.

It was 7:30 A.M.

The next frame of the unfolding picture was almost too good to be true. Twenty-two NVA took up positions in two lines, one behind the other. At this point, another NVA walked smartly out of the hooch to a position facing the two lines of soldiers who were standing at attention. Without ordering the soldiers to stand at ease, the leader spoke to them in a nasal, high-pitched voice. He looked at what were probably notes written on a small piece of paper that he held in his hand. The discourse by the superior officer went on for at least ten minutes. I guessed the NVA soldiers were getting their dose of communist political rhetoric for the day. When the superior finished speaking, he saluted his troops; whereupon the troops saluted back and held their salute until the superior had nearly reached the porch of the hooch. Again the whistle blower blew a signal note on his whistle and some of the soldiers departed for the sentry stations, while most went into the hooch, probably to begin cooking.

Soon I could smell the familiar burned stench of overheated co-
conut oil used over and over again to cook food. Several of the NVA
came out on the porch to eat food from their tin cups and talk. When
they were finished, they carried food over to the cages to feed the
POWs. God knows what kind of slop they fed those poor guys. I
watched the two NVA pass cups through the bamboo "bars" to the
eager hands of the prisoners. Then another NVA made the rounds
with gourds of water, placing them just outside the cages where the
POWs could reach through the bamboo bars and dip their cups into
the gourd after they had consumed the food from the cups. They
were akin to animals: very dirty and very hungry and thirsty. I guessed
some had been held long enough that it didn't matter to them what
they ate or drank. I wondered how long those Americans had been
in captivity, and I particularly wondered about their physical and
mental condition.

Because the POW camp was small in area and because there was
no bamboo stockade constructed around the facility, we all agreed
this POW camp was just a "holding" camp in Cambodia. We believed
prisoners, captured across the border in South Vietnam, were held
there until they could be transported to permanent POW camps in
North Vietnam.

Two of the POWs in the cage nearest to my position remained sitting with their backs propped up against the bamboo bars at the back
of the cage. Because the cage was shaded by overhanging tree
branches, it was difficult to see them clearly. I assumed they were ill
or injured and could not get up to receive the food and fill their cups.
The ambulatory POWs fed them and carried water to them. It was
apparent we would have to carry some number of the POWs out of
their cages to the extraction helicopters. If some were mentally ill
from abuse, we might encounter problems just getting them to
come out of the cages. When the helicopters landed, we would have
to have all the POWs out of their cages and loaded on the helicopters
in five minutes or less. The longer it took to load up and extract, the
greater the chance that NVA reinforcements would arrive, especially
if there were any in positions beyond what we had reconned the day
before. I decided that when our team regrouped in the evening, I
would recommend South Vietnamese or U.S. Marine A-1 Skyraiders

be brought in as we were loading POWs, to bomb the entire perimeter of the camp to kill off any infiltrating NVA who may have been attracted by the sound of our helicopters. It would have been hell if we risked our lives to save the POWs only to end up in a firefight and lose some of the POWs or our teammates, including me. I favored being on the safe side while we were in such a very open and vulnerable position during the loading operation.

From my observations I noted that twelve of the NVA soldiers carried 7.62mm AK-47s, eight carried what appeared to be old Enfield .303s, and two were armed with what appeared to be 9mm pistols. Judging from their stature and the ragtag, mismatched condition of their uniforms, it was apparent that these were not regular NVA soldiers. Most looked to be between the ages of twenty and thirty; however, as with most Asians, it was difficult to judge their age, even when you were standing face-to-face with one. Their faces did not seem to age much until reaching at least fifty years of age.

At 2:00 P.M., shortly after a change of the POW guards stationed in the huts, a column of people dressed in the usual black pajamas walked into the field from a path leading from the jungle on the north side of the POW camp. Their entry point was about seventy-five yards from my position. There were eight people in the line, including six in black pajamas and two who were wearing olive drab flight suits, standing several inches taller than the others. I knew immediately that these were newly captured American pilots. Because they approached from the general direction of the Prek Chhlong, I presumed they had parachuted from crippled aircraft somewhere and were brought in by boat from the Mekong River to the POW camp. One of the pilots walked with a stick for a cane and was limping badly.

As they came out of the jungle shadows into the sunlit field, I could see that the left side of the second pilot's face was covered with blood. He stumbled along, and it was obvious that he was in pain, perhaps even delirious.

A guard standing in front of the operations hooch ran up the steps and went inside. He reappeared shortly after and pointed out the approaching column to two other armed NVA guards from the hooch. The two armed guards jogged out to meet the approaching men, and gestured to an unseen point in the field beyond the hooch. The two NVA guards led the column along a path into the field and proceeded to open two cages in the ground, about twenty yards from each other. The pilots were kicked, prodded, and shoved into the cages, which were then locked. The guards returned to the hooch and the black pajama-clad men who had delivered the pilots departed along the same path from which they had entered.

Because of the horrid treatment of these American prisoners, the same anger came over me that I had felt the day before when the NVA guards had carried the POW to the hooch, hog-tied to a bamboo pole. These were my "brothers" being mistreated in total contravention of the Geneva Accords, which governed the handling of prisoners of war. The NVA were clearly acting inhumanely—but so did we at times. I was anxious to get this day over with and hit the NVA guards with a knockout punch. As quickly as possible, I wanted to load the poor POW bastards into helicopters and get them to hospitals where they could be helped by doctors and nurses and restored to health. Every minute we delayed in getting these men extracted increased the risk that one or more of them might die before we could get them to safety. There was no way for any of us to tell what kind of physical ailments the POWs had, but for some it did not look good. I was getting antsy and had to force myself to concentrate on the positive outcome of this unexpected discovery. When we pulled this off we would end the torture and suffering, and prevent the eventual deaths of these pilots at the hands of the NVA. I visualized the game plan for freeing the POWs: the helicopters arriving on time, the freeing of the POWs from their cages, the discovery of more ground cages containing POWs out in the field, the takeoff, and heading to a safe haven.

Nothing particularly eventful was observed for the balance of the afternoon. No prisoners were interrogated. They were fed around 5:00 P.M., having been given no lunch or liquids to consume since breakfast. At 5:30 I wormed my way several yards back into the jungle and began to move cautiously toward our rendezvous point. Ben was already there when I arrived. He was resting against a tree in a sitting position, and he barely acknowledged me with a minor nod of his head. I could have been an enemy soldier sneaking up on him and he would not have given more than a nod. I immediately sensed there was something wrong with Ben.

I said in a hoarse whisper, "Hey, man, what's up?" There was no response. I moved closer to him. The smell was repulsive. There was a puddle of vomit covered with feeding flies next to him, and the stink of diarrhea wafted in my direction. Instantly I knew Ben had either been injured or contracted some form of dysentery. I could not see if his face was pale because of the camo paste he had put on earlier. He tipped his head back against the tree and inhaled deeply. Ignoring the smell, I knee-walked even closer and asked Ben what he needed. He responded, "Brown Bombers, got the dysentery real bad. I'm in rough shape, man. Real weak. Got any Brown Bombers?" In our small first aid kits we usually carried about six pills that we affectionately dubbed Brown Bombers. They were small, light-brown pills prescribed for diarrhea and vomiting. I pulled out my kit, dislodged two of them from the pillbox, and gave them to Ben along with his canteen of water. He was too weak to raise his hand to receive the pills.

John approached during this process, and I quickly explained the situation to him. Both of us knew we would be in trouble without a full complement of our team able to take on the NVA guards and load the POWs. This was a major problem. George and Tom then joined us. I told them I was assuming command in Ben's place, since I was next in rotation for command. I put the two pills inside Ben's half-opened mouth and followed it up by giving him a mouthful of water. He swallowed weakly, and I prayed the pills would get into his stomach and stay there.

I pinched the skin on the top of Ben's left hand. When I released the small clump of flesh it was very slow to return to a smooth position on his hand. From this it was clear Ben was dehydrated. I had to make a decision on whether to try to extract at first light, or get Ben to safety and return some other time to free the POWs. If we went on with this mission, Ben would be a lead weight tied to our ankles. He could not assist us in knocking off the NVA guards, nor could he help load the POWs. Even if we could accomplish this without him, we would have to think about getting him into a position where we could carry him to one of the last helicopters to arrive. If we went on with the mission undermanned, we might fail to get everyone out before enemy reinforcements arrived. Furthermore, without medical attention to inject fluids into Ben's body, we might lose him—worse, he might become delirious during the night and give away our position by shouting.

I had to make some decisions fast.

Directing George and John to pick Ben up, we retreated another hundred yards south to where we could gather in safer cover and discuss our options. En route, Ben developed the "dry heaves" associated with dysentery. He had nothing left to throw up except the pills, but his stomach was contracting as though trying to expel its contents. He tried to keep the heaving sounds muffled, but he could not hold it back. He retched noisily at least a dozen times before the contractions finally subsided. He did not appear to have thrown up the Brown Bombers. All the while I was thinking about the best course of future action.

Leading our short column in retreat, I finally found a small clearing where we could regroup, attend to Ben as best we could, and formulate our plans. John mentioned that in his dehydrated condition Ben had probably lost the desperately needed potassium and other minerals from his system. There were no bananas growing in the area that we knew of, but Tom said he had some potassium tablets in his first aid kit. Bananas are a good way of getting potassium directly into the bloodstream quickly. Potassium pills are coated with a hard red shell and have to be dissolved in the stomach and then find their way into the bloodstream to be effective. We fed three potassium pills to Ben. He had a difficult time swallowing them because they were large and he was too weak to handle the quantity of water needed to float them down his throat. Moreover, the more water we gave him the greater the chance his stomach would begin to contract again, trying to expel the water and pills. Eventually we had to get more liquid into Ben or risk his going into a coma.

My thoughts became preoccupied with the catch-22 nature of our situation. Once the other men from the team had made Ben comfortable, they joined me in a sitting huddle. Obviously we were not going to chance losing Ben. Yet we knew we had to free the prisoners, and we knew we had a fight on our hands to get it done. Tom and George were very concerned that we needed more help to accomplish the objective of freeing the prisoners, since we could not count on Ben to help us. John and I agreed. When one of our number could not participate in an action of this type, it was like having a chair with a missing leg.

With input from the other three, I decided that we needed to engage in a radio communication with operations again. We had to explain the need to bring in additional manpower on the helicopters in order to carry all POWs out to the helos.

My plan, which I discussed with my teammates, involved engaging the NVA guards after they lined up in formation for announcements and political propaganda in the morning. It was finally agreed that there were twenty, possibly twenty-four, guards in total. We could not agree on the exact number of POWs, although we thought the number was between twelve and sixteen including possibly two or three in belowground cages out in the field.

After we killed off the enemy guards, we would immediately call in the Skyraiders, which would be followed by the helicopters from their holding patterns. The first helicopter would bring us six more men to help with the transfer of the prisoners. John and I would be responsible for carrying Ben out of the forest to the last departing helicopter. We refined the plan as the daylight diminished. Soon we could no longer see each other, though we sat only a few feet apart. Those lightweight night-vision goggles were still only marvelous military gizmos of the future.

We radioed our plan to a duty operations officer assigned to monitor our mission. After we had repeated very precise coordinates of our position and a description of the "scene," he indicated that we would get our A1s, helicopters, and reinforcements. We advised him of Ben's failing condition.

At first light we picked up the limp but alive body of Ben and stealthily worked our way back toward the POW camp. Ben had not dry heaved during the night, but was still limp as a wet noodle. The smell of the feces in his trousers lingered in our nostrils. It was 6:45 A.M. when we could first see light between the trees, indicating that the field and the camp were just ahead. Sighting a very large-diameter tree ahead, we carried Ben to that point, figuring I could easily locate that tree and Ben again after the helicopters had arrived.

I debated whether to take Ben's M2 rifle with us in case we needed it, but concluded that if all hell broke loose Ben might be able to use it to defend himself. We had plenty of ammunition.

John raised the operations officer on the radio to confirm that the helicopters were holding three miles south and that the Skyraiders were ready. We received the radio frequencies needed to talk to the waiting pilots. The last words from the ops officer were "Good luck, gentlemen. Out."

We moved quietly into position at 7:05 A.M. and waited for the drama to unfold. My heart was pounding and my adrenaline was flowing. I prayed I had made the right decisions leading up to this moment. If the NVA guards lined up at 7:30 A.M. as they had the day before, the extraction should be completed in ten minutes from that moment, or less . . . if everything worked out as planned.

At 7:30 A.M., on schedule, the NVA guard blew his whistle twice. The guards jogged out of the hooch to their line formation, joined by the soldiers from the guard huts. Then, as before, the superior officer marched out, stood at attention in front of his troops, and began his nasal, high-pitched diatribe. From our earlier plan we knew which of us was required to take out which guards in the formation. As we lay in wait, each of us mentally divided the NVA line up into four groups, which meant that each of us had to concentrate fire on about six NVA and make sure that we hit each of them. To my right was Tom. John and George were lying six feet and fifteen feet to my left. My teammates keyed off me. When I moved my Stoner into position to aim, the others did the same, taking a count of "four," then commencing firing in bursts of three rounds per squeeze of the trigger. At moments like this, there is no time to think about what you are doing. You just concentrate on the job at hand and follow the plan one step at a time. You just *do it* and have no regrets.

Twenty-three NVA went down in less than five seconds of concentrated fire that echoed through the forest. My first volley went into the back and head of the superior officer, followed by three more three-shot bursts into the five NVA guards directly in front of him. When the firing stopped, my next vision was a phenomenon I had never witnessed before: the humid air directly over the shredded bodies of the NVA guards had turned into a pink haze in the morning sun. I did not take time to think about this until later in the day, when I concluded the pink haze had been caused by the vaporized blood of the NVA mixing with the nearly one hundred percent humidity.

John yelled over the radio to bring in the Skyraiders and the helicopters. We leaped from our positions and charged into the open, each of us running directly at those NVA guards who had been the object of our momentary wall of hot lead, shooting single shots at any body that moved or twitched. Our bullets had torn large exit holes in the back of their bodies. When we reached the downed guards a few of the NVA were still moving. We finished the task quickly to prevent them from using their weapons during the POW extraction. Tom ran over to the operations hooch and tossed two fragmentary grenades in the open door in case anyone was inside.

Then John, George, and Tom headed toward the open field and the aboveground cages. I hung back to direct the helicopters inbound, having tossed a can of green smoke into the clearing as we charged out of the jungle. There was no wind to carry the smoke, which was used to indicate whether wind would be a consideration in the direction of landing for the helicopter pilots. I could hear the roar of an aircraft engine, and suddenly a Skyraider appeared overhead at an altitude of about three hundred feet. The jungle to the west exploded into a rolling ball of orange flames, followed by dark gray and black smoke from four napalm bombs. Then the same occurred to the north, the south, and the east, all within seconds of each other. The Skyraiders pulled up, rolled over, and returned for another run, and another. The jungle just disintegrated in a fiery heat all around us. It was a truly awesome sight. Hollywood could not have done it better.

As the fourth Skyraider departed to a holding pattern, a line of helicopters appeared through the smoke above the jungle. It was a beautiful sight. It was an equally splendid sight when I saw four more helicopter gunships commence circling around the POW camp just inside the ring of fire. These helicopters had been ordered in to cover the extraction and put down any enemy reinforcements who might appear. But it was doubtful an enemy platoon would attempt to get through the ring of fire.

My teammates shot out the rusty locks on the three cage doors, while I directed the first five helicopters in to a line-abreast landing. Six American soldiers in unmarked camo uniforms jumped from the lead helicopter and helped to load and buckle in the POWs. The ambulatory POWs helped each other carry those who were unable to walk. I saw Tom enter a cage and pick up one American in a fireman's carry (over his shoulders), and start jogging toward a waiting helicopter. When the thirteen POWs who were in the aboveground cages had been loaded into four helicopters, they took off. I was certain each helicopter carried a medical corpsman aboard to tend to the needs of the POWs as they flew to hospitals in South Vietnam.

Through the smoke hovering east of the POW camp, I saw the four Skyraiders just in case we needed some more heavy-duty fire support. John had given me the HF radio pack, and I called in the last two extraction helicopters. Tom and George had run out into the field with four of our reinforcements to try to locate any of our pilots who were confined in the loathsome belowground cages. They found three occupied cages and had to carry each pilot to the fifth helicopter because none were able to walk unassisted.

At this point I turned around and headed for the forest to find Ben. I would be joined by John when he finished his job in the field. Ben had slumped over from his sitting position where we had left him, lying on his side, not moving. I instantly feared he was dead, but I hoisted him up on my shoulders anyway, and began to jog under his 170-pound body toward the field. It was tough going, and I was relieved when John arrived to carry Ben the remaining fifty yards to the last helicopter, where we joined George and Tom, guarding our extraction. We never saw the support troops again. They had extracted aboard the fifth helicopter with the POWs taken from the belowground cages. We were all out of breath, our lungs heaving following the ordeal.

The copilot of our helicopter was looking back at us over his right shoulder, and I gave him the signal with my thumb to lift off. The modest G-force of the liftoff forced me to lie down on the deck, as I had not had time to buckle into a seat. With both hands I hung on to a piece of tubular steel that supported a sling-seat. We rapidly ascended straight up, then heeled over and raced off to the east toward South Vietnam.

We had freed POWs and could only hope that they all made it to safety, and would physically and mentally recover from their ordeal.

Unquestionably, this mission was one of the highlights of all the missions that I participated in as a member of FRAM 16, and I am certain my four other teammates would agree, if they were alive today. Of both greatest mission value and deeply moving personal satisfaction was the saving of POWs from certain torture and probable death. They would go home to their families after a time of healing in American-operated medical facilities. Those of our team who had direct contact with the POWs, while releasing them from the cages and bringing them to the helicopters, spoke of being kissed, hugged, and thanked profusely, and of the tears of joy that streamed down everyone's faces.

As my own tears fell on the deck of the helicopter, so did my youth. It was an incredibly moving experience for all involved.

We were not informed where the freed POWs were taken in their helicopters; however, they were obviously flown to a major U.S. military medical facility in South Vietnam. We were flown to an unknown base for refueling and immediately on to Udorn Air Force Base.

After two weeks of hospital-administered therapy and medication, Ben recuperated from dysentery and dehydration and rejoined the team. Most important, none of us was injured, wounded, or killed in this action. I found great satisfaction in this success and the rationale for the mission. Moreover, I am certain each member of the team felt unspoken professional pleasure that we had successfully retaliated against our enemy, who had shown no mercy toward the injured and ailing American POWs. For their evil transgressions against other humans, the judgments against and death sentences of the NVA guards were carried out at the hands of FRAM 16.

Bill Dunn met us at Udorn. He was our welcoming committee. He congratulated our team and told us we were real heroes. He said our reward would consist of a big steak and potato dinner with all the booze we cared to consume. Three days later we were allowed to go on R&R for a week in Bangkok, Thailand; each with $100.00 in cash and all other expenses paid by someone unknown to us.

Once again, upon our return from a successful mission, there were no parades, no bands, no medals, no congratulations from the White House, and no articles on our mission printed in U.S. newspapers. We were CIA operatives, and we were operating in a place forbidden under the Geneva Accords. If we had played by the rules and not ventured into Cambodia and Laos, we would never have found the POWs.

Perhaps the most incredible aspect of this mission was that if we had inserted two hundred yards east or west from the point on the second insertion, and/or if our patrol toward the Prek Chhlong had required us to maneuver right or left by only a short distance to avoid large stands of bamboo, underbrush, standing water, or other natural barriers, the POWs would certainly have been transported into North Vietnam, or shot if too sick or injured to make the journey.

Chapter 7

Mission of Abnormal Risk

It was early August 1966. Of the original sixteen men in FRAM 16, ten were dead and six were left to gather in a Quonset hut on a small air base in Nakhon Phanom, Thailand.

The June and July rains had been unusually heavy. The smell of mud, rotten vegetation, and human excrement never left our noses. A-team was exhausted and decimated from a second mission in southern Laos, where they had lost Don Willard and Peter Ragsdale. We were all internalizing the nagging question of our immortality. I guessed I was about the healthiest of our team at that point. My other comrades seemed to have a range of minor injuries that might have precluded mobility in certain maneuvers.

All I wanted was about forty-eight hours of nonstop sleep followed by a dozen thick, juicy hamburgers, two gallons of fresh cow's milk, and I'd be a well-oiled machine again. I had gone too long maintaining mobility and alertness on Dexedrine capsules (nicknamed "Black Beauties") and other pills.

We were planning the next mission out of Nakhon Phanom, overlooking the Laotian border. Some higher-up in Washington wanted to know specifically which nation was supplying SAMs (surface-to-air-missiles) to the North Vietnamese Army (NVA). We were reportedly losing an increasing number of fighter aircraft, including F-102s,

F-105s, F-4s, A-4s, and others, to these surface to air missiles. The NVA were getting better at firing them accurately. The beam-rider guidance system for their SAMs seemed to have improved significantly.

The micromanagers (politicians and military people) of the war back in Washington and in Saigon probably felt that with the risk of just a few lives, they might get the answer and be able to point the finger at the SAM suppliers. Our Washington political leaders were probably thinking that they could win a few propaganda points with the rest of the world if they could name the offensive source of those missiles that were knocking down our planes. In the team's opinion, no one had the guts to tell President Johnson or Secretary of Defense McNamara that such information was not worth the lives that would have to be risked to get the information.

When the word came down that our job would be to find the source of the missiles, Tom Reed, had the best idea.

"Hell, man," he said, "just tell our jet jockeys to look out their damn canopies and read the writing on those Roman candles when they whiz by. Why waste us when they've got those guys already as close as anyone will ever get to the SAMs?" We all chuckled and agreed out loud with Tom.

Steve Williamson, our resident brain trust, a graduate of Cal Poly, posed another question that had no answer.

"Why does anyone care who is manufacturing and delivering those SAMs? They are successfully being used to knock out our fighter aircraft every day. Someone just needs to go in and blow up every SAM site in North Vietnam, and when they build more, knock 'em out again. Finding out the source country—obviously it's either China or Russia—doesn't stop the SAMs from carrying out their functions!" This time there were no comments from around the room. Each of us retreated into our own thoughts. There were no hotheads in FRAM 16.

Silently, however, each of us worried about the risks involved with trying to get close enough to a North Vietnamese launch site to see the markings on the SAMs. What if there were no markings on the missiles? Those SAM sites were all heavily guarded and trapped. It might be just our luck to get all the way into a SAM site, only to find out there were no markings.

Doc Peterson, an internist working for MACV, gave each of us a thorough physical examination around 12 August. One at a time, we allowed ourselves to be poked and prodded, fingered and felt. He listened to our tickers and groped us all over.

Bill arrived from MACV headquarters, Saigon, in the early afternoon of 16 August with the briefing outline for the mission. He was dressed casually in starched khaki pants, the usual blue oxford button-down shirt, rubber-soled brown shoes, and a brown leather belt—no jacket, no tie. Beneath his armpits were large rings of sweat that likely were the result of being on an Air America DC-3 (C-47) that had no air-conditioning for the comfort of its passengers while taxiing. Bill opened the briefing by saying the next mission would be a one-man task. Great! We almost always worked in small teams. This would be a switch.

"Our friends with Air America are going to fly one of us into southern China to get some intel [intelligence] on the SAMs," he said.

I thought, "Sonofabitch! Southern China! That's freakin' no-man's-land. You get your butt in there and . . . well, no American we had heard of had ever been in there and come out to tell about it." I began to shiver a little in spite of the ninety-degree temperature. My nerves and lack of sleep, I guessed, were the contributors. It appeared to me to be a suicide mission. I wondered if the other team members would notice me shaking. I forced myself to stand up in the briefing room, and loudly said to Bill, "Who the hell is the dumb-ass bastard who came up with that moronic mission?" I tried to make myself appear somewhat out of control with anger by tossing my metal chair across the room, smashing into the plywood wall. No one blinked. These were the really cool guys. We'd been through more than our share already. It was okay if one of us showed moderately violent emotion from time to time.

"I don't know," replied Bill. "But congratulations, Big Guy, you're the lucky one who's going in there and coming back out to tell us a neat war story. Doc Peterson reports that you are in the best condition of anyone on our team."

"Bullshit!" I said disrespectfully. "That's a suicide mission and you damn well know it, Bill. Kiss my ass!" I glared at Bill for several seconds. Nothing was said. Bill impassively looked back at me. He folded his arms across his chest, never blinking, with those ice blue eyes looking directly into my own. It was like a classic stare tactic between two boxers listening to the referee at center ring before the big heavyweight fight.

Bill, using his well-mastered technique of deflective psychological maneuvering, calmly said, "Hey, Big Guy, if you're too scared we'll have to find us another man on this team for the job." He said this with a wry smile and calmly sat down on a chair in front of the wall map, waiting for my response, arms still folded across his chest. I admit to being very frightened then, and stormed out of the briefing room, my lower gut rolling over inside, and headed for the latrine.

I returned about fifteen minutes later. I had stopped shaking, but my brain was racing. I was able to accept the fact that this mission was probably for real and a large number of people had already planned out the tactics and strategy. Everyone in the room was quietly kibitzing, waiting for me to return. The team members each knew I'd be back and take the mission.

"Okay," I said loudly, marching into the briefing room. "What's the deal, Bill?"

"We have excellent SR-71 aerial photos of roads and rivers leading to the Chinese–North Vietnamese border," Bill began. "We have picked out an ideal location on a little plateau above a major road from which you can observe the trucks bringing supplies to a river that flows down to the NVA depots around Hanoi. From here in Nakhon Phanom the Air America guys will fly you in a stripped-down DeHaviland DHC-4 Caribou [also known as the U.S. Army's CV-2] to the airfield in Long Tieng, Laos, used by the Air Force's Ravens for their forward air control [FAC] work. You will refuel at Long Tieng and wait for the desired weather reports at the LZ in China. The Caribou has a range of about nine hundred miles with additional fuel in rubber bladders installed in its cargo area. You'll fly entirely over Laos, directly over Phong Saly, the northernmost village of any size in Laos. It becomes quite mountainous as you get farther north in Laos and is also very mountainous in southern China, with some peaks to ten thousand feet or more. The DHC-4 will be equipped with the newest available flight director system [FDS] for terrain avoidance."

I got up from my chair and casually walked over to the large wall map. I'd never heard of Phong Saly. When Bill pointed out the village on the map, I noted that Dien Bien Phu, in North Vietnam, was about sixty miles southeast of Phong Saly. Dien Bien Phu was where the Vietminh defeated the French in a bloody battle in early May 1954. The Vietminh (Communist North Vietnamese) signed a cease-fire with the French in July 1954, creating the division between North Vietnam and South Vietnam at the 17th parallel. The French pulled out and the United States gradually took up responsibility for advising the South Vietnamese Army on their defense of South Vietnam, beginning in 1955.

Bill had stopped talking while I mused over the map. After a few seconds I said, "Hell, man, that area's probably covered up with Pathet Lao and shit-head communists workin' for Ho Chi Minh. What kind of triple-A guns do they have in those mountains?"

Bill responded, "You'll be flying at night and in the clouds, my friend. No need to worry about triple-A (anti-aircraft artillery). We sent a flight of fighters into that region of northern Laos yesterday and there were no radar lock-ons indicating the presence of missiles for radar-guided triple-A. We'll do a few more flights in there before you depart to make sure they haven't moved radar guided weapons in there. It's very unlikely, anyway.

"SR-71 photo recon shows Chinese deuce and a halfs [2-1/2 ton trucks], and a few larger trucks, are filling the roads leading south from factories around Kunming, China, down several routes to a river, known in English as the Red River, near Gejiu."

He walked over to the wall map and, using a pencil for a pointer, indicated the area of southern China he was talking about.

"From here they float the war materials south, down the Red to the North Vietnam border. Now,"—he paused to swig on a Coke bottle, then continued—"we've been pulling a few air strikes a week over North Vietnam on the larger riverboats cruising on the Red. We've sunk or damaged several hundred tons of small boats carrying war materials to the distribution centers around Hanoi. But we don't think the NVA are stupid enough to take the chance of our planes hitting boats carrying their SAMs on the river inside North Vietnam. Somewhere at or near the Chinese border, we think, they unload critical ware, like SAMs, from the boats and load them onto Ho's trucks for the overland haul to Hanoi."

It was unbearably hot and humid in the briefing room. The two overhead fans didn't even begin to cool down the metal Quonset hut. Or maybe I was breaking out in a premission sweat. I took off my sweat-drenched black T-shirt. John whistled mockingly at me. The others chuckled. I was quite proud of my tired old body. My muscles rippled everywhere. You couldn't tell where my skull ended and my shoulders began. Just a solid side of beef on either side of my neck. I flipped the group the bird and, with a snarl, called 'em all a bunch of pussys. Bill ignored my comment and continued with the preliminary briefing.

"We are going to drop you from the Caribou from fifteen hundred feet. This will be mountain country northwest of Gejiu, about forty miles south of the twenty-third parallel, and about twenty-five to thirty miles north of the China-Vietnam border. You'll be in a very sparsely populated area, according to the aerial photographs, and be just above the road leading down to the border. The road is dirt-surfaced outside of Gejiu, and hopefully muddy from the recent rain. The mud on the road slows the trucks, which will permit you access to some of the vehicles to look for SAMs."

Suddenly the mission took focus for me. I would be dropped in southern China, expected to mount a few Chinese trucks mired down in the mud, see if I could find SAMs onboard, determine whose SAMs they were, radio this back, and be extracted from China. It was obvious that this would be an incredibly high-risk mission for me, wherein the odds of success made for a lousy bet.

Bill continued the briefing. "We initially considered doing a HALO [High Altitude, Low Opening] jump; however, we have no way of accurately predicting winds aloft in China. We need supreme accuracy for your landing. You'll make a short free-fall from fifteen hundred feet and open your chute. Recon shows the landing zone to be a grassy, fairly flat and small plateau, moderate to heavy forestation as you approach the mountains on the east side of the plateau, and, again, sparsely populated. The Caribou cannot land to deploy you and your equipment. As I said before, the mountaintops in the area rise to ten thousand feet. Are we clear so far?"

I didn't look up to respond to Bill's question. My job was going to be very tough. Just flying at night into the LZ would be perilous due to the mountains all around. The mission already sounded like the usual poorly planned boondoggle manufactured by Washington politicians who never fought a real battle, let alone a guerrilla war. Reconnaissance and intelligence were often unreliable. The data, which often flowed through so many hands, was filtered through inexperienced brains, and passed down until it reached the people who had to depend on its accuracy for their lives. So we frequently risked our lives conducting missions based on bad intelligence.

We all examined the high-altitude SR-71 photos. The photo interp (interpretation) people had labeled areas and objects in the large aerial photograph. Using magnifying loops, they claimed to be able to see a red hair in a rusty railroad yard. I was always convinced they made up two-thirds of what they claimed to see, squinting through their magnifying glasses at the aerials. I could not see and identify half the objects they referred to in briefings. Bill droned on.

"Now, you may have to hole up in Long Tieng for a few days to maybe a week until we see that the weather is ideal for your cover. We'll be carefully watching the weather while you are there. We want you to drop into the China LZ thirty minutes to an hour before dawn, through a low overcast, hopefully in light to moderate rain. You'll immediately turn on your pilot's emergency transceiver and wait to get your position back from the Caribou pilot. The pilot will be in communication with a couple of Navy A-3s, or Air Force RB66-Cs, aircraft that will have been maintaining a radar cross on Caribou after you leave Laos and penetrate China. They will be flying just south of the North Vietnam–China border, at about thirty-five thousand feet. From the Caribou, shortly after you are down and clear your parachute, you will get back your position relative to where we want you to set up your observation post. That will be the last inbound voice contact you will receive. You should acknowledge by pressing the talk-switch three times, separated by a two-count, followed by three more dits. If you are badly injured in the landing or anticipate near-term capture by the Chinese, immediately respond to the Caribou pilot's transmission with the FRAM emergency code, one dit, pause, four dits, pause, and one dit."

"Yeah," I thought to myself. "I get busted up, and they want me to think they'll be in to get me out! Like hell! The brass would never authorize an injured/wounded extraction from an LZ in China. Who do they think they're kidding?"

I'd be just another write-off. I carried no identification, no dog tags, and since I didn't exist on any personnel roster available to the public, there wouldn't be anything to tell the folks at home.

If badly hurt or in jeopardy of capture by the Chinese, the big boys at the Company would expect me to chew my pill, after first digging myself a shallow grave. That was a distressing part of our training we all prayed we'd never have to implement. There would be no way to walk out of southern China. Better to bite the pill and be gone in five seconds or less.

Bill continued, "Using the helium weather balloon and wire antenna system, you will have subsequent communications directly with the A-3s [or Air Force RB66-Cs] using your larger high frequency transceiver and battery pack. You will also have an ADF [automatic direction finder] radio to provide a position fix. You'll use these systems later when you are set up in position for the extraction."

I let out a loud sigh, slouched down in my chair, hung my head over the back rest, and shut my eyes. From that position I said, "What happens if the A-3s don't pick up my position? Or wait a minute, Bill: Let's assume maybe I can get a look at those missiles and determine the country that is shipping them to the NVA. That's a big *maybe*. I radio that data up to the A-3 aircraft. At that point Washington has their damn intel. That's all they need from me. Why should they risk pilots, crewmen, and an aircraft getting me out of southern China after they have the information they want? Or what if I can't get the information? Will they risk pilots, crewmen, and aircraft to extract a nonproductive operative?" I was shaking nervously again—just slightly.

Frankly, I had no prior experience of this, nor did I know of others who had experienced unwillingness by the U.S. military to make every effort possible to recover Americans from inside enemy territory, even at great risk to other American lives. But I was concerned about my extraction from China. It was obvious that the circumstances of this mission were quite different from any others, and I could not completely rely on historic precedents. The difference was that I would be in China, and any rescue effort would require further intrusion into the airspace and land of a sovereign, unfriendly nation; a nation that was known to have strong, militant feelings against the United States. Furthermore, China was supposedly a nation that was not involved in the war to the south. That was all part of the squishy side of international politics.

As one side of my brain begged that question, the other side was rapidly and perhaps guilefully pondering how I could *assure* my own extraction from China. Somehow I'd have to figure out how to guarantee my survival and return after the mission had been accomplished. My mind seemed to be racing at Mach 3.

I really believed in the overall "mission" for which I had been trained. But when boiled down to essentials, FRAM 16 might be considered by the war planners to be cannon fodder. China and Russia were known to be supplying food, medical supplies, war materials, and weapons to the NVA. Chinese and Russian writing could be seen on all sorts of captured material. But during aerial recon flights and occasional jet fighter dogfights, our pilots were warned to avoid incursion into Chinese airspace. To do so might invite a swarm of Chinese soldiers and aircraft to openly join the fight with the North Vietnamese against the United States and South Vietnamese. This, theoretically, might herald the beginning of World War III. At least this was the conventional wisdom passed down to the fighter and bomber pilots.

If the Chicoms (Chinese Communists) shot down a U.S. aircraft inside Chinese airspace and possibly captured its crew, this could cause an international incident. China would probably call for a meeting of the Security Council of the U.N. General Assembly and claim the United States had violated its territory, and attempt to set the stage for legitimizing a retaliatory strike.

What could I do to assure my extraction without directly disobeying an order or appearing cowardly? I decided to put the pressure on Bill in front of the team.

"Why would you guys want to come back in for me, Bill?" I asked.

"What do you mean?" replied Bill, his voice showing some annoyance.

"Obviously, if I determine whose SAMs the NVA is using and get that intelligence back by radio to you, you have no need for me anymore. I've done the job. There's no need to risk any more lives or an international incident. So you leave me in there."

"Shit! We've *never* done that to you guys in FRAM 16 before. There is no basis for you to suggest that! You guys are some of the real unsung heroes behind this war effort. You can't think for a moment that we would leave you in there!" Bill said in a loud, angry voice.

None of the team members looked up. Each stared at the floor or toward the ceiling. They knew I had a valid point. They knew the risks. An American captured in China carrying military weapons, could indeed touch off a national security incident, even though the world already knew the Chicoms were supporting North Vietnam's war effort.

I had very little information about the overall war effort or the motives behind certain military actions, and I had no real knowledge of the international community's view of the U.S. involvement in Southeast Asia. But from my very limited perspective as a military operative, I simply felt frustrated over the apparent general dysfunctional planning affecting missions assigned to FRAM 16 and other units, like the UDTs, SEALS, certain Special Forces, and Ranger teams, with whom FRAM 16 had sporadic contact. I chose to blame it on the war management people. We had heard rumors that over five thousand U.S. soldiers had been killed by the middle of 1966.

Because of the limited scope of our knowledge concerning the war in Vietnam, and particularly because of our not being directly involved with planning relating to the big picture, we habitually bitched and moaned, as well as joked, about everything. It helped us maintain our sanity. Every soldier, sailor, and airman does this.

"Okay, Bill," I said, "how are you going to get me out? Are you going to send in a Jolly Green Giant helicopter to an LZ, let me lazily climb aboard, and fly me out? How will you get the Jolly out before we're jumped by Chinese MIGs? I would imagine there are a couple of Chinese fighter squadrons based in Kunming, to the north."

"That's all been figured in," said Bill. "Don't worry. We're going to equip you with a newly developed extraction system, send in a Caribou aircraft specially equipped with an extended tail hook, grab on to your bungee system, crank you up, and haul you inside the aircraft. It's simple and you'll be back over Laos in fifty minutes or so. Piece o' cake!"

"Nothing is simple in this business," I thought, "and when some guy says, 'it's a piece o' cake,' watch out."

"Any questions up to this point?" said Bill.

"Yeah," I said. "It seems to me that if some of the missiles are coming down to North Vietnam from China, the missiles must be manufactured in China. If the Russians manufactured the SAMs, why in hell would they let the Chinese transport them, and perhaps rip off some of the Russian missile guidance technology en route? Or maybe keep them for themselves and not for the NVA? It doesn't make sense! If Russia supplied the missiles they would most likely put them on a ship, maybe even a North Korean ship, and deliver them through Haiphong Harbor [North Vietnam's largest seaport]. The Russians and the Chinese still don't get along, unless there are some new alliances we haven't heard about."

Bill replied, "Good question. From the aerial recon photographs taken over eastern Russia, we see a greatly stepped-up use of what are believed to be drone aircraft as test targets for Russian SAMs. From inside Russia we have word they have improved their radar-beam guidance technology for SAMs, and the capability to use proximity detonation of the missile warheads. These proximity warheads are difficult for our fighters to evade, because they will explode when their internal guidance systems indicate they are within a certain kill distance of the target aircraft. In our pilot debriefs, we have learned that many of our planes and pilots have been lost to this improved technology. In the past, the SAMs would have to strike our aircraft to explode. We don't think the Chinese have this proximity-fused warhead and improved guidence system technology yet, but the Russians do.

"We also know that Hanoi is putting up a whale of a lot more SAMs against our aircraft now. The number of SAMs being fired at us is estimated at triple the number just ninety days ago. We have also pondered why the Russians (if the missiles are Russian-made) would ship them through China to North Vietnam and risk a Chinese compromise of their improved guidance technology. We can only suppose that Russian technicians in North Vietnam do the guidance system installation and programming on each missile when it is delivered from eastern Russia. Our intelligence on the Chinese capacity to manufacture greatly increased numbers of SAMs is fair to poor. But we do know that the Russians are limiting their larger freighters and warships in Haiphong Harbor right now. The Russian presence in North Vietnam is mostly in the form of technicians and advisors. For their own reasons, they are refraining from any troop commitment, and we hope it stays that way.

"What else, Big Guy?" said Bill.

"Is this recovery system you are talking about the same system as the Fulton Recovery System being manufactured by All American Systems?" I asked. "Is it the system the Navy has been testing wherein the recovery aircraft is equipped with two large twenty-five-foot-long probes that extend in a *V* from the nose of the aircraft? Then the person being recovered floats a balloon on a steel cable about a hundred feet above him. As I understand it, the recovery aircraft flies in, traps the cable tether of the balloon between the probes, and hauls the person up until he can be pulled in from the aft cargo compartment. Is it something like that?"

"Well, Big Guy, the direct answer to your question is no. The system we're going to use with you is new and being tested by Air America and the Air Force. They think it is superior to the Fulton Recovery System; that is, there's no balloon drifting above the ground to alert enemy troops to your position, and no possibility that an errant gust of wind will blow the balloon out of position when the pilot is attempting to trap it. Another difference is that you will not have to put on a special flight suit to be extracted. You will simply put on a lightweight, rubberized nylon top and bottom, which zip together for water- and wind-proofing, and they'll wind you up fast. You'll reuse your parachute harness in the system. Otherwise the two systems are similar."

"Okay," I said. "Has this new system, as you call it, ever been tested with a human?"

"No. Not yet. They have been working with sand bags that have a total weight of 175 lbs., and the reports are that it works quite well."

"Why can't we use the Fulton Recovery System, which has been fully tested, as I understand it? Why not go with something proven, rather than something that is still in the test phase?" I asked.

"Frankly," replied Bill, "we think this new system is better than the Fulton System, and, as I said before, we like the idea of not having to float a balloon in daylight above your position."

What I heard Bill say, and what I believed to be the truth, were quite different. I believed the real problem was the CIA and Air America couldn't get their hands on an aircraft modified for the Fulton System in time for my mission and the subsequent extraction plan.

"Okay, man, let's get into the detailed brief," I said.

Bill took a deep breath and told the other team members to sit tight and critique the fine details of the plan as he went through it. The briefing lasted another hour and fifteen minutes. I argued at one point that a jump from fifteen hundred feet was too high. I preferred to make a static-line jump from an absolute minimum altitude because there would be no chance of wind currents causing me to drift away from the chosen LZ, which would be disastrous in the dark. Pressing my point, I restated the problem, saying that since I would be jumping in near zero visibility, a jump from fifteen hundred feet would not improve my chances to steer my descent to a point that I could not see in the dark. The rest of the team joined in agreement, and Bill agreed to work out this detail with those responsible for planning the mission.

The meeting ended after I asked one more question. "Bill, tell us something. Has this bungee extraction ever been tried, using those 175 pounds of sand bags, in extremely adverse weather conditions, and where the pilot had very limited or no access to navigational aids?"

"No."

Chapter 8

Point of No Return

On 20 August, in a Quonset hut at Nakhon Phanom, I laid out my gear for the mission. I selected my trusted rifle, a Stoner M23 (M63A1) with flash suppressor; a vest that carried four clips of 5.56 x 45mm rounds (thirty rounds per clip); four fragmentary grenades; a custom-made Smith & Wesson 9mm semiautomatic pistol with silencer; two clips of subsonic 9mm cartridges; survival knife with six-inch blade; 10 x 50 binoculars; Pentax SV camera with 135mm lens; two compasses; two red smoke canisters; fifty-foot climbing rope; a Jumar rope ascender (a tree climbing device); folding shovel; black pajamas made of light twill and similar to the Vietnamese peasant wear; black rubberized nylon rain jacket and rain pants; black boonie hat; camouflage paste kit; poncho with liner; first aid kit; black tennis shoes; jump boots; food rations for eight days; canteen; P-38 can opener; aspirin; some kind of pain pills in three strengths; three syringes with morphine; malaria tablets; Brown Bomber pills for diarrhea; and halazone and iodine tablets for water purification.

John Schneider, a tall, dry Southerner, walked into my billet and said that approval had come down for me to jump at six hundred feet or less. I was very relieved over this. We discussed the mission over a couple of San Miguel beers.

In the late morning Bill and an Air Force technician delivered the bungee extraction system to me. When ready to be extracted from southern China, according to the plan, I was to set two aluminum rods upright, then attach anchor cords with aluminum stakes to brace the aluminum rods, and fifty feet of 5/8-inch bungee cord. The extraction aircraft was to fly in and approach my position at fifty feet above ground level, at an airspeed of eighty-five to ninety knots. The specially configured DHC-4 Caribou would have already extended a hundred-foot bungee or nylon cord, braced near its end by a heavy aluminum shaft equipped with small steering vanes. Passing through the aircraft's rear entry ramp (which was to be removed), one end of the bungee cord was affixed to a winch attached to the interior ceiling of the aircraft and braced on legs extending to the aircraft deck. The opposite end of the bungee cord would be tied to a large swivel with three snap hooks. The aircraft would fly in, use the hooks to snare my bungee rig (to which I was to be attached by my parachute harness), and fly off with me dangling behind in the air like a marionette until I could be winched inside the cabin of the aircraft.

I went outdoors with the Army tech and several teammates and together we set up the system beside our Quonset hut. As my teammates watched this process, they taunted and teased me about the system not working . . . that I would be left to rot in China, and so on. It was the usual tongue-in-cheek kidding, but underlying the lighthearted kidding was a genuine concern for my safety. I expressed my deepest concern over the hooking system that was to grab the horizontal bungee. A set of three snap hooks, similar to a grappling hook, would be dragged behind the plane, tied to the end of a bungee cord. The opposite end of the bungee cord would be connected to an electric winch inside the plane. Just above the snap hooks, the bungee would be stabilized by the attachment of a twenty-five-foot by one-inch-diameter aluminum rod on which preset steering veins would be installed. According to their tests, this device, although crude in my estimation, would assure that the hooks could be "flown" in to snap on to the horizontal bungee of my extraction system. During the winch-up process, the crewmen on the plane would cut away the lashings that tied the twenty-five-foot aluminum rod to the bungee cord, just before the rod reached the winch. If the rod ever reached the winch, the winch might jam. The whole system looked jury-rigged to me, and my confidence sank to a new low.

Bill had no negative reports on the success of the tests on the extraction system, which was of no comfort to me at that point. He passed off my concern for the danger of the extraction method by saying, "Hell, if the system didn't work, they would not have us using it." I found this to be a dumb statement and of little consolation.

As was typical of so many missions, there were gaps in intelligence which perhaps we could have used to our advantage if it was more complete. Time, in fact, was of the essence, so literally and figuratively I would be flying by the seat of my pants, clinging to a bungee-cord-of-hope that I would return to friendly territory alive.

Bill came back again to deliver three black weather balloons, a 15"x 2.5" steel cylinder pressure-filled with helium, a battery-powered ADF transmitter beacon, antenna wire with spool and crank, an HF radio and a battery pack, and a small, hand-held emergency radio used by downed pilots. We went over the use of this equipment for two hours, ending with my setting everything up blindfolded to simulate the work of setting up the transmitting system in the dark. I passed the test.

My parachute and shroud lines were constructed of black nylon for the night jump. There was no need for a reserve parachute. In such extremely low altitude jumps, if the main chute failed to deploy properly, a reserve could not be deployed and opened before I hit the ground.

Much of my gear was stowed in a black jump pack of heavy nylon (forty-three inches long by twenty-two inches in diameter), which would be tethered by two twelve-foot nylon lanyards clipped to my webbed belt when I jumped from the Caribou. I would exit the aircraft for the static-line jump holding the jump pack in front of me, release the pack as the chute deployed, and let it dangle below me during the brief descent.

Finally, I set out the small, waterproof, stainless steel cylinder with two "death capsules" in case I decided to check out and meet my Maker. I was not about to be captured alive in China. No one could ever explain to me why there were *two capsules* in the tin. One pill should do the trick. Perhaps someone decided that two capsules were required in case one became nervous over killing himself and dropped the first capsule. Why not just use a gun? That would do the deed, unless you had run out of ammunition.

At 7:00 A.M. on 23 August, it was lightly raining outside and very humid inside the corrugated metal Quonset hut. Most of the other Quonset huts on the base were occupied by U.S. Air Force personnel and transient military specialists. Theirs were air-conditioned—ours was not.

Bill and all of my teammates were up early to see me off. I was flattered and pleased to see these guys turn out for me. A huge lump grew in my throat as each of them gave me a bear hug, slapped me on the back, and hugged me again. Nothing of a melodramatic verbal farewell was said between us. Just "Safe trip, man." "Go for it." "Bring home the bacon, man." "See ya' next week, Big Guy." and so on. Each of us knew, deep inside, that this mission was exceedingly dangerous. After the storm of firefights in the last few months, these men were past being the sentimental or religious types.

Previous missions assigned to us had always involved at least two team members. Through our training and experiences, we had developed a supreme trust in one another. We were each the extra set of eyes and ears for the other. It was a totally integrated team, which is very tough to explain to anyone who has never experienced this level of complete dependence. Being out there alone in southern China was going to be different. We all knew that. Especially me.

I was weary, since I had been unable to sleep that night. Amid the fading shouts of support from my teammates, I boarded the twin-engine cargo aircraft and began the mission. I decided not to take any "speed" pills to keep me awake and alert. Perhaps I could catch some shut-eye along the way. I hoped I could sleep better that night at our layover in Long Tieng.

We lifted off at 7:30 A.M. and headed northeast, about 100 miles to Long Tieng. The Caribou was loaded with boxes from floor to ceiling for the military special ops, FAC pilots, and the Meo tribesmen who worked with them at this highly secret air base at Long Tieng. I dozed off in a sling seat for about half an hour, and was awakened by the change in the rpm of the aircraft's engines and simultaneous groan of the wing flaps, followed by the sound of the landing gear being extended.

We landed hard and taxied up to the small operations bunker, where I was met by a blond-haired, blue-eyed man wearing khaki pants and a navy blue golf shirt, obviously another CIA case officer. He might as well have been a clone of Bill. My escort carried my fifty-five-pound gear bag and led the way to a concrete bunker a hundred yards away. I had my parachute pack slung over my left shoulder and my Stoner rifle on my right shoulder. After he explained the drill for food and drink in Long Tieng, I thanked the man, and he said, "Good luck, Big Guy, see you on your return trip." That was all that was said between us.

That evening I joined the Air America pilots and several Raven pilots at a hooch called "The O-Zone" for drinks and chow. I could say nothing about my mission into China. When asked what I was doing in Long Tieng, I simply said that I was working on a mission up north. No one pressed me for details. The Ravens flew tiny O-1, single-engine, tandem-seat spotter planes. These Air Force men and their Laotian observers flew some of the most dangerous missions of the war. They flew at exceeding low altitudes to visually locate concentrations of enemy forces in Laos and South Vietnam, flare-mark the enemy positions (so fighter-bombers could wipe them out), and perform the BDA (bomb damage assessment). All the Ravens were fairly rowdy, many wearing loud Hawaiian aloha shirts, khaki pants or blue jeans, sporting all forms of facial hair. Several had long hair below their collars.

This night they were somber because one of their number had just been shot down in his tiny cloth-covered aircraft. The NVA found the downed plane and apparently executed the pilot and his observer. One of the other Raven pilots had monitored radio transmissions from the downed pilot who had safely landed dead-stick (engine shut down) in a field. He managed to live for about ten minutes until the NVA apparently found and shot him. No word concerning the Laotian observer, nicknamed "Tiger-baby," was ever obtained.

Three days later, on 26 August, as I slept fitfully on a cot in my assigned bunker at 5:30 P.M., the base radio operator received a coded message from Bill that the cloud cover at 5:00 A.M. tomorrow would be down to below one thousand feet at the LZ. It should be raining, and winds would be out of the east at five knots or less. Shortly afterward I went over to the radio bunker and spoke cryptically with Bill.

He said, "We go tonight, Big Guy." My stomach went into a knot, and the knot swelled up into my throat. It was ninety degrees, yet I felt a chill. I tried to push the fear away. It was very tough for me this time. I secretly hoped they would abort the mission at the last hour, as happened frequently with our missions.

"Bill, are you sure we have to go through with this?" I asked. "This is a potential death trap for me, and whether I am successful or unsuccessful, our war effort will not be affected the slightest bit. I just don't like the odds. I give myself less than a ten percent chance on this deal." It was my final, fearful plea, fueled by increasing stress and basic fear.

"Look, Big Guy," said Bill. "We don't ask questions. We have our orders, we plan the tactics, and we're going to do the best we can. We'll probably never know why this information is required. It's just like a lot of other things. I know how you feel, and I know you'll get the job done for us. You're the best we have."

I left the radio bunker to notify the Air America pilots.

Shortly after midnight I reconfirmed the weather conditions over my LZ near Gejiu with weather ops in Udorn. It remained operationally desirable. I boarded the Caribou after the usual nervous shaking of hands in a brief meeting in the cockpit with the Air America pilots and a crewman, who were probably every bit as nervous as I was over the mission.

"Poor bastards," I thought to myself. "If we go down inside China there is no extraction plan to get four of us out." The olive drab–painted Caribou bore no markings; the pilots and crewman wore olive green flight suits and green crash helmets. Like me, they wore no dog tags, no insignia, and carried no other personal effects or identification.

I boarded the aircraft at 2:45 A.M. as the engines coughed and wound up. The aircraft's interior had been completely stripped of cargo except for the four large rubber fuel cells. We roared off the runway, headed north-northwest toward the Laos-China border. The cruise speed of a Caribou was about 160 knots—max speed of 215 knots. We flew at first at an altitude of fifteen hundred feet over Laos. As the crow flies, the distance from Long Teing to the LZ was four hundred miles. From time to time, as a safety precaution when flying through Laotian valleys, the pilots decreased the altitude of the aircraft to one thousand feet, or banked to change the directional heading fifteen to twenty-five degrees right or left of the prime heading. There were no known unfriendlies with radar or missiles in the area of our flight path. The purpose of the evasive maneuvers was to avoid continuous radar tracking by some uncharted radar outpost operated by the North Vietnamese or Chinese. However, as we approached the mountainous area of northern Laos, the pilots had to increase altitude for a short time to ten thousand feet. It had been raining since our takeoff from Long Tieng.

Over Phong Saly, in northernmost Laos, the Caribou pilots made radio contact with a flight of two Navy A-3 jets cruising at thirty-five thousand feet over Laos, on station "Hosannah." In the cabin of the Caribou, several feet behind the cockpit where I sat in a sling seat, there was a jack plug and headset so I could listen to the pilots sending and receiving communications. The A-3 pilots had made radar contact with us and reconfirmed the vectors from Phong Saly, Laos, to the LZ in China.

During the flight, I was attempting to deal with fear in my usual way. I had been trained, and had partly developed for myself, a way to quickly push the fear of a mission (and other incidents that generated human fear) into a different quadrant of my brain. I concentrated on the details of the mission and replayed them over and over. Then, in my mind's eye, I took myself deep-sea fishing with my father off Key West, Florida; thought of my team's dependence on cool heads; and thought of such things as Mom's home-cooked food, women I had loved, and dry clothes. There were a few fears that were difficult for me to keep stowed away in a less-accessible part of my brain, but the worst ones had a way of forcing their way into current thought without my being able to control their progression. These fears, infrequently dealt with at any length, were of being captured and tortured by the enemy, and of being wounded and dying slowly and painfully. Unlike many, I did not fear death. In a simplistic way,

I was satisfied (rather than being fearful) that if I was hit with what some called the "golden B-B," blown to pieces, or otherwise brought down quickly, and died immediately, I would not know it. There would be no pain and no time for fear or agony. Perhaps this presence of mind helped keep me sane in the insanity of war. I recall Ed Brown's frequent statement: "I'm definitely not afraid to die; I just don't want to be there when it happens."

Weather had always been a prime factor in the success of the insertion plan, which required low clouds, preferably light rain, and low wind speed. The jump from six hundred feet or less, as revised from fifteen hundred feet, was perfect. Based on the way my parachute was configured, I was relieved at having a static-line jump at six hundred feet, which would put me on the ground in less than fifteen seconds. There was little chance that some Chinese civilian or soldier could shoot at me as I dropped in the darkness. My insistence on the change in jump altitude had been a victory for me. Bill had contacted a CIA man in Saigon and we got approval as long as the insertion was not delayed more than a week. The quarterbacks in Washington were probably in a hurry to get this information on the SAMs, because Bill got the approval back relatively quickly. The location of the weather station that would forecast the weather was unknown to us. We hoped like hell that they would be accurate because my life was riding heavily on their predictions. Bill called in again on the radio, and I heard him on my headset. I went up to the cockpit to respond.

"Big Guy, one more thing," Bill said. "We need you to take photos of the equipment if you get close enough to read the markings."

"Shit in your hat Jack!," I shouted through the microphone. "Negative, man, that's a bloody *negetive!* That flash will bring in every gook within ten thousand yards!" I was pissed, and wondered what *other* foolish maneuver they might try to get me to do.

Bill said something else, but I wasn't listening. It occurred to me that in this case it would be better for me simply to agree to perform any function requested of me. Then, depending on the circumstances, I alone would be free to elect what I would and would not do. It was my life on the line and no one could second-guess me once I was on the solo-patrol. My opinions and conclusions would be unanimous. So I acquiesced to Bill, and as I was closing out the transmission recognized that my argument wasn't worth the effort.

Chatting with the Air America pilots as we flew toward the LZ, I learned that both had been C-123B pilots for the CIA after flying the cargo plane for the Air Force. They had joined up with Air America because the pay was outstanding—better than the salary airlines were presently paying their commercial pilots.

Neither pilot had been told what I would be doing in China, so I told them. They were incredulous on hearing the objective of and rationale behind the mission. We discussed the extraction procedures for several minutes, since these same pilots would be the ones to come back in to pick me up. It didn't surprise me to learn they were not pleased at having been selected for this mission. Neither was I.

Chapter 9

Solo Mission into China

About 4:10 A.M. we flew over the border of Laos, into southwest China, without crossing the North Vietnamese border. Occasionally the pilot added power to avoid a mountain displayed on the plane's radar. We would shortly be approaching the much higher mountains that surrounded the Manwan Valley. Even if we were picked up by Chinese radar, it would be very difficult for them to deploy interceptor aircraft to locate and engage us among the mountains; there was another two thousand feet of soupy cloud cover above us. We droned on, and the pilots concentrated on their FDS terrain avoidance screens.

I munched on some canned rations, not because I was particularly hungry but because I knew I needed food in my system for strength. After eating I pulled out my camouflage paste kit and made up my face, neck, shaved head, forearms, and hands. Knowing I had to be nearly invisible, I used black, brown, and dark olive colors. I must melt into my surroundings and look like a common shrub, nearly invisible at a distance of thirty feet or more. "Don't fuck with a falcon unless you can fly," I murmured to myself as I closed up the camouflage kit and stowed it in my pajama leg pocket. Comments like this, and numerous others, were all part of the mental games I played to assure myself that I would be consistently effective and productive. Fearless and immortal!

A few minutes before 5:00 A.M., the copilot called back to me via the radio intercom that the crewman would open the tail ramp of the aircraft in ten minutes. My heart leaped into high gear and pounded against my chest wall. Following the insertion plan, I was to hook up for the static-line jump when the ramp was open and I heard the engines throttle back. When the green light on the left side of the rear bulkhead was illuminated, I was to step off the end of the ramp into the slipstream. The crewman brushed passed me to operate the hydraulic lever that opened the ramp. As the ramp lowered, I could see nothing but pitch blackness out the rear of the Caribou.

It's an extremely eerie feeling when you jump into any area knowing that you probably won't see the ground until perhaps the last thirty feet, maybe less. Then you pray there will be no trees or large rocks in the LZ. The pilot was probably communicating then with two RB-33 or A-3 pilots cruising high above North Vietnam, setting up the precise triangulation for the jump zone. The crewman returned, patted me on the shoulder, and shouted, "See you on the return trip. Good luck, man." He climbed up into the cockpit jump seat and I was left alone. The engines were throttled back noticeably.

Hefting my gear pack, I moved aft to the ramp aft and hooked up to the quarter-inch steel wire above my head for the static-line jump. Then I walked nervously to within five feet of the end of the ramp. The engines (though throttled back) and wind noise were loud, and I wondered if the Chicoms on the ground somewhere below heard the noise and sent out a warning. I had already checked my gear and parachute three times prior to takeoff, making certain I left nothing behind. I set the pack down on the ramp and tightened up the parachute straps between my legs and over my shoulders. The pilot made a gradual turn to the left and leveled off. At 5:10 A.M. the pilot throttled way back for a moment. That was my signal to jump. The gooseflesh on my neck and back suddenly seemed the size of pencil erasers. I thought momentarily of my mother, my father, and my sister, and leaped off the end of the ramp, dropping my gear pack at the same time. The pack fell the length of the two lanyards attached to either side of my webbed belt. I felt it yank slightly on my belt as my pack and I fell the length of the static line.

My parachute static line, attached to the wire inside the Caribou fuselage and to my parachute, caused my parachute to be pulled from the pack and open automatically in about four seconds. It jerked me around hard as it billowed open with a rather loud, hollow slap. Seconds later I saw the earth rising to meet me . . . *no trees!* Hitting the ground, which consisted of mud and waist-high grass, I rolled left and, while still lying on my side, grabbed the left riser and began to haul the parachute in as quickly as possible so that the canopy would spill its wind and collapse. Thankfully there was no surface wind to slow the process of gathering in the chute. I scrambled to get out of the harness. About twenty seconds had elapsed since I had jumped from the Caribou and collapsed the parachute.

Flipping open the latch on top of the gear pack, which had landed nearby, I hauled out my Stoner M63, positioned a shell in the chamber, and selected automatic fire. Then I shifted to a crouched position in the tall, wet grass and listened. Nothing. The dank smell in the air was similar to that of a freshwater bog—slightly rotten vegetation. It was raining lightly. I pulled out my ADF radio beacon and turned it on for two long minutes, went through the prescribed dits and dahs for the Caribou pilots, using the key on the microphone built in to my emergency transceiver. Even though it was unlikely, I silently prayed the Chinese wouldn't pick up on my location by using a radio direction finder. If the A-3s failed to have their tracking gear switched on to pinpoint the position of the Caribou when I exited, I'd have a real problem with extraction. According to plan, the Air America pilots were to maintain radio contact with the A-3s throughout the drop and for a period afterward, until my position could be accurately established.

I waited in the mud and grass, listening for the pilot of the Caribou to transmit my grid position. The pilot waited to hear a response from the A-3 pilots flying at thirty-five thousand feet just south of the Vietnam-China border. I prayed my angels were on station Hosannah.

"Bat Boy, Bat Boy; Blue Bird here. You are one-quarter mile west of the Clubhouse, say again, one-quarter mile west of the Clubhouse, take heading 080 magnetic, say again, 080 magnetic. Out."

I clicked the microphone button three times, paused, and three times again as prescribed in the briefing, indicating I had received the information and was safely down.

The Clubhouse was the code name for the location at which the SR-71 reconnaissance aerials and other detail maps indicated I would station myself to observe Chinese truck traffic on the road heading toward the China–North Vietnam border thirty-two miles due south of my position. From the LZ, I used my compass to establish a course heading of 080 degrees to the observation position, which was supposed to be a large stand of trees, according to the aerials.

Quickly gathering in my chute, I shoved the harness and shroud lines deep into the center of the gear pack where my rifle had been stowed. The canopy of the chute didn't stuff fully into the gear pack. There wasn't enough room in the pack for that, and I had to drag most of the canopy behind me as I headed toward my objective. I loosened the shoulder straps on the gear pack, which allowed me to put the pack on my back similar to a conventional backpack. When ready, I straightened up and pulled my compass out of my top sleeve pocket along with my red-lens penlight. Shining the light through my fingers to avoid possible detection, I found north on the compass and set up the bearing. There was so much mist and light rain in the air that I couldn't pick out any landmarks to track on. I couldn't see more than ten yards in any direction.

Within my limited visual perimeter I was sure of only one thing: I was out in the open, and other than twenty-four-inch-high grass, there was no cover in sight. I moved as fast as I could.

I took off in the darkness on a heading of 080, jogging where possible. I stopped every fifty paces to check my compass heading, since the darkness precluded my seeing any trees or other landmarks. In less than twenty minutes of slogging through the mud, I made out the silhouette of trees—six feet in front of me.

Minutes later, after feeling my way around the trees, I climbed beneath some low-hanging branches and rested on my pack. At about 5:45 A.M. it was raining moderately, and there was just enough light to move about and select a tree for a temporary hide above the ground. Minutes later I had tossed a line over a tree limb, rigged the Jumar rope climbing system, and was up a tree with my pack, rifle, and private parts intact. I liked it in the trees; particularly, large deciduous trees such as the one I had climbed into. They were my comfort, my cover. The leaves were of an oval shape like a beech tree. The tree had particularly dense foliage. I felt moderately secure as I waited for more light. The temperature seemed to be a tolerable sixty to sixty-five degrees; quite pleasant in fact.

Sitting back, I rested in the crotch of a large branch and the trunk, twenty feet above the ground. My adrenaline had been rushing for the last several hours, and I was whipped. From any viewpoint (except that of a Chinese), I was in no-man's-land with no way to walk to safety.

As I sat there in the grove of trees summoning a recovery of calmness, I detected a distant, intermittent droning sound of squeaking brakes and loud mufflers, well north of my position. It was similar to the sound of heavy bulldozers clearing land. While curious about the origin of the noise, I was frustrated that I still could see nothing through the mist of the early dawn. I elected to use the time productively by cutting up a three-foot-square section of my parachute along with ten sections of nylon risers, each about twenty-five feet long, for future use. Then I rolled the parachute into a tight ball tied with the remaining shrouds, and climbed up the tree to a crotch in the branches some fifteen feet above me. It was well camouflaged by the leaves and branches.

It began to get light around 6:30 A.M., but I still could not see more than seventy-five feet. By 9:00 A.M. the mist had lifted enough for me to begin to get my bearings in the immediate area. I was on a knoll that appeared to overlook a valley. There was supposed to be a mountain range about six miles across the valley, east of my position; but I couldn't see it through the fog. The droning sound continued, though it was getting louder. It was obviously heavy, mechanized equipment of some sort.

By 10:30 A.M. the mist or fog had lifted, and I could see down into the valley, which looked to be about five hundred feet below my temporary position in the tree. The grade-slope to the valley floor was about ten degrees. There were a few leafy trees, scrub vegetation, and foot-tall grass on the slope. I concluded that the trees were sufficiently few in number that my view should not be materially hampered as the mist continued to clear—at least I hoped not.

"Son of a *bitch*," I said to myself gleefully. There was the dirt road, about thirty-five feet wide, running north-south along the base of the knoll on which I was positioned. It was then I discovered the origin of the droning sound. It was a line of at least twenty Type 62 or 63 light amphibious tanks, if I correctly remembered my brief training on that subject. If they were amphibious light tanks, I knew that each held a crew of four. The main weapon was an 85mm or 105mm gun, and each tank had a 7.62mm machine gun and 12.7mm antiaircraft machine gun. These relatively small tanks were Chinese made, very maneuverable, and capable of speeds of up to twenty-five mph on hard, open ground. They were copies of the Soviet PT-76 light amphibious tank. The North Vietnamese already had a few of these tanks operating, and they were obviously headed to resupply Ho Chi Minh's troops. I momentarily wished I had one of my teammates there with me to share the view. I was in perfect position to call for an air strike on the tanks, but American planes would obviously never be authorized into this area!

As the line of tanks passed, they were followed by several stakebed trucks, which I observed through my binoculars lumbering through the mud, carrying what appeared to be Chinese Type 56 field guns. The lightweight field guns came in two models: some bored for 70mm shells, others bored for 85mm shells. Each truck had three field guns riding uncovered on the truck bed. I counted fourteen trucks, two of which pulled canvas covered trailers. That was a lot of firepower headed south, to be used against ARVN and U.S. troops.

From my bird's-eye view, I sat there in my tree with my eyes pressed to the binoculars, pulling passive recon in a light rain. What I was observing was exactly what we had all hoped for. The road bed was being churned into a muddy river by tanks and other vehicles. As the old saying goes, the mud was "too thin to plow, too thick to drink." I was pleased that the recent nearly continuous rains had exacerbated the road traffic congestion. The tanks seemed to have no difficulty navigating the mud at about ten mph; but the trucks were having a very tough go of it.

About 2:00 P.M., Chinese soldiers or North Vietnamese conscripts (I couldn't tell which), pushing supply-loaded bicycles, could be seen slogging along the road in groups of two to twenty. I was too far away to hear their voices. Perhaps seventy-five to one hundred of these primitive vehicles were in my view at the time, probably carrying food, munitions, medical supplies, and small weapons of every description down to North Vietnam. They were also having a very tough time negotiating the mud. But there had been no vehicles passing by of a size capable of carrying a rack of fully assembled SAMs.

At 4:00 P.M., after reapplying camouflage paint, I rappelled down from my observation post, carrying only my Stoner, black vest with ammunition, and a first aid kit. I should have patrolled the area at first light, which I would have done if I hadn't been so curious about the tanks and trucks parading past my post. I wanted to patrol the entire grove of trees to the rear and sides of my position to determine if there were any signs of unfriendlies in the area. My careful patrol lasted just more than an hour, and I saw nothing to cause me concern that my position might eventually be compromised; however, I reminded myself that the rain would have quickly blotted out any human or animal footprints. I returned to my tree post to watch the activity on the road below, until about thirty minutes before it was too dark to see.

Pulling my food sack, black nylon net hammock, black rain jacket, and poncho from the gear sack, I rigged up for the night. I ate three cans of some kind of rations seemingly unfit for vultures, then set my alarm watch, which gave me a wake-up call by vibrating against my body. After tucking the watch in my chest pocket, I buttoned the flap closed. I checked the water bag, which I had earlier hung out on tree branches to collect rainwater. It was critical to gather as much rainwater as possible, because you are taught to never drink free-flowing water from streams or rivers in these areas. Free-standing water was muddy and subject to infiltration by animal feces. Water in Asia was always considered polluted by Westerners, due to the use of human and animal excrement as fertilizer, which in turn washes into streams and rivers. Systems to process sewage in Asia were still future luxuries.

At 8:00 P.M. I eased into the hammock, placed my trusty Stoner on my chest with the barrel pointed toward my toes, rechecked for a chambered round, covered my body with a lined poncho, and tried to sleep. I was quite sleepy, but was annoyed by the light rain falling through the tree branches above me, dripping loudly onto my poncho, which I had pulled over my head.

I fell asleep after nearly an hour of trying, and woke up again around midnight with a painfully full bladder. Lying on my back under the poncho, I slid my pajama trousers down to my knees. Then I rolled left, holding on to my rifle, and hosed the forest floor through the thin strands of nylon netting of the hammock. Normally it is dangerous to urinate on the ground directly below your tree. If the enemy were patrolling about, they might smell the urine, look up in the tree, and you're history. But the rain was coming down steadily by then, and I figured it would quickly dilute any residual odor of the urine. Having relieved myself, I settled back into the hammock for another several hours of sleep.

At 6:20 A.M. on the second day, my vibrating alarm awoke me. I struggled stiffly out of the hammock onto the adjacent tree limb, rolled the hammock into a ball about the size of a softball, and stowed other gear. Then I rappelled down from the tree, still stiff and sore from staying in one position for almost nine hours. I wanted to patrol the area once more to look for alternative places to hide, reassess avenues of escape and evasion, and look for signs of activity or life, footprints, animal droppings, or anything that would indicate I might have company. Being quite hungry, I thought frequently of hamburgers, French fries, and cold milk. A cold beer would have been nice, but was too much to hope for here in Chinaland. I would eat after the recon.

Patrolling, I scanned other trees and dense shrubbery that could provide me cover in case the enemy decided to venture up the hill for some reason. I felt confident no one would ever see me from the road below; however, failure to plan well for escape and evasion caused the death of many fighting Americans. There was always the chance that I could be discovered by the enemy approaching through the trees west of my position. But I didn't expect this to happen because this area appeared to be rolling pasture land, according to my earlier recon and the aerial photographs.

I found the perfect tree about one hundred feet north of my observation tree. It was about sixty feet tall and looked like an American maple. It had a large branch down low on the trunk, which I could grab on to and climb up quickly without the use of the Jumar rope climbing system. The leaves were thick enough to provide great cover. I would have moved my observation post into this tree had it not been for the lack of a clear view of the valley floor. I was comforted by the discovery of this new find so close to my observation tree. If the enemy approached for some reason, I could evade with my gear in about forty-five seconds.

On returning to my post, having checked all approaches to the tree grove, I scanned the valley road below. No activity. I climbed back up into the branches and took a few moments to set up my gear bag and other equipment, which would permit a very rapid evasion if necessary. I planned to take my hammock and water bag (now nearly full) down every morning before leaving my position. I took a large drink of rainwater from the water bag, and I settled back against the tree trunk and watched. I made several notes on a pad about observations of the valley road the previous day. Particularly important were events that were observed in conjunction with the time of day. Today I would take time to use the sweep hand on my wristwatch to determine how long it took for a vehicle to drive through the mud from one point to the next. These facts would bear heavily on my timing in approaching one of the vehicles.

By noon, only a few bicycles and less than ten small trucks went by on the road below. It was a slow day for interprovince transportation in southern China. I had hoped for more rain. My spirits heightened over the prospect of a successful mission if the rain, and its effect on the muddy road, continued.

In the late afternoon, as the daylight diminished, I ate some more canned chow. It was cold meat chunks in thick gravy with the texture of prunes, and it smelled like three-day-old fish. But when you are hungry . . .

Suddenly, just thirty minutes before last light, I was jolted out of my somewhat relaxed condition. "*Damn!*" I murmured "This is my second night! I've got to transmit my position and condition tonight! How the hell did I almost forget?" I looked at my watch. It was 7:15

P.M. I was due to transmit at 9:30 P.M. I still had plenty of time; however, my concern over having nearly forgotten this matter caused me to dig frantically in the gear bag for the three waterproof bags containing the radio equipment needed for the transmission. I strived to remain calm. Had I failed to transmit at the appointed time, I might be considered a dead nonhero of the Vietnam conflict. There was little doubt that a friendly search party would not be sent in to recover me. I convinced myself then I was okay on time remaining, and not to panic. I took half of a speed pill to assure that I would be alert for the next three hours.

Rigging up the antenna, upper sideband HF transceiver, and low-frequency Automatic Direction Finder (ADF) was simple but time consuming. Sitting in my tree, I eased the three bags of radio gear, my rifle, and the Jumar system down to the ground. After shoving my poncho in the back of my trousers, I rappelled down and headed off to the west end of the grove, a distance of perhaps a hundred yards.

It was almost completely dark when I got to the spot that I had determined from my morning patrol would be the best point from which to transmit. I would set up the communications system entirely by feel. The rain had stopped. The mist had gathered again like a bridal veil around my hilltop. The temperature was about sixty-five degrees Fahrenheit, wind from the northeast. Perfect. I set to work.

First I briefly turned the transceiver on, making sure I had a tiny green light on the monitor illuminated, indicating battery power was sufficient. I pulled out one of the three black weather balloons and commenced the arduous task of blowing it up. The balloon when fully blown up was about thirty-six inches in diameter. After several minutes of gradual blowing (not wanting to hyperventilate from overly deep breathing) I had filled the balloon to approximately three quarters of its air capacity before adding helium gas from the steel cylinder. I added the helium until I could feel a positive upward tug, then I tied the balloon off at the nipple, and put a steel balloon clip on for safety. Then carefully I anchored and taped the top of the antenna wire to the steel clip on the nipple. My thigh was resting on the spool of antenna wire, and I was critically aware that I could not move my leg, since the balloon filled partly with helium might have lifted the entire spool into space and I would be S.O.L. (Shit Out of Luck). I checked my watch for the twentieth time. Thirty minutes to go.

Somewhere, further west, I heard a rooster crow. "Now it's well after dark. Why is a friggin' rooster crowing? Roosters aren't supposed to crow before dawn," I thought. "Must be something different in these Chinese birds. Wonder how far that rooster is from me? Where there's a rooster there's gotta be several hens; and where there are hens there are eggs; and where there are eggs there are people! Damn!"

I couldn't worry about it right then, other than to have it serve as a reminder that I might have unexpected visitors in my neighborhood. It was a certainty that if I were detected somehow by the Chinese (civilians or military) I would not have the smallest chance for escape. Eventually they would find me.

At 9:20 P.M. I placed the ADF instrument next to my left leg and the UHF transceiver with wire leads ending in alligator clips next to my right leg. I lifted my leg slightly and slid out the antenna spool, gripping it between my thighs. Slowly I unwound the spool to let out the balloon (which pulled out the antenna wire), being careful not having to stop the progress abruptly for any reason, for fear of having the balloon break loose from the antenna wire. The light wind caused the balloon to move away from my position, about fifteen yards from the trees, and float above the field.

It was not difficult to know how far the balloon had been let up into the sky, since back in Cambodia the technicians had whipped some cotton twine around the antenna wire at the hundred-foot point. When I felt the twine between my index finger and thumb, I stopped the spool and set the catch lock on the spool sprocket to prevent it from unwinding farther.

I reflected for a moment that I was about to reach a very major turning point in the mission. If the transmission was successful, I had a good chance of being extracted safely. This, of course, assumed that the bungee extraction system worked as advertised. There would not be an extraction if it could not be confirmed by our people that I was still healthy. I shook with nervousness as I applied the alligator clip from the transmitter to the antenna wire. I turned the battery power switch on the transmitter to the green light position and clicked the microphone twice. The small blue transmitter light winked on and off indicating that I was broadcasting. If I could only have the confidence that the transceiver and the high gain amplifier were also working. . . .

At 9:30 P.M., I put the earplug in my ear, cleared my throat, lifted the microphone to my lips, and mashed the transmit button.

"Blue Bird, Blue Bird, this is Bat Boy, at the Clubhouse and okay. Copy?"

Nothing! No reply! I waited three minutes and transmitted again. During those minutes I prayed that those fearless jet jocks would be up there, just below the China–North Vietnam border. They'd better be up there, damn it!

I tried again. Nothing.

"Should I haul the balloon back down and see if the connections and frequency are correct?" I wondered. Suddenly, the HF transceiver came alive in my earphone. I was so startled by the sound of a human voice, I nearly whizzed in my drawers.

"Bat Boy, Bat Boy, reading you five-by-five, at Clubhouse and okay. Good evening, sir."

The transmission was purposely short; merely a repeat of my transmission was all I could expect from the A-3 pilots. I needed to stay off the airwaves because there really was no need to carry on even the smallest chitchat. However, I admit that I would have liked to stay on the radio for a little longer. It was my only link to friendlies at that time. More so than in past missions, I felt very alone, isolated, and vulnerable. I was precluded from making a more lengthy transmission because the Chinese might have a radio direction finder turned on and could possibly get a fix on my position. I felt a strange combination of emotions consuming me. I was near elation that I had made contact with Blue Bird. On the other hand, I had that ever-present feeling of being incredibly *alone* and estranged. It was just me and God out there—and approximately six hundred million Communist Chinese who would have loved to capture my butt and put it in a public wok for stir-fry.

I was quite weary from the effort coupled with stress over the last couple of hours. The speed pill I swallowed earlier had not had much effect. After winding in the helium-filled balloon, I attempted to remove the clip attached to the nipple of the balloon. For some unknown reason the clip had become bent and locked, and I could not open it. Obviously I could not carry the inflated balloon around with me, nor was I comfortable just cutting it loose and letting it take off into the sky. I elected to put the point of my knife in the balloon nipple, just above the clip, to start a slow leak and slowly let the pressure out of the balloon. I stuck my knife in once again and made a larger hole, obviously trying to avoid the loud sound that accompanies a popping balloon. Might wake up the ol' rooster again. Later I would wish like hell that I had tried harder to remove the clip from the nipple of the balloon, let the air escape, and save the balloon for future use. I did not worry about this at that point because I knew I still had two unused balloons remaining in my pack.

I unhooked the dead balloon and shoved it into my shirt, not wanting to litter the Chinese countryside with remnants of my visit. Quickly I felt around in the dark, located the remaining equipment, and loaded it all into the three nylon bags. Standing up, I turned around and looked into my tree grove. I could not see five feet in front of me. In my haste I had not planned well at all. I would go nowhere among the trees and underbrush in the dark.

I made the decision to walk around the south side of the grove until I felt the ground taking me down the knoll toward the valley floor. Then I would turn 180 degrees around, take about fifteen paces, turn right ninety degrees, take about ten paces, and I should be very near my tree. Certainly, using a flashlight was out of the question even when using the red lens.

I set off very slowly, trying to feel the trees and shrubs on the edge of the grove. It was tough going. There was no background light. Nothing but blackness. "It would be my luck to run into a wild boar out foraging in the night and set him to squealing through the fields, or worse yet a poisonous snake," I thought. I walked slowly for about ten minutes. Several times I thought I felt the ground begin to dip. However, I always walked a few more feet past the dip to see if it continued downward. I was feeling for trees on my left side at the same time.

Frankly, I was getting worried that I would not find my tree at all in the darkness. Suddenly I felt my back lurch with each of four strides, indicating that I was definitely going downhill. "Great. Now turn around, 180 degrees, take ten paces. No, take two more paces, make it twelve. Now turn right and take ten paces."

On the sixth pace I walked right into a tree with my left foot and nearly fell backward on my butt. Funny how it's always darker under the canopy of woods than it is when it is pitch black under the sky. You know black is black. But some black must be darker black than other black. I continued to bump along in the grove a short distance until it finally dawned on me that, I was not going to find my tree.

"Damn it," I said aloud.

So close and yet so far away. I had not wanted to leave behind any identifying mark on the tree, but I could have planned better on how to locate my observation tree! I also realized that I would not be able to get my rope climbing system installed in the dark. I was aggravated over my poor planning. One makes mistakes when stressed.

Finally, after a few more instances of bouncing off trees in the rain and dark, I decided to shuffle my way along until I found a low-branched tree, then climb under the limbs and lie on the ground for the night. I curled up on my side around the radio gear and my rifle, then covered myself and my gear with the poncho. Resting my head on my arm, I was asleep shortly.

"No more poor planning, fruitcake," I said to myself as I awoke shivering from the damp cold of morning. It was just before 6:00 A.M. The rain had stopped sometime during the night. My radio gear was still protected and dry. There were no sounds around me and no mechanical noise from the valley. It was still quite foggy beyond the grove, as I moved to the edge. The valley was obscured. Gathering up the gear, I located my tree nearby, set up my climbing system, and hauled myself up into my tree. Carefully I stowed my radio gear in my waterproof gear pack. Then I checked the breech of my Stoner for dirt and moisture, checked the clip, and generally made sure everything was in working order. I caught a few more winks in the hammock, after I set it up, and woke up to sunlight—something I'd not seen for several days. The sunlight gave me grave concern. I needed the elements of rain, fog, and mud in my favor to accomplish my mission. I packed up the climbing system, rappelled down from the tree, and headed for the southern point of the grove. On seeing that the sun had simply shown through a brief break in the overcast, I was relieved. A short time later it clouded over again, and I continued to watch the road.

There is an old response given by experienced pilots when asked to describe what it is like to fly: "Hours and hours of boredom, punctuated by moments of stark terror." Many of the FRAM 16 missions fit this description perfectly. It is during the periods of boredom when combatants let their guard down—when they take a nap, when they daydream deeply, when they have a period in which they mentally escape from stress. Often these letdowns are times when the brain grows tired of being on alert and we inadvertently surrender to complacency. This can be a very dangerous time for anyone in a hostile area, whether in a war zone or in an area of wild, carnivorous animals. It is a lot to ask the mind to remain on alert for long hours at a time. My teammates and I used a variety of tactics to remain reasonably alert, particularly in times when we had to remain still, in position, watching for enemy activities or any form of change in whatever we were observing. We keyed on keeping our blood filled with oxygen by breathing deeply five times every three or four minutes. We thought this kept our brains alert . . . slow, long breaths in; slow, long exhales. Shifting positions—whether sitting, squatting, kneeling, or standing—every five minutes. The brain can also remain alert over long stretches if it remains exercised.

I would exercise my brain by planning strategy and tactics. "If this happens, my first course of action will be to . . .", or "If I see this, then I will do . . .", or "If the enemy discovers me and my position, I will . . ." I would find solutions, run them through my mind visually many times, and trust that by doing this planning I would be able to simply react to potential threats with rapid measures that would keep me alive. Sometimes I would exercise my brain by picturing memorable events—of my past, and particularly my homecoming. But this brain exercise was much less effective because it potentially took me too far away from the immediate situation of survival. I had the most difficulty remaining alert for long days and nights when I was comfortable that my position was well hidden and there would be no reason for the enemy to approach my location. Call it complacency. If you become complacent, you may die.

After long hours of remaining still in an observation situation, I would occasionally move to the rear of my position, get well hidden, and exercise. I usually did push-ups, sit-ups, leg raises, stretches, and squats to keep limber and relieve cramps and soreness. I never jogged or sprinted except back at a safe U.S. base. If it was not possible to leave my observation position, I would work on flexing and contracting specific muscles, beginning with those that were most cramped. My flexes were always slow and measured, so as to not attract any attention by my movement. Always in the forefront of my mind was preparedness for a quick escape or quick defense, leaving behind as little trace and trail as possible. Hence, a successful mind game to remain alert is to force yourself to believe that you are in jeopardy, moment to moment. However, this game is very difficult to play for hours and days on end.

I rarely conjured up visuals of being captured, being wounded, or being tortured. Simply stated, I believed that if I remained alert and prepared, I would not suffer the consequences of failing to be prepared; which thus did not cause me to visualize any unlikely negative consequences. That is basic "circular reference logic."

I looked north, up the valley, and then gradually swung my binoculars southward. There were no vehicles or bicycles to be seen on the road. The rain was still holding back. I thought I could smell French fries cooking somewhere, but I knew my mind was playing tricks on me. After about five hours of sitting with my back against a tree, watching the road, very bored, I recognized that same sound of heavy equipment rolling. It was 1:30 P.M. A light rain had started again.

Chapter 10

Bull's-Eye

My binoculars were aimed northward as I continued to monitor the arrival of the truck and bicycle traffic on the muddy road. For the next three hours only a few small stake-bed trucks moved on the muddy road. At about 4:30 P.M. I detected the throaty exhaust sounds of heavier vehicles approaching from well north of my tree observation position. Moments later two large, ten-wheel trucks appeared, laboring to get over the hill. Within ten minutes I counted twenty-five to thirty trucks, with common olive drab canvas tarps covering their beds. They were rolling very slowly and carefully down the hill, sliding and plowing through the deep mud that covered the roadbed. By the time the lead truck of the convoy was directly below my vantage point, I could see an additional forty-five trucks of varying sizes stretched along the road for about a half mile. It began to rain much harder. Visibility immediately dropped to about a quarter mile or less.

The two larger trucks that I had seen earlier were well out of my view to the south, beyond the crest of another hill. It was 5:10 P.M. when the sound of the convoy, all driving in low gear, slowed and stopped. Suddenly it was very quiet except for the din of the incessant rain slapping on the tree leaves around me. I watched through my binoculars intently, though it was difficult to see because of the rain dripping onto the front lenses. Nothing was happening. The truck engines were turned off.

Why had the trucks stopped? Why were the drivers remaining in their trucks? Some of the heaviest trucks had pulled up on the east side of the roadbed where there appeared to be slightly less mud. I waited. Nothing moved for over thirty minutes. I was confounded. While I was not concerned for my immediate safety, since I knew the enemy would not have reason to climb the hill to my position, I was extremely anxious to know what was going on down on the road. The rain slowed somewhat, and I observed a uniformed soldier on the road in the distance, slogging through the mud, walking north against the traffic flow. He opened the passenger side door of each vehicle, appeared to say something to the driver, closed the door, and repeated the process until he passed over the far hill to the north. On receipt of the message from the soldier, each driver climbed out of his truck, closed the door, and began walking south on the edges of the road, which had been least churned up by vehicles. Panning my binoculars quickly back and forth along the line of trucks, I noted that two of the drivers who had climbed down, had remained beside their vehicles, not joining the others drivers. *Why?* I observed the men carefully. Each truck appeared to have only one occupant—a driver. All the drivers were wearing uniform caps, with shorts and shirts of light tan or medium olive green. It did not appear these were military people, but rather civilian conscripts. Perhaps they were North Vietnamese conscripts. I could see no insignia on their uniforms or caps, and no weapons. They laboriously plodded around the muddy slush, over the south hill to my right, beyond my view.

"What the hell is going on now?" I wondered. The last driver disappeared over the hill to the south. When would they return? Why had they left? What about the drivers who had remained behind? My mind was confused with unanswered questions. I watched intently. The two drivers who remained were driving the largest canvas-covered ten-wheel trucks. Both trucks were towing a canvas-covered, twenty- to twenty-five-foot-long trailer, which were now parked almost directly below my position. These two trucks were spaced six trucks apart from each other. The drivers stood by their front bumpers smoking cigarettes, and appeared unaffected by the light rain. I observed the drivers communicating by waving heartily to each other, but they did not seem to want to join together for a conversation. After finishing their smokes, each driver climbed back into his truck. It was 5:50 P.M., which meant it would be dark in another twenty to twenty-five minutes, as the sun set over the mountains behind me.

I contemplated the fact that what had happened on the road below might be a godsend. Now I would not have to attempt to board trucks and investigate their contents while they were moving. Boarding a moving vehicle would have been very dangerous in the dark and slippery mud, and this tactic was at the bottom of the list of my alternatives.

I concluded that the most likely reason the drivers had dispersed over the hill was because one or more of the lead trucks, now out of sight, had gotten mired in the mud somewhere farther south. The drivers may have been summoned forward to help with the task of pushing and pulling the vehicles out of the muck on the road. The two remaining drivers may have been staying behind to guard a special cargo. Could the cargo be SAMs? Why would they bother to guard a truckload of SAMs in this apparently safe area?

I committed to my objective at that moment, having concluded that conditions might never be more favorable for me, with so many of the drivers leaving their trucks, and it being nearly dark. It was truly a stroke of luck that the convoy had actually stopped! This is what all of us had hoped for under the best of circumstances as the mission was being planned. I concluded that the trucks whose two drivers had remained behind were of a size capable of carrying missiles—if there were any missiles in the convoy. The trailers pulled by these two large trucks were also of a size sufficient to carry a rack of two to four SAMs. I mentally marked the relative positions of the two vehicles from which I had seen the two drivers climb out for a cigarette break.

After climbing down from my tree observation post, I quickly dug a small hole with my hands in the dark muck beneath the tree. The hole immediately filled with standing rainwater. I stirred the puddle several times, loosening the dark earth around the edges until I created a muddy soup. Then I cupped my hands together, dipped them into the mud and, using the mud as an abrasive, commenced scrubbing my face, neck, and head to remove all traces of the camouflage paste. While carefully scrubbing and concluding with a washing of clear rainwater, I decided I would not wear my black boony hat on this recon. I needed to look like a Chinese . . . at least I did not want to look like a Caucasian! None of the Chinese would have camoflauge paint on their faces. None would be wearing a soft boony hat, certainly not a black one. Most wore medium tan uniforms and a matching soft hat with a short, round brim. I had on custom-made black pajamas, which I believed would pass inspection at a distance in the dark. However, the fact that I was six-foot-two and weighed 175 pounds did not help to promote a disguise. The typical Asian man was about five-foot-five and weighed 135 pounds. To the Asians, someone my size and with a large nose (by comparison), was borderline "giant." Before leaving, I strung a few lengths of parachute cord between the trees at the edge of the grove to aid my return in the dark.

Carrying my trusted Stoner rifle on its sling over my right shoulder, with one ammo clip locked in and one clip in my right thigh pocket; my 9mm semiauto pistol with silencer in a shoulder harness inside my shirt top; the K-bar knife in my boot beneath my pajama bottoms; a penlight flashlight in my shoulder pocket; and with my heart pounding in my chest, but making a great effort to appear nonchalant, I walked out of the tree grove and down the hill—just as though I was out for a Sunday walk in the park. The downhill distance was about five hundred feet.

There was a light, chilly rain still falling and it was almost dark. I guessed it was about fifty-five degrees Fahrenheit. With good luck, the windows of the two occupied trucks might be steamed up from the drivers breath. After ten minutes I made it down to the drainage trench beside the roadbed, jumped over it, and walked right up onto the muddy road . . . as though I was supposed to be there. I walked with supreme confidence. I was immortal! I was not cannon fodder! I had a *crucial* mission! I was an invicible winner! I ate nails for breakfast and breathed fire on my enemies! For all my confidence, my stomach was in a knot! I was fighting fear as never before. My mouth was competely dry, as only fear can make it. I was very much alone, and had only myself to rely on for anything that might occur.

I passed three trucks and approached the fourth, which had the trailer in tow and a driver in the cab. Pulling the passenger side door open with my left hand, I drew my revolver from the shoulder holster inside my pajama top with my right hand, while simultaneously taking a step up on the running board of the truck. The Asian driver had obviously been asleep. In my thoughts, I hoped the driver of the other truck down the line had also fallen asleep, though his truck was well back from my position.

The driver was mumbling and groggy in his attempt to gain perspective on his visitor. I could just make out his form in the driver's seat. The mild, silenced thud of my pistol firing was the last sound he ever heard. I was aware of a rush of wind inside the truck cab as my pistol fired, and my ears were blocked momentarily.

Continuing the fluid motion with which I had opened the cab door and stepped up on the small running board, I climbed into the cab, keeping my pistol pointed at the driver, closed the door, and sat next to the soldier I had just executed. On entering the truck, I made every effort to give the appearance to any observer that I was another driver, just visiting for a while. I needed to be confident that if another driver had seen me walk up to the truck, my actions would not give me away. Everything had to look normal.

Glancing out the rear window of the truck cab, I could see that the truck-bed tarpaulin prevented my viewing the cargo area. I waited five minutes. The smell of cordite from the exploding 9mm shell permeated the cab of the truck. My enemy, slumped against the opposite door, never moved.

Nearly three decades later I still vividly remember that moment. I had already killed several enemy soldiers in firefights prior to this, but never one this close. Some soldiers can kill their enemy and never feel remorseful. I met soldiers in Southeast Asia who I believe actually took pride in and achieved a "high" by killing the enemy. Two Special Forces soldiers whom I met in Long Bin boasted loudly about how they had slit an enemy's throat and performed surgical atrocities on his body. They laughed heartily as they graphically described the gurgle sound in the enemy soldier's windpipe as his life's blood squirted from his sliced carotid artery. It wasn't easy for me to understand their glee over having killed another human. I found no joy in it. In the midst of a firefight, or in the case of this driver, however, there is no time to be remorseful over killing. You pull the trigger, the enemy succumbs, and you are already three strides ahead, fully consumed with covering yourself; your teammates; and your escape, extraction, and return to safety.

The NVA, Vietcong, and Pathet Lao were usually very experienced soldiers whose mission was to kill Americans, South Vietnamese, and their allies. They were often ruthless killers with little apparent concern for their own lives. They delighted in cruelly executing American and South Vietnamese soldiers, even those whom they found wounded and unable to defend themselves. For me, any enemy soldier was a target. Always, when I fired, I wanted each bullet to make a clean kill. I rarely fired my rifle on automatic, because I felt I could be more effective with well-aimed single shots or, at the most, three-shot bursts. The enemy intended to kill me and my countrymen. My task, driven by self-preservation *in its most primitive form,* was to kill them before they could zero in on any one of us.

But in the case of the truck driver, it was different. He was asleep as I opened the door. I could not take a chance on him hitting the horn, pulling his pistol, or somehow attracting attention to my presence. Moreover, I could not simply try to knock him out with a gun butt, tie him up, and leave him in the cab, because he would obviously tell his returning compatriots there was an enemy in the area. I could be tracked down and killed. In essence, it was either him or me. One of us would die, and for me it had to be him.

My subsequent rationale for killing this driver was simple and acceptable to me. He was logistically supporting North Vietnam. If you willingly supply the enemy, offer him shelter, food, or other aide, you die as one of the enemy. Did I think about the truck driver's family and their sorrow? No. Yet I still never found pleasure in killing the enemy, except when I knew they had wounded or killed one of my teammates, in which case I killed with some satisfaction. The killing was necessary.

In the dim light of the truck cab, several moments after firing the pistol, I glanced down toward the seat and saw the dead soldier's clenched right fist resting on the dirty, oil-stained, cloth-covered bench seat. About a minute after I had pulled the trigger, I glanced down on the seat again and saw the soldier's hand twitch open slightly, his fingers beginning to slowly extend from his fist. This movement startled me, and I reacted instantly by pointing my pistol at the man's head, prepared to fire. I stared in the gloom at the soldier's face, wondering if he was really dead, or just wounded. The slightly bloody entry wound was a visible dark spot on his right temple at the hairline.

"No way could you be alive. No way," I muttered aloud.

Replacing my pistol in the holster inside my shirt, I remained in the cab for another three minutes, and then opened the door, climbed down, and stepped onto the muddy roadbed. Holding the door open, I pretended to say good-bye to the driver. I even bowed a little, as many Asians do. After casually closing the passenger door, I made my way to the rear of the truck, untied the rear flap of the tarpaulin, and climbed inside . . . just like I was intending to pull an inspection of the cargo. I could not be certain that there was no one in the truck only thirty yards behind, or in some other part of the convoy watching and sensing something wrong. But it was now dark. The tarpaulin over the trailer behind the truck blocked the view from the rear. The rain had stopped.

I was a lucky son of a bitch. My ultrasimple deductive reasoning, regarding vehicles that appeared to be of the proper size to carry racks of SAMs, had brought me to the right truck on the first try! As the tarp closed behind me, I reached out in the total darkness of the cargo area and hit my knuckles on hard sheet metal. I groped and felt around the object.

"Bull's-eye!"

It was most certainly the fin of a SAM missile! Feeling about rapidly, I confirmed there were four SAMs loaded on a rack, two above and two below. I whipped out my penlight, shined it briefly through my fingers on the SAMs, then moved farther inside the cargo area, and immediately saw Cyrillic writing stenciled on the side of the top missile. The characters were definitely not Chinese or Korean.

"*Russian*," I said aloud, with a great sense of pride of accomplishment and good fortune. For an instant I wondered if I could get away with sabotaging the missiles, which would clearly be used against our fighter pilots in the next few weeks. But that might prove foolish and time consuming. Plus the fact that I knew practically nothing about missile construction, and therefore knew nothing about how to sabotage them, short of blowing them up, which was obviously out of the question. I had decided much earlier not to photograph the missiles and did not carry the camera with me. How would I have carried a camera without its being obvious?

Excited, I climbed back out, retied the tarp flap, casually looked back down the line of trucks, and walked back to open the passenger door. I pretended to thank the driver for his permission to make an inspection, and closed the door. I then walked south, past three vehicles. It was completely dark by then, and I had great difficulty making out the shapes of the trucks ahead.

When I reached the third truck in the line I turned right. Because of the darkness, I had to carefully climb down into the flooded drainage ditch, the water in the ditch flowing strongly southward. Clawing my way up the opposite bank, I started up the hill to my refuge in the tree grove. The time was 6:25 P.M. I was now quite confident that I had not been detected. It was too dark—my kind of night. Several times I slipped on muddy erosions in the hill, tripped and fell over rocks and small shrubs that I could not see as I struggled onward. I skinned and scraped my shins and forearms. But I never acknowledged pain; I was too excited by the success of the mission. I began visualizing my extraction from this no-man's-land in China.

Trudging up the hill for almost twenty minutes, I hoped I'd hit my tree grove en route. As the ground leveled out at the top of the knoll I was quite out of breath—the juices had been flowing hard over the last hour. Feeling along with outstretched arms, I hit the grove of trees right on the nose. More good luck. The rain stopped as I reached the crest of the hill. I thought I could see a little better now in the dark.

In preparing for my return to the grove, I had cut off a few lengths of parachute shroud lines, tied the ends together, and tied one end to a prominent tree at the very front edge of the grove and stretched the rest of the line directly to the tree that had the lowest branches, where I would spend the night. As I returned in the darkness, I felt for and found the cord quickly. Then, cutting the cord from around the large tree, I guided myself, hand over hand, along the line and climbed up into the low-branched tree. I was totally whipped, and my breath came in short gasps, partly from exertion, mostly from excitement. I concentrated on slowing my breathing and heartbeat.

Planting my butt on a wide limb ten feet above the ground, I leaned back and wedged myself between two limbs above my seat. It was perfect. Unless I lurched forward in my sleep, it would be unlikely I would fall out. That was always a danger. Normally I tied myself into a tree before sleeping. But I couldn't find the strength to tie myself in. I was too tired. I even forgot to cut the parachute cord from the tree; I just left it in a pile at its base. I hoped no one would discover it.

I spent a restless night, mainly because I was hungry and the tree limb I was sitting on was uncomfortable. My rations were over in my observation tree. I had flash-nightmares about Richard Shell and Ed Brown being shot in their backs by Vietcong as they tried to extract from "Dung" Island.

I had met Richard's family: mother, father, and two sisters in Pensacola. They were so obviously proud of him. What must they be feeling now that their only son was gone—if they had even been told. Making matters worse, his death could not be confirmed because the bodies were never recovered. I awoke from the nightmare, sweating in spite of the chilled air and not immediately remembering where I was.

At first light I climbed down out of the tree, slung my Stoner over my shoulder, picked up the pile of parachute cord, which was undisturbed, and headed back to my observation tree for a delicious "snack-in-a-can."

It was misty down in the valley. No sounds of trucks or tanks, only the quiet, parked convoy. For breakfast I opened two cans of chicken with noodles and a can of something called berry pound cake. Strangely, for once, it tasted good. I drank heavily from my water cache and washed down a Dexedrine together with three aspirin tablets. My skinned-up shins and elbows were very sore. Using water from my cache, I gently washed all the mud and muck from my limbs, hoping to prevent infection by spreading an antibacterial ointment on the cut places. Gradually my head cleared. Momentarily I congratulated myself on a successful mission, then I began to mentally address the extraction plan.

I knew the body of the dead driver would be found at some point; however, I could not predict what the Chinese would do when that event occurred. Would they patrol the area to attempt to find the killer? Would they call for helicopter gunships to patrol the area looking for the assassin? I hoped they would assume the truck driver had an enemy among the other drivers and had caught a bullet.

"Never mind," I mumbled aloud, "it doesn't matter what they think, I need to get out of here now!" Using parachute cord, I lowered all my gear and empty ration cans to the ground and rappelled down. With the gear pack on my back and my Stoner slung over my shoulder, I headed to the edge of the grove. Heading west, away from the road, I worked my way along the edge of the grove. It was 6:45 A.M.

My objective was to get at least two miles away from the grove, find an open area with at least a half mile of unobstructed approach, plus a quarter mile clear field beyond the extraction point. I worried about being able to find such an ideal setting. Examining the route ahead of me, another concern grew: I would be frequently exposed for periods of time as I patrolled.

Just prior to finally exiting the area of the grove, I emptied my gear pack of everything except the absolute essentials. If the need came for me to start evasion, any extra weight and the soft earth would combine to slow me down, making me an easier target. The task of unloading, burying the few nonessentials, and then reloading critical gear took about fifteen minutes.

With that task completed, I sucked in several breaths of misty, cool air and headed west. The aerial photos that I had reviewed were a foggy memory. It started to rain again. I was happy about that. Still I had to take care not to develop hypothermia, and I wore my rain jacket and hat to retain a little heat in and around my body.

Hiking along with difficulty for nearly an hour through puddles and waist-high grass and brush, I finally took a break in a small grove of trees. Shedding my gear pack, I spread my poncho out and lay down flat on my back to regain my strength, wondering if I would find the ideal extraction location. Then it hit me! What if the visibility remained at zero-zero? A heavy mist hung at perhaps sixty feet over my head. The Caribou pilot could track in on my ADF signal—augmented at the end by my voice transmission for directional corrections—but for the last half mile inbound to my position, the extraction would require the precision of eye contact from the aircraft pilots to my position. I doubted if there would be more than one attempt to lift me out. The sound of low-flying aircraft in this zone would certainly be unusual and thus sure to attract the attention of the Chinese.

After an hour of rest, I donned my gear bag and rifle and headed west-southwest. The rain had let up. The mist had risen to about 150 feet above the ground. This gave me moderate concern, because I would be in the open as I patrolled further in a totally unfamiliar territory. I had no topographical maps and nothing that would aid my orientation except my memory of the aerial photographs, a compass, and instinct.

I had walked for another forty-five minutes, and upon reaching a good-size grove of trees I looked back over my path of travel and realized I had been tracking a fairly straight line for almost a mile, perhaps more, without any tree cover.

"This is the place!" I confidently told myself. The track I had taken consisted of grasslands with occasional small hills. The grass and scrub was about two feet deep everywhere. I had maneuvered around the higher hills for cover, but I had not been thinking about the straight line of the open area I had just traveled. Although I had been walking generally westerly, there was also a good approach for an aircraft from north to south, which would be preferable for the extraction because of the high mountains about four miles farther west. In a north-to-south approach the Caribou would pull up into the cloud cover after hooking me, and would not have to turn sharply to avoid the mountains, as it would if the approach was east to west. Quickly I planned the next strategy, but I was tired and stressed out at this point.

I would install the bungee lift apparatus on a small hilltop, facing north. The plane would fly in, skimming the ground, and extract me from the top of the small hill.

Heading into a nearby tree grove, I soon found a very protected area to camp for the remainder of the day and through the night. If I was lucky, I could be extracted in a day or two. Maybe. There was plenty to do before I could think about that. I patrolled the perimeter of the grove just inside the tree line for about twenty minutes, looking for any evidence of life. On reaching the south side I smelled something rotten. Perhaps it was a dead animal. I moved along slowly, staying concealed in the trees and underbrush, smelling the air like a bloodhound, and literally followed my nose until I discovered it. The grass in the field just outside the grove was matted down in an irregular rectangle area of about thirty by eighty feet. I observed some dark spots or piles in various places and went out to investigate. Fresh water buffalo or cattle droppings, I guessed. The smell was very rotten.

"They must have eaten some bad cauliflower or cabbage," I thought with a chuckle.

Actually, I was quite worried because where there are domesticated water buffalo or cattle, there are farmers. Chinese farmers. Unfriendlies. I moved out and completed my patrol, satisfied that I was alone for the time being.

After dark, I went through the process of setting up the transceiver and balloon antenna apparatus for a scheduled radio transmission at 10:30 p.m. As before, I blew air into the balloon to partially fill it before adding the helium. I was sitting in the dark on soggy ground, feeling a slight pressure build in the balloon. Suddenly I realized it was taking too long to fill it. Pinching the nipple of the balloon, I squeezed what air remained and heard a faint hissing sound and quickly realized the balloon had been punctured by something—probably something sharp in the gear pack. I clutched with near panic. What if the third—and last remaining—balloon had also been punctured?

I forced myself to remain calm. In the dark, I dug blindly through the gear pack, which was not well organized since I had hastily dumped it earlier. Finally, I located the other balloon and began to blow it up in earnest, hyperventilating in the process. Thank God it held air. When the balloon was about two feet in diameter, I attached the nipple to the helium cylinder and opened the valve slowly. The helium hissed in. The balloon began to tug as the helium generated lift. I forced the metal clip onto the balloon nipple and held it close to my ear to determine if any air was escaping. Wonderful. No leaks.

Being satisfied finally that my balloon was not going to leak, I completed the process of hooking up the cable and aerial. Then I tethered the steel cable to a strap on my gear pack, using it as an anchor until just before time to transmit.

The constant humidity and warm weather always brought out mosquitoes the size of skinny buzzards. They chowed down on me like a royal banquet, and I scratched like mad. I sorted through my gear pack trying to find the pouch containing the Avon Skin-So-Soft cream that we used as an insect repellent. The Avon product was imported into Vietnam by the gallon. I found the pouch, pulled out the plastic squeeze bottle, and smeared it over every exposed part of my body. I smelled very sweet from the Avon, but the mosquitoes were totally turned off by the smell. The smell would dissipate.

I waited until 10:10 P.M., then moved out of the trees to a position about twenty-five feet into the field, and gradually let the balloon rise up on the cable into the darkness. The wind was calm. The night remained overcast. The rain had stopped for a while. I unwound the crank until I reached the cord wrapping that indicated the balloon was a hundred feet above me.

At exactly 10:30 P.M. I commenced my transmission. My heart was already racing double-time, as usual. Would our planes be up there over North Vietnam? Was all the equipment working? Were the batteries sufficiently charged? Was the transceiver working? Was the balloon leaking? I switched on the ADF transmitter, paused ten seconds, then switched on the transceiver.

"Blue Bird, Blue Bird, this is Bat Boy, copy?" I spoke nervously into the microphone. No reply came for nearly four seconds. Then light static and an American voice!

"Bat Boy, Blue Bird's on station. We have your position. Over."

With near jubilation I said, "Roger, Blue Bird, Bat Boy has the data. Ready for extraction. Bulls'-eye! Bull's-eye! Over."

The A-3 pilot responded, "Bat Boy, we copy your bull's-eye. Say your condition and location of unfriendlies."

"Blue Bird, condition five-by-five. No known unfriendlies within four miles east, repeat east, of my AO. Open area for extraction approximately one mile, approach from north to south, no obstructions.

"When can I expect extraction? Over."

"Bat Boy, stand by one," the pilot said casually.

I had turned off the ADF transmitter to avoid possible detection by the Chinese and huddled over the transceiver for the next minute. The wait was intolerable. I was sweating profusely, in spite of the cool night air, still wondering if MACV/SOG would really try for the planned extraction of my worn-out, nervous body.

The pilot came on again. "Bat Boy, we are working on your situation. Transmit at T time plus one point five, next day. Bat Boy, say nation of the birds you found. Over."

I paused for a moment, and responded, "Blue Bird, I say again, bull's-eye! Over."

I intentionally did not identify the origin of the missiles.

"Roger, Bat Boy, we are picking up bogeys on radar now. Need to haul outta here. Out."

The radio went quiet. Just a faint hiss of static. I felt quite alone, very isolated and vulnerable. I switched off the transceiver. All was quiet.

As I cranked the balloon down, I began to plan. T time plus one point five tomorrow meant I was to transmit again at 10:30 P.M. (T time) plus one and a half hours. That would put the transmission time at midnight. At that time I would hope to receive instructions for extraction.

I had been reeling in the cable for about ten minutes or so, not thinking about the balloon, when I felt it hit my head lightly, signaling that it was all the way down. I reached up and very carefully pulled the balloon into my lap. The balloon was wet and slippery from the mist in the air. I made certain I had a firm grip on the nipple, just above the clip, and unhooked the wire cable. The balloon was tugging at my hand. I maintained a hold on the nipple and removed the clip, placing it between my teeth for safety. Loosening my hand slightly, I began to let the air escape slowly. The nipple vibrated, making a flatulent sound as the air came out. I stood up, still holding the nipple, waiting for the air and helium to be expelled. Suddenly my grip on the wet balloon slipped. With a vibrating sound, the balloon took off. I lost sight of it immediately in the dark and could tell only by the sound that it was headed up into the fog above me. Once all the helium was expelled, the balloon would fall to earth, somewhere.

I was extremely upset at my mistake. Little errors can cost your life in combat. I knew the balloon would expel its air (my air) and the helium quickly through the half-inch diameter nipple. But I could not see in the dark field more than about two yards. The sound of the balloon ceased somewhere above my position, but I could not determine where the sound had ceased relative to my position. Where would I find it? The balloon was black, the night was black and frankly, the moment was also black, for me. I had escaped death many times before. But this time it might be the devil's undoing of my otherwise immortal body.

I stood there in the field, my radio gear between my feet, the balloon clip still in my mouth, and tried valiantly to get my mind back into a survival spirit again. "Stay cool, fool," I admonished myself. I rapidly considered my options.

I could wait until morning and hunt for the balloon in the field. If I could not locate it, I could climb a tree tomorrow and haul the antenna cable up with me, climb back down, hook up the antenna at the base, and make the HF radio transmission. The problem with the second choice was that I had not seen any tall trees in this particular grove. The communications techs had told me I'd need only twenty-five feet of antenna, but a hundred feet was better to get the transmission out. Did they *tell* me that? Or was I just forgetting the torrent of instructions they peppered at me in preparation for the mission? I was tired and becoming confused. That's a lousy condition to be in when you are touring around in the enemy's backyard.

I decided to hunt for the balloon at first light. If that effort failed to produce it, I'd find the tallest tree, climb as high as I could while pulling up the cable, and try to make the antenna work.

Still standing in the field, I used my penlight to aid my vision picking up my radio gear. I gripped the pen light with the red lens barely shining through my fingers, and used it to guide me back to my living quarters in the grove. The rain was still holding off. With the radio gear stowed in its waterproof bags, I organized all my equipment for a hasty escape and evasion, if required. My hammock was slung between two stout limbs low to the ground. There was underbrush all around the hammock, which gave good security. I was about twenty yards in from the edge of the trees, and it was impossible to detect my position from the bordering field. I opened four cans of C rations as I sat in my hammock. It was not possible to tell what I was eating, except for the canned sweet corn. The rest all tasted the same to me—bad. I drank my fill of water, and buried the ration cans nearby.

It was nearly 11:30 P.M. at this point. I unrolled my light poncho for cover and prepared to sleep. Lying in my hammock, I had been visualizing the next day for about ten minutes when I realized I needed to move my bowels. Rolling out of the hammock, I laid my Stoner in it, then untied and removed my boots. I wore no socks, of course. Wet socks would eventually become wadded down in the bottom of your boots. The cool groundwater oozed up between my toes. I eased off my pajama bottoms and laid these across the hammock too. I wore no underpants (skivvies) because these also would become soggy, then the elastic waist band would stretch, and they would slip down below your waist, ending in a wad in your crotch. We believed that socks, underwear, and toilet paper were for politicians and sailors; not for warm weather combat. I removed the penlight from my shirt pocket and shined it between my fingers toward the ground, grabbed my rifle, and tiptoed around seminude, looking for a private spot away from my hammock to shit. This was not difficult to find in this part of China.

Chapter 11

Preparation for Extraction

After replacing my black pajama bottoms and boots, I covered my face, shaved head, neck, hands, and wrists with a large quantity of Avon, and climbed into my hammock. My Stoner lay on my chest, muzzle pointed toward my toes, with a round chambered, safety on, and the selector on "automatic fire." I covered myself with my poncho to shield me from the intermittent falling rain. I could hear the hum of mosquitoes patrolling my perimeter.

Since I had decided not to set my vibrating alarm clock, I awoke naturally the next morning. It was just barely light among the trees. My watch showed 6:45—I had overslept, but had seventeen hours and fifteen minutes before I had to make the next radio contact. I lay in the hammock listening to the quiet for about ten more minutes.

Suddenly I heard a sound that I could not immediately identify. It was like a human taking slow, measured steps on cold, crusted snow. No snow around here! I listened. My breath quickened—it was close. I thought I could hear more than one set of steps on the "snow." No voices. Just the very slow cadence of steps, followed by pauses for several seconds. Whatever was making the sound, it was getting closer, perhaps forty yards, just outside the perimeter of the trees.

I slithered out of my hammock like a jellyfish being poured from a bucket, and lay on my belly on the soggy ground. Though I was quite stiff from staying in one position for nearly seven hours in the hammock, I reassured myself that I could not be seen from the field. Unless the enemy decided to enter the grove, I was safe. I melded into the foliage, lying motionless for another ten minutes. The sounds continued. Who the hell was it? Soldiers? Farmers? Chinese Boy Scouts? Slowly I rose to my knees, but the underbrush obscured any view to the border of the trees.

It was important to know who was in the area causing the sounds. If it was some Chinese, I might have to make other arrangements for an extraction zone. I inched forward, walking on my knees silently, rifle ready. I knee-walked my way for about ten yards until I could see light through the trees—the field just beyond. Nothing. No human shapes. The sounds continued. After moving forward another five yards, I stopped and saw what was making the sound. The dark coats of water buffalo! I counted five of them grazing near the edge of the grove. The sounds I had heard were coming from the water buffalo grabbing tufts of grass in their teeth and tearing it off just above the ground.

Obviously, I was greatly relieved, but would they accidentally munch on my balloon or step on it with sharp hoofs as it lay somewhere out there in the field?

Did the presence of water buffalo mean that Chinese farmers or herders were also nearby? Seeing no human forms, I decided to climb back into my well-hidden hammock, and just rest and wait until the water buffalo grazed off to greener pastures. I pondered my status and listened intently for human voices that might have accompanied the water buffalo. After nearly an hour, none were heard. In the meantime, the water buffalo wandered out of range of my hearing.

During my retreat from the trees on the knoll the previous day, I had not seen any fences, and I wondered if the owner of the water buffalo just let them roam freely. It seemed inappropriate and odd, from my experience. But no one showed up to herd the animals.

Lying back in my hammock, I was shortly jolted to consciousness by the memory that I had to locate the lost balloon. Other than that,

I had little else to do before the transmission at midnight. I was not used to having free time on my hands. It gave me too much time to consider my situation and the potential dangers that might be out there. I ate some C rations. After another hour passed, I stood up and eased my way toward the edge of the trees. Then I pulled a full recon of the grove perimeter. The fog had lifted to about two hundred feet, and it was possible to see nearly a half mile away beneath the clouds.

About 8:00 A.M. I moved to the edge of the grove and looked out into the field in search of the balloon. I set up a visual grid of the area of the field where I believed the balloon may have come down. In an organized approach to the search, I mentally counted off four squares of fifty feet by fifty feet each in the field. As I paced out in the tall grass to the first square, beginning five feet from the edge of the grove, I turned around after thirty paces to survey my position relative to the grove prior to starting the search of the first grid square. Suddenly, I saw something out of place move.

Bobbing very lightly in the slight breeze on the end of a tree limb, twenty feet above the ground, at the edge of the grove, was a black object.

"Damn!" I excitedly said aloud. "That's the freakin' balloon!"

Standing below the branch, I observed the balloon carefully, wondering if a tree branch had punctured it. Since the balloon was well out of my reach, I needed a pole to bring it down.

I returned to my campsite, picked up eight two-foot sections of the aluminum pole that I would use for assembling the extraction system, and returned to the edge of the grove where the balloon was stranded. I studied how best to lift the balloon from the branch without tearing it. Finally, I assembled the pole pieces, reached up with one end, and gingerly lifted the balloon. It was easy! The balloon came down on the end of the pole, and I lowered it into my hands. I then moved a few feet back into the trees and promptly blew air into it. I blew it up to a soft eighteen inches in diameter, held the nipple tight, and began to squeeze the balloon between my arm and chest. No hissing sound. No leaks! I was elated.

Returning to my campsite, I began to check and clean my rifle and pistol carefully. This was always important in climatic conditions such as these. I removed another thirty-round ammunition clip from my vest and carefully taped it upside down onto the clip already installed in my rifle. This gave me access to a total of sixty rounds of shells, quickly. When the first clip was expended, I'd simply eject the clip into my left hand, rotate it 180 degrees, and jam in the fresh clip. I wanted to be ready for any action during the setup of my extraction bungee system. That task being accomplished, I decided to do some pre-assembly of the extraction bungee system. I did not want to haul my gear pack out into the field, remove the equipment and do a major setup in the open. That might be foolish.

Once again I administered more Avon cream to battle the swarms of mosquitoes and biting black flies.

If I was notified that night by the A-3 pilots that extraction would occur the next morning, I would be ready. I certainly would not attempt to assemble the extraction equipment in the dark of predawn.

The two green aluminum poles for the extraction assembly were each eighteen feet long by three-quarters of an inch in diameter. There were eighteen sections that fit together with ferrules, with the top section having a Y-shaped top for the horizontal bungee cord to lay across. For safety later, when carrying the poles to the field, I put two turns of olive drab cloth tape around each ferrule joint. I pulled out the coil of orange bungee cord from my pack. It was fifty feet long by about five-eighths of an inch in diameter, and looked similar to nylon mountain climbing rope, except that this bungee was highly elastic and capable of being stretched to about three times its limp length, like a huge rubber band. After marking the exact middle of the bungee with green tape, I left the cord in a coiled pile and pulled out six sections of parachute riser cord from the gear pack, each section being twenty-five feet in length. The parachute cords would be used as stays to support the poles as close to vertical as possible on the hilltop. Once the three stay-cords were tied to each pole, I wound tape tightly around the half hitches to prevent any slippage. Then I removed the six twelve-inch aluminum tent stakes from the gear bag. These were lashed to the six tag-ends of the parachute cords.

The assembly took me about forty-five minutes as I sat in my hammock in the grove. At that point I pulled a quick perimeter recon and saw nothing of concern. As I patrolled, I went over the extraction process in my mind several times.

I stopped to eat some more rations, drank water, and, in fact, took a catnap for two hours. That nap was a rare treat, and perhaps dangerous. I just needed to make the time seem to pass more quickly. When I awoke and checked my watch I still had about nine hours before my next radio transmission. I was bored, anxious, a little scared, and apprehensive.

The desk warriors at the Pentagon in Washington, D.C., would get their information shortly. I wondered how they would go about making political hay out of being able to name the origin of those surface-to-air missiles on the Chinese trucks. The odds of my being successful had not been good. Maybe there were other, overriding reasons why they risked my life to have this information, and the rationale was beyond my scope of understanding, because I only saw the war from a microperspective. The planners, like Johnson and McNamara, probably saw it from a strategic perspective.

Frankly, I did whatever I could to remain alert for those next nine hours. After doing some exercises, I probably recalled pleasurable moments of my life before the war, particularly the crew races in which I had participated in England. I did simple algebraic equations in my mind. I tried to picture old girlfriends from college days, and wondered when I would get back to the days of driving fast cars, flying planes, and chasing attractive women. I wondered how my teammates were doing, and grew anxious that on my return I would find more of them killed in action.

I stowed all gear in the large bag and checked my water and food supply. There was enough for two more days unless I decided to execute and butcher a fifteen hundred pound water buffalo and have a private barbecue for my closest friends in southern China.

Two hours before dark, I gathered up the fifty-foot coil of bungee cord, found the mid-point again, and slipped on two carabineer rings, sliding them to the center of the bungee. Then I carefully stepped off twenty feet in either direction from the center point. At those two points I tied three overhand knots on top of each other, which resulted in a hard ball of bungee about four inches in diameter. When the extended tail hook system dragging behind the aircraft captured the bungee, the two knots would prevent the cross bungee from slipping out of the snap hook that had grabbed the bungee. At least that was the theory. It was supposed to work; however, my instructors in Nakhon Phanom could not assure me sufficiently that this method had actually worked every time, even with the sandbags. Not much satisfaction there.

I prayed and wondered if He heard me and would honor my fervent request to reach safety in the next day or so. I wasn't good at prayer, but the time seemed right to pray.

At 4:45 P.M. I decided to take one more perimeter patrol. I was getting to know this tree grove even better than the one I used to recon the supply road when I first inserted. The patrol took nearly forty-five minutes. I walked slowly. Nothing moved except the leaves and branches on the trees and the grass in the field. There was no change in the weather. The fog drifted about two hundred feet above me. The temperature remained at about sixty-five degrees Fahrenheit, and thankfully it had not rained for several hours. I knew the Caribou pilot would need at least three hundred feet of ceiling to make an extraction attempt to extract me. It would be my function to act as weatherman, and to transmit weather data to the A-3 pilots who would then in turn relay the data to the air base from which the Caribou would depart.

An hour before last light, I walked boldly out of the grove, a distance of about 150 yards, and located the hill upon which I would install the apparatus. Approaching the foot of the hill, I slung my rifle onto my back and crawled to the top. It took nearly five minutes to crawl to the top, and once there I maneuvered my prone body around 360 degrees at the top of the hill, studying everything in range of sight. I could still see for almost three-quarters of a mile and saw nothing of concern with respect to security. I carefully studied the intended north-to-south approach of the extraction aircraft. Within two hundred yards on either side of the approach path there were no hilltops with an elevation as high as the one I selected.

It was critical that the sixty-foot extension of the aircraft's hook assembly not strike a hilltop and bend the heavy aluminum stabilizing bar while the aircraft was on its final approach. If this happened, the extraction would likely fail because the tail hook might not extend a sufficient distance below the aircraft, and it would pass over the assembly.

I made my way back to the grove, satisfied that everything was in order. It was tough to go back to my campsite because anxiety would again badger me. I wished I had a deck of cards with which to play solitaire! I needed something mindless to do; anything to divert my attention. When bored or anxious, I would eat. So I ate. It began to rain hard again, and I huddled under my poncho, sitting in my hammock with my feet resting on the ground, rocking myself gently back and forth, bored as hell. The rain stopped at 10:15 P.M.

At 11:00 P.M. I moved to the edge of the grove and began to set up for the radio transmission. With nervous care I blew up the balloon, added helium, applied the balloon clip, tied on the antenna wire, and tethered it to my gear pack. This was all done in the dark without the need of my penlight. It was my third assembly and I felt my confidence building.

At 11:45 P.M. I slowly unwound the balloon cable from the crank assembly. At one hundred feet I attached the clamp-on clip from the transceiver, switched it on, and rotated the volume knob. The static was unusually loud; however, a minor adjustment of the squelch knob cleared the sound to a minor hiss.

It was midnight. I palmed the microphone and punched in the button.

"Blue Bird, Blue Bird. Bat Boy here."

The response from the jet pilot was immediate this time.

"Roger, Bat Boy, five-by-five. Extraction at T plus eight, repeat, extraction at T plus eight. Code name Red Bird. Red Bird. Any unfriendlies? Say weather. Over."

"Blue Bird, Bat Boy. We copy. Extract at T plus eight, code name Red Bird. Negative on the unfriendlies. Repeat. Negative on the unfriendlies. Approach is three-quarters of a mile on a one-nine-zero radial, hilltop, unobstructed. Ceiling three hundred feet, overcast, light rain. Over."

This was all good information for any Chinese listeners, if they could decipher it in time to figure out where I was located.

"Roger, Bat Boy. Copy that. Safe trip. Out."

I turned the transceiver off. It was so quiet out there I could hear my heart pounding with excitement. I knew the tough part was about to come; however, contact with the A-3 pilot gave me renewed confidence and determination. I was filled with anticipation. Or was I just confusing that feeling with heightened anxiety? Eight more hours to liftoff. Once again I previewed the extraction in my mind, seeing exactly how it was supposed to transpire at 8:00 A.M. tomorrow. God willing, I would be able to end this nightmare of a mission.

Chapter 12

Extraction from China

That night I slept fitfully. My alarm was set to vibrate at 5:30 A.M.; however, I awoke at 5:15, before the alarm, and slid out of my hammock. Shortly, I began to feel nauseated. It was the same queasiness one gets as a child before the first day of kindergarten or first grade. The feeling was caused by sheer anxiety.

I dumped the contents of my pack into my hammock. Beneath the trees it was still dark. I broke out my penlight and held it in my left hand, shining it through my fingers. I located and slipped the parachute harness on loosely over my ammunition vest. I left the ammo clips in my vest pockets and planned to jettison the clips just before extraction. It remained possible I could still find myself in a firefight prior to the arrival of the Caribou. Perhaps my enemy would be a farmer out hunting with his old rusty bolt action rifle, which had been in his family since the Ming Dynasty.

I located the roll of international orange marker ribbon among the gear in the hammock and tucked it in my shirt. Taking a long drink of water, I ate nothing. I was too excited to take time to eat. I set aside a waterproof bag containing the ADF transmitter, the transceiver, and the microphone. The coils of bungee cord were placed on my left shoulder, the Stoner on my right shoulder. Finally,

I rolled up the lightweight rubber coated nylon suit I would wear to protect me from hypothermia, and the two pole supports with parachute cord and tent stakes attached that had been assembled the previous day. I held the poles as I made my way through the underbrush to the edge of the grove with the help of the penlight with the red lens.

At the edge of the grove I stopped to listen and plan. I debated the merits of setting up the assembly in the semidarkness, or waiting until 6:30 A.M. I decided it was too dark, and I waited until 6:30 to move out and do a partial setup on the hilltop. There would be time enough to raise and stabilize the assembly when the first radio transmission from the Caribou was received. The last minute raising of the apparatus would give less time for any Chinese to spot it and move in on me.

I headed out to my hilltop, spread the apparatus out, and checked the ground for resistance to the tent stakes. I then ripped off ten lengths of bright orange ribbon, each eighteen inches long and three inches wide. These ribbons were tied with overhand knots at two-foot intervals along the bungee cord. The orange ribbons would aid the pilot in visually locating my position (after tracking in on the ADF) and discerning the wind direction. The ribbons could potentially attract the Chinese too, if there were any around. Finally, I attached the fifteen-foot-long bungee cords as shroud lines to the two carabineers sliding on the main bungee cord between the two four-inch end-knots. As planned, these bungee shrouds would hang down to my shoulders when I was in a sitting position, and they would be tied just before extraction to the shoulder clips on my parachute harness.

For the extraction, I would sit on the ground and face the oncoming aircraft for the liftoff. I would effectively fly backward through the air.

It was 7:15 A.M. I hooked up the microphone; raised the external, telescoping antenna on the small emergency transceiver; switched the unit on; thumbed the mike; and spoke.

"Red Bird, Red Bird, this is Bat Boy. Over."

No reply. I left the transceiver on and looked up at the clouds above. The cloud ceiling was at least seven hundred feet. There was no ground fog. I prayed.

At 7:20 A.M. I transmitted again.

"Red Bird, Red Bird, this is Bat Boy. Over."

Nothing!

I checked the squelch knob on the transceiver and found it in the full squelch position. The squelch facility in a radio is designed to block certain static and allow voice transmission to flow through. However, with the radio in the full squelch position I was blocking out both the static and the pilot's reply. Dumb *shit!* I turned the squelch back to receive just a slight hiss of static and tried again at 7:21 A.M.

"Red Bird, this is Bat Boy. Copy? Over."

Then it came!

"Roger, Bat Boy. Red Bird. Initiate ADF now. Over."

I nervously switched on the ADF, having intentionally left it turned off until I made voice radio contact, for fear of giving my position away to area unfriendlies.

Then I transmitted again. "Red Bird, say your distance."

"Bat Boy, we estimate we are twenty out. Say conditions. Over."

"No unfriendlies," I said. "Ceiling five hundred feet, visibility one mile. North-to-south approach. Will call when I have a visual. Over."

The Air America pilot gave me a simple response. "Roger." Like it was a piece o' cake.

I sprang up quickly to set the tall poles upright, jamming the short tent stakes into the ground by stepping on their tops to brace the main poles. The main bungee, having been taped lightly just below the *Y* at the top of the two poles, needed to have an eighteen-inch bow in it, and not be stretched tight between the poles. As I lifted the second pole into position, the fifty-foot length of bungee looked like an extremely small target for the pilot to hit at nearly one hundred mph. The orange ribbons hung limp from the cross bungee. With the extraction assembly in place, I put on the rubber suit, put on and tightened the parachute harness, moved over to the midpoint of the assembly where the bungee shrouds hung down from the carabineers, and sat down on the ground. I had my transmitter and rifle next to me. The ADF transmitter remained on. As I reached up to grasp the bungee shrouds, I heard the aircraft off to my right. Quickly I radioed to the pilot.

"Red Bird, you are estimated a half mile southeast of my position at this time. Over." I estimated this by the sound, praying I was reasonably accurate.

"Roger," said the pilot with incredible calmness. Nothing else was said. The drone of the aircraft diminished as the plane flew on before turning south into the final approach.

Each bungee shroud was then tied to carabineers on my shoulder harness clips using a bowline knot, followed by a half hitch for added safety.

I could barely hear the engines of the aircraft as it prepared a final turn toward my position. In fact, I spotted the plane before I picked up the engine noise.

"Red Bird, turn left ten degrees. Over."

"Roger," the pilot grunted.

Without using the Red Bird code name prefix, I said, "Now right five degrees. Respond visual contact. Check altimeter, fifty. Over."

There were about ten more seconds of silence. It seemed like ten months.

"I have visual contact, Bat Boy. Contact!" The pilot's voice rang out from the transceiver lying on the ground beside me.

The Caribou was hurtling toward me at the rate of about 140 feet per second, nearly 100 mph. I slipped the Stoner over my neck and left shoulder, then yanked the three clips from my vest and tossed them aside. I also ripped off the extra clip taped to the duty clip and tossed it away. It was tough to find Stoner clips, but the extra weight under the G-force might injure me. I tossed my boonie hat like a Frisbee, pulled the light rubber hood over my head and tied it under the material flat beneath my chin—wishing I had a crash helmet.

As the aircraft raced toward me it appeared to skim the grass on the field with its gear and flaps extended, and at full throttle. The sixty-foot tail hook was extended downward, at a sixty-degree angle. My heart was in my throat. I was totally focused. The steel hook assembly looked like it was coming straight at my face. The pilot expertly guided the twin-engine aircraft fifty feet above my position. In fact the hook assembly flew only about five feet over my head and hit the slightly slack cross bungee cord. The stabilizing bar slid upward and one of the three hooks clamped onto the cross bungee cord strung between the vertical poles. I did not look up. Too scared to watch.

My body was ripped off the ground and accelerated up into the air. In about two seconds I was flying at 100 mph. Zero to 100 mph in two seconds creates a substantial G-force on the body, equivalent to five or six times gravitational pull. The bungee shrouds stretched to their fullest capacity and stopped with a hard jerk. My eyes momentarily seemed to bug out of their sockets, my right boot nearly pulled off my foot, and the parachute harness ground into my thighs like steel tourniquets. The G-force also caused the webbed nylon sling on my Stoner to bind into the rubber suit and into my neck, causing instant pain. I tried not to notice the pain. My chin was forced down to my chest, and it was impossible to move it upward for at least ten seconds. I felt like I might choke on the neck of the suit.

The force of acceleration was over in about ten seconds; however, the drag of my body continued to create great pressure on the parachute harness around my legs. It was one of the most simultaneously exhilarating and yet unpleasant sensations I had ever experienced. I began to feel claustrophobic.

As planned and implemented, the hook assembly tied to the one-inch diameter bungee led up to the large electric winch inside the Caribou. The stabilizing bar for the hook assembly was cut loose from the bungee cord as the bar neared the winch inside the Caribou. The crewmen cut the lashings on the bar and pulled the uppermost end of the bar inside the aircraft as I was being winched in. The main cross bungee cord had been torn loose from the light taping on my pole assembly, as planned, and the right tag end of the cross bungee whipped beside me as I flew through the air, backwards, unlike Superman. The Caribou pilot ascended about five hundred feet into the clouds while retracting his landing gear and flaps. Within a matter of seconds after liftoff I was shrouded in clouds filled with moisture. My rubberized suit protected me only slightly. The air passing my body then, at over 120 mph, caused me to become very cold.

"Will hypothermia become a problem for me now?" I wondered fearfully.

The noise of the aircraft engines increased dramatically during the next minute as I neared the Caribou.

The maintenance crew at some air base had completely removed the access ramp that was normally used to load cargo through the rear of the aircraft. The winch, mounted on ribs at the ceiling of the fuselage, was positioned about two feet behind the rear lip of the cargo deck of the aircraft and braced on steel legs that were bolted to the deck.

The trickiest hurdle came next: getting my butt safely into the plane. The blast of air suddenly diminished to nearly nothing as I was winched out of the slipstream of the plane, being shielded from the wind by the fuselage. I tipped my head backward and looked up. The winch was rotating, winding the bungee cord that led to the clamp on my cross bungee. The crewmen cut the lashings at the end of the stabilizing bar and discarded it out the rear of the aircraft. The winch wound up the shroud line bungees attached to my parachute harness. I was beneath the ceiling of the plane; however, my body was still hanging out over mother earth.

I heard voices shouting to one another. The voices belonged to two crewmen, each being tethered to the side of the aircraft by nylon belts attached to cargo tethers on the fuselage ribs. All I remember was two humans reaching out from either side of me. Their hands met, clasped, and were pressed against my belly, guiding me backward to the cargo deck of the Caribou. As my toes struck the solid deck, one of the crewmen backed off on the winch a foot to let me down to the floor of the aircraft. Using their knives, they cut the bungee cords at the rings on my parachute harness. Still holding on to my harness, the crewman on my left shouted in my ear to turn around, face the cockpit, and walk forward to a small jump seat behind the cockpit. Removing my rifle from my neck and shoulder, I slumped into the seat and strapped in. The crewmen were right behind me. They squatted down on either side of my knees and, shouting above the engine roar, asked if I was okay or if I needed anything. I nodded my head in reply to the first question; then shook it to indicate "no" to the second. I leaned my head back against the skin of the aircraft, closing my eyes. I was totally exhausted from the ordeal.

We remained in the clouds for the entire flight, using them as a shield from enemy view. I had no discussion with the pilot or copilot, who were intent on watching their instruments and FDS in the soupiness of the clouds.

From the instant the hook assembly hit the cross bungee cord of my extraction system on the ground, to the time I strapped into the jump seat for the ride to safety, was about seven minutes. Five of those minutes were very cold.

I shivered and shook for nearly the entire trip back, in spite of the crewmen having wrapped me in three wool blankets and given me hot coffee from a thermos. I was certain that I had the beginnings of hypothermia.

I awoke with a change in the sound of the engines. I noted the two crewmen strapped into their seats across from me. I concluded we were approaching the airstrip. About ten minutes later I looked out the opened rear section of the Caribou and could see we were flying below the cloud cap. The engines were throttled back, and we were in the approach for landing at Vientiane, Laos. The pilot greased the aircraft onto the runway, the sound of the main landing gear making two slight squeaks as the rubber met the pavement. Then the nose gear hit the pavement. Immediately the pilot reversed props and went into full power. This action, combined with a heavy application of the brakes, brought us to a quick stop on the runway. We taxied to the operations building and the pilot cut the engines.

A form and face appeared beneath the open tail section before the propellers had stopped turning.

"Hey, Big Guy, whose damn missiles were they?"

It was Bill's voice shouting at me.

In jest, I shouted back, "Californian!" Bill had been born and raised just outside of San Diego.

There was none of the usual, "Hey, Big Guy, glad you made it back safely. Are you in good shape? Any blood? Any holes beside those God gave you?"

"Bull*shit!*" Bill shouted. "Get your butt out of there and let's have a beer."

I unhooked my seat belt, released my parachute harness and dropped it to the aircraft deck, picked up my rifle, walked aft, and climbed down to the tarmac. The two crewmen were already standing on the tarmac and I shook their hands, thanking them for their good work. Bill threw his arms around me and hugged me. I was appalled! Certainly I was not expecting to be hugged by my case officer. It wasn't macho.

While waiting near the aircraft tail to thank the pilots, I began to feel weak from hunger. My knees were wobbling, my head was light, and I simply wanted to eat something, then crash on anything soft and sleep for a few days. The incredible intensity of this mission had suddenly ceased. The adrenaline no longer flowed.

"That was a tough one, man," said Bill. "Now we've got to get on the radio. We need to call Saigon to tell them whose missiles those are. They're waiting in Washington for the word."

"Fuck 'em," I said, with extreme, venomous anger welling up inside me.

"Did you get a good look?" Bill asked vehemently. "I mean, did you really get next to the missiles?"

"Yeah," I replied quietly, not volunteering more information for the moment.

"Where's the cold beer, Bill?" I wanted to play with Bill's head a little, and avoided a direct answer.

"You didn't see the missiles, right, man? You really didn't get to see 'em," shouted Bill, childishly trying to use reverse psychology on me and simultaneously dying to know if I had accomplished the objective of the mission. Bill was obviously frustrated in his attempt to debrief me, to get the answer he needed and get on with the show.

"Come on, Big Guy!" Bill shouted, moving away from me as we walked toward the operations building.

"Whose fuckin' missiles were they?" He spread his arms and opened his palms as if to say "I give up!" I stopped in my tracks, turned, and glared at Bill.

I paused. "*Russian!*" I shouted back at him at the top of my lungs. "*Russian!*" I repeated.

Still shouting, I said, "*And what in the hell difference does it really make?* Call the President of the United States right now! Call Lyndon Johnson. Get him out of his warm bed. Tell him the missiles killing our pilots are Russian."

Bill's look of exasperation turned to one of relief. He took a deep breath and simply said, "You're certain? Okay."

I was angry over what I believed was the simple, politically motivated rationale behind the mission objective. I never took time to realize that I really did not know the whole story behind the need for this information. All that was certain was that I had taken an incredible risk, and gotten lucky. Oddly, I was both proud of my accomplishment and pissed at the same time. I was also dead tired.

The morning temperature was already eighty-five degrees, and it was humid and overcast. I was still slightly cold as I walked into the ops building for a beer, two burgers, and fries. They only had beer, water, and a selection of C rations in green cans, which was called food.

Bill let me sleep for three hours while he radioed in the information on my sighting of the Russian SAMs. Then he awakened me, and we took off in a helicopter for a short hop south to Udorn.

Tom, John, and Richard were the only teammates at Udorn when I arrived. Tom was still recovering from a knee injury, Richard was recovering from malaria, and John had just returned from a mission with two South Vietnamese Rangers. They had been on an observation mission near Kompong Som in southern Cambodia. One of the Rangers had been killed during the extraction.

Debriefings conducted by Bill Dunn typically followed each mission. At these occasions each team would work with Bill to develop a mission report that included every detail we observed and experienced, whether or not we thought everything important. The debrief following my mission into China took place in two sessions of about two hours each. My teammates sat in on the sessions, asking questions, prompting me, and adding some levity.

Courtesy of the U.S. Air Force, the four of us sat in the "O-Club" for several hours drinking beer and eating some great Thai food, while I told them the details of my mission into China. They were proud of me, as I was of myself. After about two hours of talk and laughter, I asked about our other teammates. John told me of a mission involving two of our team in eastern Laos. As he explained their mission objective, I noted his voice dropped to just above a whisper, and the look on his face and the expressions on the faces of Richard and Tom assured me that something bad had happened. Finally, John got around to telling me that Jerry Thomas and Peter Bells had not been recovered—meaning they were presumed dead. He

explained that their last radio transmission to the extraction helicopter indicated they were being pursued by North Vietnamese soldiers and that they were taking rifle fire. Nothing more was heard
from them. Our aircraft had overflown their last known position for
three days and had not received a response to radio calls.

Chapter 13

Combat Engagements

In the Hollywood movie productions with a Vietnam War theme we are frequently shown combat teams engaging in incident after incident, back to back. This is done to keep the audience's attention with continuous excitement. Occasionally there is a film in which there is a single combat objective and the film deals with the preparation and buildup, the development and implementation of tactical plans, accomplishment of the objective as the climax, and finally a conclusion in some format. Usually there is a gorgeous female who gets into the action, then dies in the arms of the hero or is rescued from the hands of the abusive enemy. These films have often provided a distorted view of the war in Vietnam.

Many of FRAM 16's patrols were quite uneventful in that we did not encounter any hostile action. We'd hide on the ground or in the trees, observe the enemy for a time, and report back. This describes the patrols of many combat units in Vietnam. In reality, one did not engage the enemy with great frequency, that is, there weren't back-to-back firefights. For one thing, the stress resulting from combat engagements with live bullets flying around, mortars exploding, machine guns blasting their staccato, grenades bursting, and the screams of men hit by bullets, shrapnel, or napalm, is extremely debilitating mentally and physically. In World War II, ground combat engagements with the Japanese or the Germans in the Pacific and European theaters would occasionally last for several days, even stretching into weeks. Placing men under continuous anxiety and stress reduces the effectiveness and decision making abilities as the engagement time increases. Combat leaders know this well and usually will do everything possible to give soldiers "break time" to rest, recover, regroup, replan, and reengage the enemy soldiers.

In Vietnam, engagements typically ranged from a three-minute firefight to a three-day battle. U.S. soldiers usually had the advantage of calling in fire support from fighter or bomber aircraft, or from artillery batteries on firebases located miles from the battle scene, and sometimes bombardment from ships lying offshore. With deployment of this backup, engagements were usually broken off quickly by the enemy.

FRAM 16 was primarily trained to infiltrate and gather intelligence information without engaging the enemy unless it was impossible to avoid an engagement, such as incidents wherein we were ambushed. Many of our missions were quite boring, especially when we found nothing of value to report as intelligence. In the beginning we were divided in to A-, B-, and C-teams. As we lost members of our team to enemy gunfire or booby traps, there were none trained to fill in our personnel gaps. As we lost teammates we made up for this by selecting squad members from those remaining who were reasonably healthy, making up a team of whatever number was required. Many of our missions were one-, two-, or three-man jobs. We would patrol out and climb a tree or dig a hole—whatever was required to observe the enemy and report that information back to the REMFs (Rear Echelon Motherfuckers) intelligence types who would massage the information and develop strategic and/or tactical plans.

When our assigned missions did not result in physically engaging the NVA or the VC, they were obviously welcomed. Wherever we patrolled we had to be constantly aware of our location; know how we would escape and evade if detected; avoid booby traps (many of which were quite clever in terms of concealment); quickly decide how to circumvent the enemy and approach from behind or to the side to avoid detection; and how to insert and extract without getting into a firefight. This, of course, required constant focus and critical thought and plenty of good luck. Setting up an observation position high in a tree afforded a view of the surrounding area that was often superior to being in a hide on the ground. Though we found it necessary to use the trees as observation positions, I was uncomfortable up in trees because of the occasional difficulty in quickly escaping. If I was ever more than ten feet above the ground I always had a line ready to drop down for a rappell. Sometimes mere seconds made the difference between whether you could escape and evade undetected, or not. Sometimes the branches below a tree observation position would impede a fast rappell and escape.

On one patrol in Laos, Ben White and I were positioned in trees about fifty yards apart, overlooking one of the many trails and roads that constituted the infamous Ho Chi Minh Trail. Our positions were approximately seventy-five feet west of the trail. During the first two days of our patrol, there had been an intermittent stream of bicycle and foot traffic carrying war materials southward on the trail. Very boring. We had planned to rappell down just after dark and retreat some distance for the night, and extract the next morning. Just before last light, one of the NVA, who appeared to be a young officer, stopped on the trail and began to direct the civilian laborers to move west off the trail to eat rations and camp for the night. The North Vietnamese set up their camp around and beneath the trees in which Ben and I were positioned. There was virtually no time for us to get down out of the trees and escape. When I realized what was about to happen and was still able to use my walkie-talkie to communicate with Ben, we agreed to sit tight and wait for the NVA to move out in the morning. We spent a very hungry, uncomfortable night wedged between branches in our respective trees, afraid to move for fear of knocking loose a piece of bark and having it alert the enemy below.

I listened to the nasal, high-pitched voices speaking forty feet below me while they smoked their cigarettes, ate their fish and rice, and drank their fermented juices. At midnight I had to urinate. Actually I had the urge to urinate about 11:00 P.M.; however, I held it. When it was no longer possible to hold it, I slipped off my shirt, folded it up, and placed it between my butt and the branch on which I was sitting. I must have passed at least a quart of urine, which was at first soaked up by my trousers (black pajama bottoms) and then by my shirt. It would have been nice if it had been raining hard, because I would not have had to bother urinating on my new shirt. When finished urinating, I put my shirt on my lap and unfolded it very slowly, trying to make sure any puddles were soaked up by the material, and any last drips would hit the thigh of my trousers.

It was absolutely the most tedious urination of my life! After the shirt was fully unfolded, I left it to dry on my lap. Then, when my upper torso became chilled to the point where I was into a hard shiver, I put the shirt on and buttoned it up. At first the coldness of the damp shirt was almost worse than the cool air before I donned the shirt. But within about forty-five minutes I was more comfortable. The strong urine smell helped keep me awake and maintain my balance in the tree. I have often wondered what I would have done under these conditions if I'd had a case of diarrhea. In all probability I would have been detected and shot out of the tree.

Around 7:00 A.M. the North Vietnamese packed up and hit the trail, and about 10:30 there was a break in the parade of foot and bicycle traffic on the trail. Ben and I rappelled down and moved about two hundred yards west in the Laotian jungle, where we sat down and stifled our laughter with our hands as we discussed how each of us had fared during the night. Ben's problem during the night was gas in his lower intestine—major gas. Each time he was forced to pass gas, he would muffle it in his boonie hat, pressing it to his butt with his hand. We laughed at ourselves and at each other for several minutes, to a point that our eyes watered and we rolled on the ground holding our sides.

In another incident, not nearly as humorous, we were on a lengthy patrol about fifty miles south of the DMZ near the western South Vietnamese border with Laos. After two days in the jungle, where it had rained very hard, we made radio contact with an Army firebase and were granted refuge. During the course of a conversation with the firebase commander, an Army Special Forces captain, who complained of the need to capture some North Vietnamese soldiers and bring them in for interrogation. I was operating with Tom and John on this recon mission, and we volunteered to bring back some prisoners if the captain would tell us the nearest place where he suspected there were NVA. We believed that such interrogation might benefit us as well.

That night around 1:00 A.M. we applied camo paste and exited the firebase. Passing through the recently mined perimeter of the firebase, we entered the jungle and set up camp for the night preparatory to moving out at first light. At 6:30 A.M., after patrolling only about forty-five minutes, we heard Vietnamese voices speaking in relaxed tones, at normal decibel levels. The three of us spread out and moved in. We discovered six North Vietnamese eating breakfast in a small clearing in the jungle. From a brief recon of the surrounding area it appeared that these soldiers were not part of a larger group. Perhaps they were in a lookout or forward position for a larger body of enemy soldiers. Because our movements were masked by the sound of rain hitting the leaves around us, we were able to crawl undetected to within ten yards of them. It was a "piece o' cake" to charge the unsuspecting NVA soldiers, capture them, tape their mouths, bind their hands behind their backs, hobble their ankles to permit only an eighteen-inch stride, and march them off to the firebase.

On approaching the edge of the clearing, we radioed in to the firebase and received clearance to approach with our prisoners. Once inside the firebase, the Army Special Forces and ARVN soldiers hustled the prisoners off to an interrogation tent. I followed the group out of interest and curiosity. In the tent, an ARVN captain ordered that the prisoners, who were lined up at the end of the tent opposite the entry, be stripped-searched by the ARVN guards. They could have been carrying concealed weapons, and stripping them allowed them to be completely searched. It was also a demeaning psychological technique to strip an enemy soldier, hopefully making him feel uncomfortable and vulnerable preparatory to being interrogated, and therefore more likely to "spill the beans." When the shirt was stripped off the smallest NVA standing on the left end of the line, I noted nothing out of the ordinary; however, when the trousers were stripped of this individual, I noted a difference: the person was absent a penis. I did a genuine Jerry Lewis doubletake. This was a female NVA! She had no breasts—not even a ripple of fatty tissue where her breasts should be—just nipples that might have been slightly larger than the nipples on the men. The Army captain ordered the ARVN captain to dress the woman and leave the others naked. Shortly after an ARVN sergeant began interrogating and knocking the naked NVA soldiers around with a large bamboo stick, Tom, Richard, and I left the tent with the U.S. Army Captain. Personally, I was not interested in observing the interrogation in a language which I did not speak well at all. I was also not interested in observing the torture that the ARVNs would likely employ to get information about troop locations and strength from the NVA soldiers.

So Tom and I wandered off to our tent and a short nap. John said he didn't need a nap and wandered off somewhere else. Minutes after I had fallen asleep, John burst into our tent and shouted, "Big Guy, the ARVNs are raping the NVA woman—about five of them are taking turns gang-banging her. You can hear her screams outside the tent!"

I kippered up from my folding cot, grabbed my rifle, and raced out of the tent with Tom and John right on my heels. We ran toward the interrogation tent, about fifty yards away.

My fear was that with all those ARVN soldiers raping this woman, she might not physically be able to respond to interrogation; that is, she might go into shock or just clam up. I was really pissed.

Storming into the tent, I observed one ARVN in the act of raping the female on the ground, and four others standing around making comments about the action, laughing, and keeping their weapons trained on the male NVAs. The ARVNs were all noncommissioned officers.

I have the gifted capacity to shout very loudly in a bass tone. Bellowing loudly enough to shake the tent foundations, I caused the ARVN to scramble up from his prone position on the female with the speed of light. So loud was my bellow that great fear was evident on the faces of the ARVN present, especially on the face of the ARVN soldier whose trousers still lay in a pile beside the woman, and whose erect little penis still protruded foolishly from between his shirttails. I ordered the ARVNs out of the tent and left Tom and John to guard the NVA prisoners, including the woman. With my rifle pointed at the backs of the ARVNs exiting the tent, I followed them out, marched them to the opposite side of the firebase, and lined them up facing me. I really did not know where I was headed with them, just that I was getting them away from the scene.

At this point the ARVN and U.S. Army captains arrived at my side, and I quickly explained to them what I had seen. To my surprise, after my explanation the Special Forces captain brought his M16 to his waist, pointed it at the ARVN soldiers, selected automatic fire, and hosed them down with a twenty- to twenty-five-round burst of fire. I was shocked and stood staring dumbly, with my mouth open, at the sight of the dead South Vietnamese laying five yards in front of me. For the moment I could not comprehend what had just occurred; I fought to mentally compute the situation. The loud sound of the bursts of automatic fire continued to reverberate in my ears for several seconds after the deed had been done. The ARVN captain, about twenty-five years old, appeared to be equally shocked. The Special Forces captain turned and started to walk the several yards back toward the interrogation tent, when the ARVN captain shouted his rank and last name. My immediate fear was that the ARVN captain was about to shoot the American captain in retaliation for what had just occurred. I stepped back, fingered the safety off my rifle, and prepared to fire at the ARVN captain, but I did not move my rifle up to do so. The American stopped and turned slowly around, and the ARVN walked toward him with his rifle pointed toward the ground. The two walked away together.

Later than evening I learned that four of the five ARVNs who had been involved with the rape had recently been reprimanded. On a patrol in which they had been engaged, their squad of six men was found to have departed some 250 yards into the surrounding jungle, where they sat down without carrying out the patrol beyond the cleared perimeter of the firebase. When they returned to the firebase two days later, they reported that they had seen nothing. That same night over fifty NVA "sappers" (NVA infiltrators) engaged the firebase perimeter guards in a fierce battle in which 15 ARVNs had been killed and the same number wounded. On subsequent interrogation, one of the members of the ARVN squad spilled his guts and explained that they had not carried out the patrol; instead they had laid down, rested, and falsely reported their patrol.

I surmised that the American Army captain simply felt the need, as the commanding officer of the firebase, to set an example of what would happen if orders were disobeyed. He confirmed this to me that night after the execution of the ARVNs. He was calm and cool in his explanation—just as though relating a walk in the park. Though I made no comment to the captain, it remained difficult for me to accept the need to *execute* friendly forces as an example to the others. I further surmised, and chose to conclude, that this execution had really been a reaction out of anger and frustration.

The pounding rain finally stopped the next afternoon, so Tom, John, and I departed that night to continue our original patrol to an observation position. Four days later we called for an extraction helicopter, and eventually ended up in U Tapao, Thailand, for a few days of R&R.

The primary seaport of entry for war supplies and materials for the North Vietnamese was Haiphong, located about sixty miles east of the capital city of Hanoi, on the Gulf of Tonkin. Intelligence information always indicated that this busy port was occupied by freight and tanker vessels of many nations, particularly China and North Korea. It was widely known that ships docked in this port were providing the North Vietnamese with weapons of all types, food, clothing, and advisory manpower.

In early 1966 there was a temporary prohibition of the bombing of Hanoi and the port at Haiphong, in spite of the U.S. knowledge that the supplying and resupplying of the North Vietnamese was greatly benefiting their war efforts. A plan was prepared to mine the Haiphong harbor; however, this plan was canceled shortly before it was to be implemented. A second plan was developed to plant limpet mines on the hulls of selected ships docked at Haiphong. A team of twelve UDT and five FRAM 16 members were selected for the mission, which was to be carried out at night by submarine insertion. The sub would take us through the Gulf of Tonkin to a point within five miles or so of the Haiphong docks. In three rubber boats propelled by ten-horsepower outboard motors, we would ride to within a half mile of the docked vessels, then proceed using scuba tanks to the hulls of the selected vessels, where the limpet mines would be attached. We were supposed to sink the rubber boats prior to swimming in to attach the mines. The limpet mines were designed, using delayed fuses, to blow a hole through a ship's hull up to about two feet in diameter, allowing water to flood the ship, causing it to sink at dockside. A ship sunk at its dock would render the dock useless to all future ships bringing supplies to the enemy.

The harbor was heavily patrolled, twenty-four-hours a day, by small vessels operated by North Vietnamese. From intelligence sources inside North Vietnam, it was learned that these vessels were fast and typically carried a crew of four or five men, with each boat having a machine gun mounted near the bow. We assumed they had crates of hand grenades that could be dropped to explode underwater. Grenades exploding underwater typically did not kill with shrapnel, rather the concussion caused by the exploding grenade could kill a human many yards away from where the explosion occurred.

We practiced as a team for six days in the Cam Ranh Bay area, which is located on the South China Sea, two hundred miles northeast of Saigon. At that time, Cam Ranh Bay was the home base of the U.S. Navy's Coastal Surveillance Force.

The practice involved exiting from the submarine at night, inflating the rubber rafts from the deck of the sub, motoring into Cam Ranh Bay, switching to scuba, swimming in and planting practice limpet mines on the hulls of Navy ships, and exiting to be picked up by fast, small boats operated by a South Vietnamese UDT squad. The small boats took us back to the submarine. We were never told how the South Vietnamese boats were going to get into this area of North Vietnam; however, the boat crews would be taken aboard the submarine as we extracted, and their boats scuttled. Locating these small boats during our swim out from the harbor, and subsequently locating the submarine in the dark, was going to be accomplished by radio direction finders.

There were several matters with respect to this mission that left all of us significantly concerned. Obviously, the heavily patrolled harbor could be a nightmare to circumvent in our rubber boats. The pickup and extraction by the South Vietnamese boats was of even greater concern to us. Because of the enemy patrols, and our rubber boats having earlier been scuttled, we would have to swim approximately three miles from the docks—which was planned to occur during an outgoing tide—to a point off Quang Yen where we would be picked up by the small boats. From that pickup point we had to run another three miles—through what amounted to a two-mile-wide gauntlet—out of the harbor, to a predetermined point in the gulf about two miles southeast of Do Son, to link up with the submarine again. In our conclusion, which was mutual, the odds of a successful mission with all of us returning safely were poor.

Sharks, when they are feeding, are a constant threat to humans swimming in their presence. While the Cam Ranh Bay area where we practiced was relatively free of fresh garbage (dumped from vessels), we assumed that ships in the Haiphong Harbor would not be under the same fresh-garbage dumping restrictions as the U.S. vessels in Cam Ranh Bay.

Following a team discussion of this subject, we asked for intelligence on this matter; that is, the presence of fresh garbage and feeding sharks at Haiphong.

I took the initiative to bring up this subject with the UDT lieutenant who had been selected to lead the mining mission.

"Don't worry about the sharks," he said. "The water in the harbor will be heavily stained with mud and junk. Sharks don't swim in water that has a lot of suspended soil, silt, and debris. That stuff clogs their gills and they can't absorb oxygen. It is doubtful you will encounter any sharks in that area because of the silt."

That answer was not sufficient for me and several of the others, because we knew that we could easily be swimming in water approaching the mouth of the harbor, which might not be as muddy as it would be near the docks. We also considered the fact that the ships might be dumping garbage in less silted water as they entered or departed from the harbor, not just when they were docked. The UDT people seemed less concerned about the sharks than the FRAM 16 people were, particularly me. To the UDT guys the concern over being consumed by a shark was minor compared to the problems they envisioned with respect to the insertion and extraction.

Two days before we were to make the trip on the submarine up to the Gulf, the mission was scrubbed. We were not told why, nor whether the risks of the mission were considered too great. We celebrated this decision in grand style at a military club on the base at Cam Ranh. It was not unusual for FRAM 16 teams to have their missions called off at the last minute with no reason given. We were never told of the hierarchy of people in charge of mission planning and decision-making. While we usually had premission tactical input, and our questions and concerns were usually fully addressed, we were never privy to the same knowledge as the persons ultimately pulling our strings from above.

Chapter 14

Demolition of Vietcong Radio Tower

At one of the many mouths of the Mekong River, where the mud, debris, and water flows into the South China Sea, there was a small unnamed fishing village, a short distance south of Ba Dong, fronting the South China Sea—population of about 150, give or take a few dozen. This was Vietcong country. By night the VC controlled many villages in this area. By day the residents, including the VC, raised staple crops, trapped and netted fish, and squeezed out a daily existence. Many small fingers of water cut back into the land from the sea, and were perfect shelters for the fishing boats of the residents. But many of these boats, disguised as fishing boats, were in reality used for transporting war supplies, materials, and enemy soldiers throughout the delta region and coastal Vietnam areas.

The VC had erected a radio tower in the unnamed village estimated by intelligence photos to be one hundred feet in height. The main antenna, supported by the tower, was just above the treetops. The primary construction material of the tower was bamboo. The location was at the northwestern edge of the village, slightly apart from the greatest concentration of hooches (Vietnamese living huts). The purpose of the tower was to transmit and receive radio communications between the VC boat crews regarding transport assignments, instructions, and intelligence on American or ARVN patrol boats observed in the area. The radio transmissions had been intercepted by U.S. forces, and it was concluded this was an important target. At first, when the VC radio tower transmissions were intercepted by American coastal surveillance boats, the intelligence people thought it best to take out the tower with a bombing run by planes from one of the aircraft carriers cruising on Dixie Station in the South China Sea. Subsequent photo recon revealed that the tower was strategically located by the VC near the "downtown" area of the village. Intelligence people had second thoughts about bombing the tower, because the military was already being criticized for what the liberal American media tagged "indiscriminate bombing of innocent women and children" in villages throughout Vietnam.

Several of us were resting up in U Tapao when Bill called our team together. Because of the haste with which Bill called the meeting, and the serious look on his face when he walked into the billet shack, I knew the next mission would be tough—no "piece o' cake." I was right.

"Okay, this operation is for Turkey and Big Guy," he said. After unrolling a large, detailed grid section map of the Mekong Delta region, he said, "We need you guys to get into this village near Ba Dong and take out the radio tower and the transceiver. The strike needs to be done in the next week. The UDT people and the new SEAL team are deployed in other actions for a while; hence, the mission falls to us."

Bill laid out the background, gave John and me the aerials, maps, and intel reports. We were to use C-4 explosives to knock the tower down and take out the radio shack. He indicated that we would be inserted by a fishing boat operated by ARVN river patrol forces, and dropped off on the shore just over a mile north of the village. We would be extracted from the South China Sea by helicopter when the job was done. The briefing was over in ninety minutes, and I began to prepare myself mentally for the mission.

I was always pleased to work John "Turkey" or "Turk" Schneider, a graduate of the Georgia Institute of Technology (Georgia Tech) in Atlanta. John was slightly shorter than me, but about the same weight. He had dark brown hair, ice-blue eyes that could penetrate steel, and was amazingly strong. He never complained about anything unless it really mattered to us—like poor food, lousy water, or American politicians. His father was a sheriff in north Florida. John was the best of any of us in hand-to-hand combat. As he was a genuinely nice, quiet fellow, we marveled at his ability to put down (kill) an enemy with a single chop of his meat-hook hand. While hand-to-hand fighting was unusual for us, John's talent saved ammunition, and it was far less noisy and messy. Ben White and George Townsend once claimed they had personally seen John take on three VC at the same time, someplace in southern Cambodia. They reported that John killed them all in less than one minute, with his bare hands. We kidded him that when he returned to the States he'd have to register his hands as lethal weapons and carry a weapons permit. John and I had become close friends.

Three hours after our briefing with Bill, we helicoptered out of Soc Trang, South Vietnam; refueled, ate some chow, and flew east a short distance to Long Phu, beside the Bassac River, for the boat pickup.

It was a moonless night. The ARVNs arrived at the small firebase at Long Phu about 6:00 P.M., in a fishing boat that had been captured from the VC and overhauled and upgraded for missions such as the one on which we were about to embark. Beneath the rectangular tarpaulin, which stretched over bamboo joists amidships, were two .30-caliber guns and several boxes of belted ammunition. While we did not expect to engage the enemy from the fishing boat, it was comforting to know we had the extra firepower to defend ourselves.

We had two haversacks of C-4 cubes, about eight pounds of the explosive, which could sink small warships or take down a major building, if properly placed. We had six timed detonators, rations for four days, and our weapons and ammunition. Dressed in black pajamas, both of us were fully camouflaged about the head, face, neck, and hands. We sat under the tarpaulin on boxes containing belts of .30-caliber ammo. In the darkness I could not see John, but I could hear the five ARVN crew members chatting aloud among themselves as we maneuvered eastward on the Bassac River. I guessed it was a good idea for them to be talking (and possibly overheard by passing VC boats) so that everything about our transit appeared to be normal. We had to assume that because it was nighttime, any vessels moving around us were probably occupied by VC. We cruised out into the South China Sea with no running lights.

Thankfully, the ARVNs knew their way around this area, because we could see nothing. The light from a half-moon helped us clear the various islands, and the high tide saved us from running up on the sand bars that stick out in the channels everywhere. I was impressed with the ARVNs' ability to navigate and maintain orientation in the dark. We did not communicate with them during the excursion. For that time period my only concern was that we got inserted on the beach as near as possible to the planned point of insertion.

Just prior to departing from Long Phu, I had carefully cleaned and test fired my Stoner into the Bassac River, then loaded up five clips of 5.56mm ammunition. John carried a twelve-gauge pump-action shotgun. His shells carried lead buckshot, which could do serious damage. The weapon was a crowd-killer, according to John; but we hoped we would not be chased by an angry crowd on this mission. We also carried .45-caliber pistols, knives, and frag grenades.

Eventually, the ARVN boat coxswain turned the helm over to another crew member and crawled under the tarp with us.

"We will reach the beach in about forty minutes," he said in excellent English.

"You will go up to the bow of the boat one minute before we touch the sand. When you climb off, do it quietly, and do not attempt to help us push back from the sand. My people will take care of that. Walk from the boat and into the jungle as if we were simply dropping off friends from the boat."

The coxswain then rolled the tarpaulin back to clear the view for the machine guns, and placed them on their mounts. Two ARVNs took positions at the machine guns and were prepared to fire at the first sign of the enemy. Of course, if we had to use these weapons our presence would obviously be compromised, and we would have to abort the mission.

The rest of the crew continued their friendly banter in Vietnamese as our vessel slowed and approached the beach in the darkness.

One of the machine gunners tapped us on the shoulders and said, "Go to front, sirs."

John and I moved into position and could just make out the dark outline of the trees that lined the shore, about fifteen yards back from the water's edge. As we disembarked, the ARVNs continued their charade by quietly calling their farewells to us in their native tongue. Two of them immediately followed us over the side and began pushing the boat back into deeper water.

We walked directly into the trees, then crouched down and listened for several minutes. I wondered if our footprints in the sand would attract any attention; but this was doubtful because we were barefoot. We put on our tennis shoes when we were in among the trees.

Our track to the village would be southward, about 1.6 miles. It would have been easier to walk along the beach, since the jungle was quite thick here. John and I debated this for a moment. . . . The temptation was great in spite of the exposure.

Finally, John whispered, "Look, Big Guy, it's too fuckin' dark to try to move through the jungle, man. Let's just follow the damn beach south for about a mile, then cut back into the jungle. We still have several hours until first light."

"We'll have to walk just above the water's edge, because there is too much chance the VC have set up trip wires (for booby traps) close to the tree line, figuring that would be the usual route for unfriendlies like us," I replied.

John agreed. We removed our tennis shoes and walked back onto the beach. I slung my Stoner's muzzle down and kept it moving in unison with my left leg as much as possible. John did the same with his shotgun. We walked single file, about two yards apart, so it would simply appear that we were locals making our way down the beach, not close enough to talk. The small waves hitting the beach provided background noise, which canceled most other sounds. This concerned me.

John took up the point. We had walked about fifty yards when I got the idea that I could improve on the naturalness of our appearance and presence on the beach. I concocted a limp, with my left leg held straight, appearing to have been injured. If we were spotted it would appear that we were just average VC guys, one of whom had been injured. Surely, I thought, we would not be perceived as the enemy if one of us was limping. I felt the VC would know that Americans are not usually sent on missions if they are injured. The only problem with this ploy was that John and I were both tall. We did not look like Vietnamese, in spite of our black pajamas. But the darkness concealed this.

John maintained the count of our strides, counting about thirty-two hundred strides, which represented about a mile and a half, and headed into the jungle for cover. It was 1:45 A.M. and the sun would be up in five hours. It was impossible to orient ourselves with any degree of accuracy because there were no landmarks that we could tie to our map. About fifteen yards into the jungle we found a sandy area and took a nap with one ear cocked for the slightest foreign sound. There were none. John nudged me at 6:00 A.M. I awakened instantly, alert and listening.

"Sun's coming up, sweetheart," John murmured. "I didn't want you to miss the beautiful sunrise. Room service will be bringing us coffee and blueberry pancakes in a few minutes, then it will be Miller time."

John was always full of humor and practical jokes. It made the missions more tolerable to have a teammate around who was less than intense. We ate some canned rations sitting on the sand, watching the sunrise. I thought of hot black coffee and blueberry pancakes; but the lovely waitress never showed up with our order.

As the sun cut a thin yellow line on the eastern horizon over the ocean we could gradually examine our jungle surroundings. Out on the beach I could see our footprints as they turned in from the South China Sea to the jungle. The tide had gone out a few yards. If the VC had found our prints they would have concluded that Gulliver and his brother had been there. Our feet were U.S. size eleven and Vietnamese feet are far smaller.

At 6:30 A.M. we moved inland. I took the point after selecting and cutting a four-foot-long, slender piece of bamboo. The VC frequently set mines and booby traps along trails that might be used by their enemies. The trip wire of the booby trap was usually very thin and set about four inches or more above the ground. We had also observed trip wires of four- to six-pound test monofilament fishing line or of finely twisted local vines. The point man would use the thin bamboo stick, if we were patrolling on or near a trail or path, in order to feel the vines or monofilament stretched across our track. It was possible to feel the tension of the tripper with the bamboo stick without setting it off, even before the tripper could be seen.

In the dark shadows of the triple-canopy jungle it was particularly slow going, because each time I felt resistance on the stick I had to stop and slide my hand down the bamboo to feel if the resistance was being produced by a branch or vine from jungle underbrush or from a tripper. Additionally, as we came to paths that appeared to be more heavily traveled, I had to be on the alert for the presence of toe-popper mines hidden just below the surface of the soil. *Toepopper* was a misnomer. If you stepped on one it had enough power to shred a man's foot, even with a steel shank in his combat boot. We were still wearing tennis shoes at this point and a toe-popper would have removed a foot up to above the ankle.

Our patrol would have been greatly speeded and quieter if we had chosen to use the numerous paths in the area; however, we elected to thread our way through the jungle most of the time. As we progressed and began to believe we should be approaching the VC village, we moved even more slowly—ten to fifteen yards at a time, then stopping to observe and listen for a minute. About 10:30 A.M. we stopped to take a rest break, sitting on the ground near a large thicket of bamboo. Within seconds, swarms of mosquitoes were feasting on our necks, even though we had earlier swabbed on generous portions of non–sweet-smelling deet repellent. It didn't help much as the mosquitoes committed suicide on our bodies and right through our clothing. The mosquito is the national bird of Vietnam, we believed.

We cut some ripening bananas off a nearby tree, and John and I enjoyed a fruit cup consisting of bananas and mosquitoes.

After fifteen minutes of rest we began to patrol again. After having progressed another one hundred yards or so we heard voices. A woman. Then a man. Then a baby crying. Then silence. The sound came from the same direction toward which we were patrolling. We judged the people were another fifty to seventy-five yards in front of us.

After several minutes of slow going we made the outline of a hooch. Staying well out of sight of it, we patrolled slowly in a westerly direction, and began to observe the palm frond and banana leaf roofs of other hooches along a tree line. Shortly, we heard more voices. We stopped and crouched low.

Aerial photo recon showed the radio tower to be approximately 250 yards inland from the ocean. I figured we were about that distance inland already. But we still could not see the tower, and heard only occasional voices to our south. We continued patrolling west until finally we could see no more hooches or hear any voices. I guessed we were then about seventy-five to eighty yards northwest of the perimeter of the village. The jungle was dense. It was 3:30 P.M. and it began to rain.

Sitting on the ground in the thick underbrush, we began to plan our next moves and listen. The fishermen had probably left the village to go fishing or to haul war materials. But the women, children, and dogs should have been making some noises. The rain may have been canceling out the sounds. We decided to move back southeast of our position, and had progressed nearly one hundred paces, when we heard a man's voice speaking above the sound of the raindrops. The voice was so unceasing that I guessed he was giving a speech of some sort. Maybe that was why everything had been so quiet several minutes ago. We moved forward, three paces at a time. The male tenor voice stopped, then started up again, then stopped, and we heard the murmur of several voices. We could not see any hooches or the radio tower. But as we crossed over a well-used path in the jungle leading to the village, we both glanced east up the path, then found cover on the other side.

We crouched just beyond the path for a moment, and I looked up through a thin break in the jungle canopy. The top of the bamboo structure of the radio tower appeared through the break, and I nodded over at John, indicating with my index finger that I wanted him to follow my line of sight. He saw the tower too. We grinned at each other in brief acknowledgement.

Our objective had been located, and the immediate task was to sufficiently recon the area to determine the best approach to knock it out. First we needed to recon the guard situation around the tower. We also had to determine the position of the radio equipment shack relative to the tower. I whispered to John that we should wait until

nearer dark, and suppertime for the villagers, before patrolling farther. He nodded in agreement and we moved farther away from the
trail to pull a little R&R.

With the smell of cooking oil as our signal, we moved out. It was
5:45 P.M. and getting dark in the jungle very quickly. The rain had
stopped two hours earlier.

The village dogs, which can give away your hiding position very
quickly, are usually less of a problem during mealtimes as they are fed
the scraps. About thirty minutes into our ultracautious recon I picked
up a hint of a different smell. It was slightly sweet and pungent.

"Opium," whispered John. I nodded back, smiling.

At that point we observed the backside of a long hooch, raised
about seven feet above the ground on multiple bamboo support
columns, located fifteen yards from the south side of the radio tower.
Three or four VC were lounging in bamboo chairs near the left front
side the hooch.

"The hooch must be the radio shack," I thought to myself.

It was the only structure I could see located close to the foot of
the tower. I concentrated on cementing a visual image of the radio
tower construction. It had four legs of stout, six-inch-diameter bamboo at the bottom. Strong cross members and X members were
lashed to the legs with what appeared to be twisted vines or perhaps
a type of rope. The pattern of the cross members was generally uniform as far up as I could see. Climbing the tower did not appear to
pose any difficulty for us. We only needed to climb up fifteen to
twenty feet and tie in the C-4 explosives. I wondered if the lashing
material holding the bamboo together was rotten. Would it hold us
when we climbed? Should we just blow up the base of the tower and
be done with it? No. We needed to get up to the second group of
cross members in order to have the cutting blast of the C-4 create a
whipping acting on the tower. We needed to demolish most of the
larger support members in the blast and cause the tower to fall and
break up. Otherwise the VC would have it rebuilt and operating
again in a week.

We inched our way about 150 yards back into the jungle as it was
getting dark. Some underbrush had been pounded down by villager

foot traffic, and we had no trouble moving away. The voices of the VC around the radio shack were muted, but we occasionally discerned their high-pitched laughter. They were relaxed and certainly not suspecting there were two green-painted villains lurking a few yards away, preparing to blow up their hooch. After discussing the situation in whispers for a few minutes, we moved several yards apart and were left with our own thoughts as we ate rations and set up for a night's sleep.

In reflecting on this mission now, many years later, I wonder how John and I withstood the intense pressure. This was not a Hollywood movie unfolding here, where the good guys from "Delta Force" always win in the end. This was a real life-or-death proposition. War is about life and death. Either you kill enough of the enemy—knock him to his knees, bomb his home and his workplace, obliterate his supply lines, and bring him to the surrender table—or the enemy does that to you. There is nothing complicated about this. The tenseness of these situations is very difficult to impart to those who have not personally experienced it. Unlike football, hockey, or basketball, this game is extremely dangerous. To win and survive, you employ what you have learned from training and other experiences. You rely on your wits and instincts; you constantly visualize your success, and you have a supreme confidence in your ability and immortality. Risk evaluation is a constant process of updating all the facts of the operational situation. The more information you have, the less you have to leave to luck. But luck is always part of the calculation of the situation.

There we were, two tough hombres, getting ready to take down a one-hundred-foot bamboo radio tower, at night, in the midst of a Vietcong village, with an unknown number of armed defenders between us, getting the task accomplished, and getting ourselves out of there safely. We had a long way to go.

The bark of two dogs was an unwelcome alarm clock for John and me the next morning. We were both awake in an instant. The barking was heard again—about 150 yards from our position, we guessed. We heard a male voice shouting two monosyllabic words. The barking stopped. In a crouched position we waited and listened.

It was 6:30 A.M. when we heard the sound of a shrill mechanical whistle. I thought I could hear the sound of many men speaking. Wanting to take advantage of the opportunity to do some reconnaissance, we hid our backpacks and haversacks of C-4, and we moved southeast toward the south side of the village. The open area of the village was already getting brighter in the sunrise, but it was still fairly dark in the jungle where we were. About seventy yards from the radio hooch, we stopped and listened. Very faintly we heard a male voice speaking in a monotone, as if reading. He halted between groups of monosyllabic words as if thinking about the next thing to say. John tapped me on the shoulder and motioned for me to move with him behind a large tree trunk.

John said, "Look, this village has gotta be crawling with people, women, kids, dogs—the kids and dogs making this daylight recon dangerous. We need to do another night recon and confirm the security setup. Maybe we ought to back off, wait for dinnertime, move in closer and locate a good hide, check everything out carefully, pull back, and strike tomorrow night."

I whispered, "I haven't seen any good hides close to the tower, have you? The underbrush is smashed down for several yards into the jungle from the cleared area of the hooches. The tower may be equipped with a trip alarm that we couldn't see in the dark. There could be dogs prowling around at night; maybe even sleeping under the tower or the radio hooch. But I agree, we don't have enough information yet, and we're liable to get our asses shot off if we don't get it."

"There's a sizeable clump of banana trees thirty-five to forty feet from the northeast corner of the hooch. Did you see that? If the clump is not too dense, maybe we can get into it. Don't worry about the tarantulas in the banana trees, they don't feed much at night," said John.

Neither of us liked the idea of being so close together in the banana grove if a firefight broke out, because we had been compromised by a child or dog. We decided to move into the banana grove after dusk and try to find another hide where we could split up. If not, then I would drop back into the jungle and, John or I would do the observation alone.

We backed up to the position where we had spent the night before, broke out some C rations and had a lovely brunch in the jungle. I catnapped for a while and it began to rain again. In the mid-afternoon we checked all of our equipment and thoroughly checked our weapons for dirt or mud buildup. We would take the C-4 haversacks with us for the recon, just in case we had an opportunity to blow the tower that night. I had a one-hundred-yard roll of dark-green heavy twine, which we would use to find our way back to our jungle resting position after the recon was completed.

We reapplied camouflage paste, and at 5:30 P.M. I motioned to John that it was dark enough to move out. The sun was setting behind us and did not filter into the jungle. I tied the twine to a sapling, John took the point, and I unrolled the twine as we moved along a few yards at a time. Within fifteen minutes we could see the roofline of the radio hooch. We could also see the dark outlines of the banana trees near the corner of the hooch. On closer examination it appeared to be too small a clump to hide us both adequately, so John moved forward with great stealth to a holding position in the jungle north of the banana trees. I remained forty yards west of him, under the cover of a fallen tree trunk.

In our respective positions we could not see each other. The camouflage worked well. It was 6:45 P.M. The villagers began to cook dinner, and the smells of fried fish wafted around me. It made me feel hungry, as usual. We remained in our respective positions until 11:30 P.M., at which point John was to work his way into the banana grove, remain there for up to two hours, then work his way back to my position.

When he rejoined me later around 1:45 A.M., John told me that he had been unable to get into the banana grove because he feared being seen—the area between his holding position and the banana trees was just too open. Further, he said that between 11:45 P.M. and 1:30 A.M. he had seen only one armed guard posted outside the hooch. Most of that time the guard sat on the steps of the hooch, or walked around the shack and the tower at infrequent and unpredictable intervals, occupying himself by chain-smoking and whittling a stick with a pocketknife. His weapon was the usual AK-47. Around his neck he wore a tube-shaped silver whistle on a string.

We were both confident we would have no trouble laying the guard to permanent rest, and I hoped that the next night there would still be only one guard.

Rolling up the twine, we moved slowly away from the village and reached our campsite in about fifteen minutes with no difficulties.

"This is going to be a piece o' cake, Big Guy," John whispered to me. "Ya know, it would have been so easy to take out that guard back there, climb the tower, and blow it tonight. What did you see?"

"No dogs and no kids after 7:40 P.M. Couldn't see much after that time. These people go to bed early; no lanterns. I didn't even hear any VC on the porch of the hooch. I couldn't see clearly enough to tell if there were trip wires on the tower," I said.

"Well, there weren't any that I could see," said John. "What about blowing it tonight? Conditions might change if we wait until tomorrow night."

I paused for a moment or two, and then agreed that we should strike tonight. Continuing to whisper to each other, we agreed that the C-4 should be set at the joint of the first level of cross support members with the four legs of the tower. But we would first wire two explosive charges under the hooch, since we believed the radio equipment was housed there. The timers on the charges under the hooch were to be preset for forty-five minutes, and on the radio tower they would be set for forty-six minutes. We felt this would be ample time for us to start the timer for the charges on the tower, climb down and activate the charges under the hooch, escape, and travel up the beach at least a mile or so.

I whispered, "You want to flip a coin to see who takes out the guard?"

John replied, "It's dark. If you flip the coin, how am I going to see whether it's heads or tails? Listen. How 'bout I'm thinking of a number between one and ten? You guess first and I'll guess second. Who ever gets closest to the number I'm thinking of, wins."

I decided to play out his lighthearted game. "Okay, smart-ass, let's do it your way. You thinking of a number?"

"Yeah."

"Okay, lucky seven," I whispered. "What number did you guess?"

"Five. And the number I had in mind was six. So we're both one number away. Want to try again?"

"No, idiot. That guard has my name on his shirt, and I just sharpened my knife two days ago. I'll take him out and you cover me," I said.

"Okay, if you insist," said John. "But if you screw up and that gook makes a sound when you're trying to cut him, I'll waste you both with a twelve-gauge shell."

We chuckled quietly to ourselves over this banter.

In the previous lighthearted exchange, we were discussing which of us would have the opportunity to take another human being's life. That is a rough thought to any civilized, rational person. But, as is often said, war is irrational. You do what you have to do to protect yourself and your comrades, get the job done, and maybe go home alive someday. If the enemy is in the way, you eliminate him. With our training and the proper frame of mind, there was no mental problem with my slicing the throat of an enemy while I was en route to an objective. Thirty years later, I could not even kill a deer or a duck. But this was Vietnam, where killing was the job. You didn't think about it, much.

It was 2:30 A.M. We had already preset the timers on the detonators and would install them in the C-4, which would be wired in series—one set of two blocks wired under the hooch and another set of four to be wired on the legs of the radio tower.

We moved into a position behind the long hooch. It was very quiet except for the sound of snoring above us from the sleeping radio operators. I smelled the cigarette being smoked by the guard, and could see its occasional glow when he inhaled on it as he sat on the steps of the radio hooch. John remained behind the hooch, and I moved to the northeast corner and waited.

After standing there for nearly an hour, I heard the guard make a sound as though he was stretching. It was 3:30 A.M. I heard him scuffle about on the sandy soil and grunt as he stood up. The slight sound of his footfalls indicated that he was walking around the hooch toward me. I drew my knife with my right hand and leaned up against the hooch. He passed by me only three feet away; so close I heard him breathing. I took two steps in stride behind him, silent as a cat. Grabbing him by clamping my left hand around his mouth, I jerked his neck back sharply to my left shoulder, shoved my left knee into the small of his back, and cut his throat powerfully from left to right, through to his vertebral column. The only sound was a muffled grunt and a gurgle. I held on to him for some seconds until I felt his muscles completely relax, then I dragged him several feet under the hooch.

John was at my shoulder as I came out from under the hooch. We said nothing to each other, but immediately went to work setting the charges on the beams supporting the floor. Then we both climbed the tower. I was filled with adrenaline and breathing heavily. We climbed easily in our tennis shoes. On reaching the first cross members we wired up the C-4 and installed the detonator. John finished before me and signaled me with a *"S s s s t"* sound. I *"S s s s t"* back at him when I was finished. At that instant I activated the timer on the detonator. Then we both climbed swiftly down from the tower and moved over to the backside of the hooch, feeling around for the C-4 charges under it.

Locating the detonator, John activated it, and together we crouched behind the hooch and listened for two minutes.

John nudged me and we moved out, walking east along the tree line of the jungle toward the beach. We passed two hooches that were thirty feet from the tree line, forded a small, dry streambed, and prayed we would not wake any dogs that might be sleeping under the hooches. It was almost too easy. We moved along silently, covering about 250 yards before reaching the beach—all the time listening for any sounds around us, and listening to the sound of the small waves washing up on the beach. There was enough moonlight to barely see where we were going, and we finally felt soft sand under our feet.

The detonators had been set to blow when we were well up the beach. As we were walking in the salt water, the small waves flowed in and washed away our footprints immediately. After progressing about a mile up the beach—nineteen-hundred paces by my count— I murmured to John that we had covered a mile.

In a low voice he said, "I make it about twenty minutes she blows."

We promptly headed inland toward the jungle and progressed only ten yards before encountering so much underbrush that further progress in the dark was impossible. Within twenty minutes of stopping we heard a loud explosion—the radio hooch going up. Less than a minute later we heard a second explosion, signaling that the tower had blown up. The amount of C-4 used by us was definitely overkill; but why not use it?

It was music to our ears and we smiled to ourselves in the dark. We were too far from the village to hear any shouts or screams; however, we commented to each other that the villagers were probably running around yelling and screaming, trying to figure out what had happened. It must have been a helluva rude wake-up call.

We progressed northward along the beach just over a thousand paces, finally reaching an estuary of the Delta that was carrying millions of gallons per hour of muddy water out into the South China Sea. This was to be our transportation to safety. We were most ready to get the hell out of there, but I was not looking forward to the swim ahead.

Chapter 15

Foiled Recovery and Near Death

After consuming most of our remaining rations and relaxing on the sand for a few hours, John and I waded out into the muddy water and manually inflated the small life belts that we had carried in our packs. Then we slipped the life belts up under our armpits. It was 4:45 A.M.

Using the frog kick, and remaining shoulder to shoulder so as not to lose contact in the darkness, we swam our way in a northeasterly direction, attempting to swim out into the most swiftly flowing part of the estuary. Unknown varieties of rotting vegetation were constantly bumping into us. Broken vines twirled themselves around our extremities. Judging by the horrible smell, the river was definitely a cesspool of every type of discard, including human excrement and rotted garbage. Sharks were not a concern because they would stay well away from the mud-filled water that would surely clog their gills. Nothing but leeches could survive in this watery trash. I tried not to think about it, and kept my lips pursed to avoid swallowing some rare, exotic disease-bearing amoeba or bacteria.

From aerial reconnaissance, the heavily mud-stained water was shown to extend out for a distance of about a mile before the brackish water of the estuary finally began to be absorbed by the ocean water and gradually became clearer. We were supposed to reach that point by 6:15 A.M. and expected a helicopter extraction shortly thereafter. The extraction helicopter was being supplied by an aircraft carrier, courtesy of the U.S. Navy. The helicopter was set to come in every morning at the same hour, beginning with our first day, until we were retrieved.

Silently I dreaded the probability of sharks patrolling the area where the water became clearer and less silted. What a helluva way to die: bleeding to death from an unseen enemy that gnawed your leg off at the hip and left you to bleed or be consumed, one bite at a time, by other sharks.

John and I spoke very little to each other as we let the outgoing tide carry us to our extraction point. Our speed slowed as we got farther from the shore and the current slacked. By 6:00 A.M. we had stopped trying to distance ourselves from the shoreline. The line of the rising sun on the horizon was now visible to us. John pulled a flare canister out of his pack and stuffed it into his shirt, where it could be quickly retrieved when we spotted the helicopter.

Just before 6:30 A.M., as dawn was first breaking, we could hear the droning of what we believed was a helicopter. It was coming in from the north of our position. Then we saw it. There was sufficient light to use smoke to signal our position, and John pulled the D-ring on the smoke end of the canister. He held it in his outstretched hand, allowing the red smoke to drift out over the water. There was very little breeze at that point to disperse the smoke—it hung around us like a cloud just above the surface of the ocean. Almost immediately the helicopter pilots saw the smoke and turned directly toward us. It was a wonderful feeling to see that old gray Navy H-19 heading toward us. We would be safe in another ten minutes or so.

Moments later, the helicopter was hovering above and a crewman let the horse collar down to us. The collar was fastened to a steel cable connected to a winch that was extended out from the starboard side of the helicopter. When the collar hit the water it was closest to John. He grabbed it, slid his arms through the opening, pulled the collar down under his armpits, and gave a hand signal that he was prepared to be retrieved. I remained in the rotor wash, which splashed water all over me, and watched John take the seventy-five-foot ride up to the hatch on the side of the helicopter. The crewman reached out and placed his gloved hand around the wire as if to guide it, and just as John's waist reached the bottom of the hatch, the crewman pulled in on the wire, helping John get a foothold on the bottom of the hatch. Then he grabbed him by the shirt and pulled him into the helicopter.

When John had freed himself from the collar, the crewman activated the winch, dropping the collar down to me. In normal procedure I would have slung my rifle over the front side of my body before inserting myself into the collar. But I forgot to do this in my haste and excitement until I was in the midst of putting the collar under my armpits. Not wanting to delay the extraction for even a few more seconds, I signaled that I was prepared to be hauled up. My Stoner crunched into my back under the collar. I tried not to notice the pain that it created on my ribs and shoulder blade.

I was within about twenty feet of the bottom of the helicopter when I looked up to see how much farther I had to go. The noise of the rotor engine was extremely loud to my unprotected ears as the helicopter hovered above. A split second after I looked up, I saw three-eighth-inch holes appearing in a straight line along the side of the helicopter progressing rapidly from near the tail forward toward the hatch. I knew instantly the holes must have come from the automatic fire of a machine gun somewhere—probably from a small riverboat, and I did not have time to determine where the shooting was coming from. The sound of the rotor and engine drowned out any sound of gunfire.

The helicopter heeled to port, swinging me on the wire under the fuselage. Then it lurched to starboard; and, as I swung out from under the helicopter, still looking up, the crewman fell out of the hatch, grabbing onto the wire with his left arm, clutching his belly with his right hand. His hand was drenched in blood, and blood was gushing out from between his fingers.

I saw the pain in his face, his open mouth trying to scream, his eyes tightly shut, and heard him scream briefly above the roar of the rotor engine. The toe of his boot smashed my forehead sharply at the hairline and dragged down my nose, causing me a major shot of pain. I thought my nose was being ripped off as I slipped out of the rescue collar like a piece of oiled, wet spaghetti, and fell about sixty feet into the ocean, landing flat on my back.

For an instant, as I fell, I experienced a sense of resignation: This is it, it is all over, I am not going to survive this mission; and I welcomed death as freedom from battle. My rifle dug into the flesh of my back as I smacked the water, and I lost consciousness. Fortunately, I had not deflated my small life belt before entering the horse collar. It was still up under my arms when I regained consciousness a few seconds later, coughing and retching salt water. The pain in my back was intense, and the more I coughed the more the pain increased. I looked around quickly for the helicopter, but it was merely a dot (about the size of a fifty-cent piece) on the morning horizon as it disappeared to the northeast.

Next I looked around for the source of the automatic weapons fire. I was just a mile offshore and it was quite obvious that a VC boat must have somehow sneaked up undetected, and fired on the helicopter as I was being hauled up. I prayed I would not see a riverboat heading my way to finish me off. I was defenseless, and knew I would never be able to get my rifle off my back to defend myself because of the intense pain in my back. The slightest movement of my arms set off waves of agonizing pain.

There were no riverboats within my 360-degree field of vision. The mere jostling of the light waves on the surface made me wince frequently with pain, and I felt myself losing the will to survive. How long could I survive alone in the South China Sea, a mile from shore with the tide carrying me east, out to sea, foot by foot? I looked at my watch and noted with dismay that the crystal had broken. Obviously it was useless. The hands were stopped at 6:35 A.M. Then I remembered how this had all begun, and I looked around for the helicopter crewman who had knocked me out of the collar. His body was nowhere in sight, and he was probably dead. Would his blood in the water create a shark feeding frenzy?

As I was suspended in the water by my life belt, I contemplated my situation and how, by some great blessing, I might be able to survive. Miraculously, the life belt air chambers had not been punctured by my rifle and it had not deflated on impact. I would never have been able to remain afloat, let alone swim, without that life belt. A second miracle: My half-filled canteen was still attached to my belt on my left side. Painfully, I removed the canteen and took two long swallows. There was not much I could do except hope the Navy would send in another rescue helicopter. Meanwhile, I continued to hope that a VC boat would not cruise by and finish me off—or worse yet, haul me out of the South China Sea and torture me. The pain in my back was so intense, I probably would have told the enemy everything they wanted to know and half of what they did not need to know. I was physically a mess and mentally exhausted. I twitched my toes inside my tennis shoes to assure myself that my injuries had not caused paralysis.

I bobbed around for several minutes, searching the horizon for a rescue aircraft. Suddenly, from the northeast, I heard the increasing sound of a reciprocating engine aircraft. Rotating myself around with my feet, I saw the equivalent of a heavenly angel; it was a venerable AD Skyraider! The pilot was diving almost directly at me, pulling up at about one hundred feet off the water and passing about seventy-five yards east of my position. I tried to lift my right arm to wave, but the pain forced it back to the water. I could not even signal my position. But as the Skyraider pilot pulled up, I believed I saw him rock his wings. A minute later he returned, this time only fifty feet above the ocean, and flew almost directly overhead—so close, I could see his helmet and his face. I thought he saluted me as I looked on. Beneath his wings were two rocket pods and several small bombs. With his machine guns and rockets, I knew he was loaded for bear and I was in good hands, except perhaps for the sharks.

Soon the first Skyraider was joined by a second, and they set up a circular cap above me that seemed to last a long time—at least an hour. I relaxed in spite of the awesome pain and drank two more gulps of water. It was a great day to be alive. Finally the sun was up and shining on me. It is strange how circumstances can sometimes change from totally rotten to awesomely good in a short period of time. I was indeed blessed and almost forgot about the pain in my nose and back. I thought that if I ever got out of this salt water, I would never go near the ocean again. I would move to Kansas or Oklahoma, where no tidal waves could ever reach me. I would gladly put up with the dust and drought, the frigid winters, the boring mile upon mile of farm crops growing; but if I would never see the salt water again, that would be sufficient. I didn't even care to see a fresh-water pond or lake.

John flashed into my mind's eye, and I wondered if he had survived the machine gun shelling of the helicopter. I hoped he was aboard an aircraft carrier just over the horizon having thick black coffee, scrambled eggs, ham, grits, and sweet rolls. The Navy sailors always ate well, especially those stationed on a carrier. It occurred to me that the helicopter might not have made it back to the carrier. What if the enemy shells had penetrated a vital fuel or hydraulic line? I wiped that thought out of my mind by watching the Skyraiders continue their lazy circles just east of me.

It seemed like several hours passed; I couldn't be sure. Two new Skyraiders arrived and relieved the two that had arrived first. The departing A-1s both flew in low over my head to check me out, waving their wings on approach and departure. I nodded my head; however, I suspected they could not see me move. But they could see that my head was erect, and I prayed they would know I was still alive. The ocean water was relatively clear now, because I could see from the surface down to my knees. I looked around for shark fins on the surface.

I began working to detach my rifle sling, because I felt I might be able to reduce the pain in my back if I could release the rifle. It took me about ten minutes before I could loosen the sling sufficiently to get it over my head. The effort was incredibly painful. I knew I probably had some broken ribs, because it was so painful to inhale air, and I hoped nothing was damaged internally, such as my lungs. I thought I might have collapsed a lung. Deciding not to release my rifle, I took a turn of the sling around my left arm. I could always hold my rifle pointed up to improve the visibility of my position if the waves and swells affected the view of my head bobbing on the surface—at least I hoped this would help. I had a smoke canister in my pack, but I knew I could not retrieve it, because it would involve too much use of my arms—and the pain would prevent me from doing so.

Wondering why it was taking so long for the Navy to dispatch another helicopter to come pick me up, it occurred to me that there was no way I could get myself into the collar to be extracted. I knew the pain would cause me to pass out and wondered how I could signal that to the helicopter pilot or crewman. I decided that when the helicopter arrived, I would put my face in the water and make every effort to appear disabled or dead. In that way, I hoped the pilot would quickly order the crewman to lower a wire stretcher into the water, and perhaps have the swimmer-crewman jump in to help load me into the stretcher.

With that decision having been made, I stuffed my Stoner between my chest and the life belt, leaving the muzzle about twelve inches above my head. Then I rested and drank the remaining water in my canteen. It could not be that much longer to wait.

Sure enough, within about half an hour after putting my rifle into position, I heard the friendly *whomp-whomp-whomp* sound of the rotors of a helicopter. As it came to hover above me, I didn't look up; rather, I dropped my face into the water, then raised it up slowly, then dropped it back into the water. Several seconds later I saw a Navy swimmer coming toward me in the choppy water created by the rotor downwash.

"We're here to get you, man. Are you hurt?" asked the swimmer, yelling with his lips close to my ear.

I nodded my head but said nothing. The swimmer signaled toward the helicopter and ten seconds later a chicken-wire stretcher appeared at the end of the cable. The swimmer removed my treasured Stoner and my backpack, dropping them into the depths. Then, skillfully, he dove with the foot end of the stretcher, carrying it down to my feet. He wrapped a stretcher strap around my ankles, and surfaced next to me, supporting me under the arms. I let out a yell of pain.

On the swimmer's signal, the crewman in the helicopter activated the winch that took up the cable slack, and the swimmer guided my upper body into the stretcher and buckled another strap across my chest while the stretcher bobbed just on the surface of the water. The swimmer signaled the crewman to take me up. The swimmer was left in the water. As I was taken up, I caught a glimpse of the Skyraiders passing low between us and the shoreline, continuing to guard against any VC boat that might have a chance to fire on us. Seconds later, the helicopter crewman pulled the stretcher and me into the cabin while another crewman let off on the winch to give enough slack in the cable to allow this to be accomplished. The crewman quickly unclipped the stretcher from the cable, shackled on the horse collar, and dropped it down to retrieve the swimmer. While this was being done, the cabin crewman knelt down, covered me with a blanket, and put his mouth next to my ear.

"Where are you hurt, sir?"

"My back is broken up. No open wounds. Need some morphine quickly," I responded. "Lotsa pain, need morphine now."

The crewman scrambled forward to the cockpit, and I assumed he wanted the pilots to radio back to the aircraft carrier my request for morphine. Several minutes later, as the helicopter was headed out to sea, the request was granted, probably by a doctor on the carrier, and the crewman plugged me with a syringe of morphine. A great peace and comfort came over me within less than ten seconds, and I went to sleep immediately in spite of the crewman's efforts to keep me awake. The last thing I remembered was the crewman attaching an oxygen mask to my face.

I awoke very briefly as the roar of the rotor engine increased and we hover-landed on the carrier. Then I was vaguely aware of being transported in the stretcher to the carrier's sick bay. On arrival I was transferred to a gurney and rolled into a brightly lit examining room where two orderlies, using blunt tipped scissors, proceeded to cut off my black pajamas. As this process was nearly completed, three Navy physicians gathered around me. I was offered water through a flexible straw and I drank deeply. After several minutes of questions and answers about how my injury had occurred, the oldest physician ordered X rays from the base of my skull to the base of my spine. He also issued an order to the X-ray technician to treat my case as a broken back, which probably meant that I should be moved tenderly. Six men, including the corpsmen, placed their hands under my body and lifted me from the stretcher, putting me back onto the gurney. I was still painless from the morphine, a bit groggy at this point, and preferred just to take a nap rather than be put through a set of cervical, thoracic, lumbar, and sacral X rays. Three corpsmen prepared to lift me onto the X-ray table.

"Hold it, men. I want at least five men to lift me to the X-ray table. I don't want my body to bend even half an inch or you may cut my spinal cord. Don't try it. Get some more men in here."

I was surprised at the vehemence of my order to the corpsmen, wondering where I had summoned the strength to raise my voice. Anyway, it worked, because two more orderlies appeared, and I was moved to the table without bending my spine. Rolling me over on my chest was quite painful. The morphine was wearing off already. The X-ray equipment buzzed as they took four X rays from my neck to my butt; then two more of my front rib cage. After placing me back on the gurney, I told one of the men to tell the doctors I was going to need some more morphine in a few minutes and to have it standing by. As they rolled me to a holding room, I wondered if they had sterilized me with all the X rays taken.

Fifteen minutes later I was rolled into another room, used for analyzing X rays, which was darkened except for several backlighted screens on one side of the room. The physicians were putting the developed X rays up on the screens. They began at my neck and examined each vertebra and disk carefully. These X rays were followed by two thoracic shots. Even to my untrained eye I could see the ribs on my left side did not have the same balanced alignment as those on my right side.

"Okay. We have two ribs fractured here and possibly a third green bone fracture here. These two are pressing on the left lung, but it does not appear that there is a puncture—just some minor bleeding," said one of the doctors.

"Look at this lumbar shot."

From my vantage point I could see the broken ribs. In addition, I clearly saw that two transverse processes on the left side of two of the lumbar vertebrae were snapped off and hanging.

Pointing with his finger, one of the doctors commented matter-of-factly, "Okay, we have two lumbar processes broken, possibly exposing nerve ganglions here and here. It appears we probably have compressed disks, here and here."

This was followed by some technical medical discussion among the doctors before they turned to speak with me.

"Young fellow, it appears you have some broken ribs, which will heal in a month or so. You'll have to be careful in your movements so these do not puncture your lung. But you also have two compressed disks, and two lumbar processes that are broken downward, possibly exposing some nerve ganglions. Now, you told us you remember hitting the water flat on your back?"

"Yes, sir," I replied.

"Well, the strange thing we see here is that your ribs are broken *inward,* but your lumbar processes are broken *downward.* If the lumbar processes had broken inward, we might expect some paralysis, which you don't seem to have."

"No paralysis, sir."

"Well, even with your rifle being mashed between you and your impact with the water, it is difficult to understand how the ribs were broken *inward* and the lumbar processes were broken off *downward.* Is it possible you have had two separate accidents?"

"Hell, sir, I've been knocking my body around a whole lot for the past several months. You learn to live with the pain. I can't be sure if I hit my back hard enough in another incident prior to getting knocked out of the horse collar this morning. By the way, sir, I understand the chow aboard a carrier is pretty decent. I haven't had a square meal in several days. Since I don't have any major holes in me where the food I eat would pass through, how's about ordering me up some baked armadillo steak, grits, broccoli, and sweet whole milk? Some morphine would be fine for dessert."

The doctors roared with laughter and ordered me some food from the mess deck. Then they got those serious looks on their faces again.

"We're going to let you eat some chow now, and then we will have to see whether we need to put you in traction. We will examine the X rays further and make that determination. Meanwhile, we want you to remain flat on your back. That will make it tough to eat, but that's the way it will be until we get finished reviewing the X rays."

Before they rolled me out, I asked, "Do any of you know how my partner, John Schneider, is doing? He was onboard the first helicopter that took automatic fire. I guess that helicopter came from this ship?"

The doctors looked at each other and then gazed downward. I knew without pressing that the worst had happened.

"The helicopter was pretty badly shot up. The pilot was killed along with the crewman who is presumed dead—the one who fell out and hit you on the cable. The copilot and your friend were both wounded. The copilot was losing blood from his wounds as he flew inbound, and he lost it about two miles out from our deck. The helicopter went into the ocean from one thousand feet of altitude and sank before our rescue helo could get out there. There were no survivors."

My best friend in FRAM 16 was dead. I could not deal with it right now. It was as if someone stuck a dagger in my heart. In a pleading voice I asked again for more morphine. But the doctors agreed that I should be on Demerol, which is far less potent than morphine, just to see if I could handle the pain level without resorting to more morphine. Having never had Demerol, I could only hope it was as satisfying as morphine. It wasn't. I needed something to help me over the loss of John.

For the first time in my adult life I had to be fed by someone else. An orderly sat on the edge of my bed and spooned me some mushy meatloaf, green beans (overcooked, of course), and mashed potatoes. The galley was out of fresh milk, and I refused to drink the canned stuff, which tasted like it had been laced with boat varnish. I drank orange juice through a straw instead.

By the time I had finished the meal the Demerol had taken effect, but it did not diminish the mental pain at the loss of John. Fond memories of him floated in my brain. Though the physical pain had decreased only slightly, I still managed to fall asleep very quickly and slept for about seven hours. When I woke up, I pressed the "call button," asking the orderly who answered the call for a bedpan. Defecating in a bedpan while lying fat on your back is a lousy experience. I should not elaborate. After sipping two cups of water, I slept for another six hours.

A doctor woke me about 7:00 A.M.

"We have decided to get you over to Clark Air Force Base for further evaluation and treatment, my friend. They have an available bed or two, and are much better suited for treating injuries to the spine. You will be better off there than anywhere else right now. So we'll get you on a S2F COD (Carrier Onboard Delivery) flight, shoot you off this bucket, and get you out of the combat zone and into the land of beautiful female nurses and other neuromedical types."

"When do I leave?" I asked.

"You'll load on the hangar deck in about an hour and a half," the doctor replied. "We're going to put you in a traction harness so the effects of the catapult shot will not hurt as much. Regardless of what we do, you may feel a jolt of pain from the cat shot, but we hope there will be no damage to your spine or the nerve ganglions. Meanwhile, we'll order you up some breakfast, then give you some more Demerol. We'll gather up your gear and get you aboard. Is there anything more I can do for you?"

"No, sir. But . . ."

"What is it, fella?"

"Was there no chance of recovering my teammate's body from the wreckage of the helicopter? I mean, isn't there some way?"

"Afraid not," said the doctor. "I imagine that helicopter went down in very deep water. We've been told that our rescue helicopter reported no bodies and no debris from the crash site. I know it is really tough on you, but he's gone now."

I sobbed. The doctor left me to my tears. My tears were of anger, sorrow, and helplessness. There was nothing at all I could do. I would have to contact his parents by telephone from Clark. They would probably have already received one of those terrible telegrams, delivered by a uniformed military officer, that stated he was "missing and presumed dead."

At 7:30 A.M. one of the doctors and five orderlies came in and transferred me to a padded stretcher. They installed the traction equipment at either end of the stretcher and stretched me out. It was very uncomfortable. Then they issued me four Demerol pills in a pill jar, covered me with a gray woolen blanket, slid my X rays under the blanket, and started me on my journey to Clark.

Amid stacks of mailbags and boxes that were tied down with nylon straps, the orderlies loaded me into the reciprocating twin-engine S2F. The crewman aboard the plane checked the straps that anchored me in, then told me he would dispense the Demerol as needed during the flight. He closed the side hatch and buckled himself into a jump seat behind the cockpit. The S2F was then rolled over to a port side elevator to be brought up to the flight deck. When the elevator stopped, I heard the reciprocating engines start. They sounded like a large Model-T Ford starting up; coughs and wheezes, then a catch, followed by a roar and vibration. We taxied forward toward the catapult after the pilots had gone through the preflight checklist and engine run-ups. I could not see anything outside the aircraft. The traction equipment completely limited my movement. I could move only my arms and eyeballs.

The pilot taxied the plane into position for the cat shot. The crewman shouted to me over the roar of the engines.

"All set, sir?"

I didn't respond. There was no use in my trying to shout. Within three seconds we were airborne. I felt only a slight amount of pain, mostly discomfort from the traction equipment, especially on my neck. Several minutes after takeoff, the crewman came over to me and kneeled down beside me. He removed his crash helmet and asked if I was okay. I told him I was fine, no pain, but that I needed him to loosen up the neck halter of the traction device. Hesitating for a moment, he let off on the click winch two notches. It felt much better. He suggested I wave my arm in the air if I needed anything.

Sleeping most of the way to Clark was the best method of not having to deal with the recent events and my condition. I really was not particularly concerned that I might not fully recover. Those thoughts did not occupy my mind. But, when awake, I mourned John and my other teammates who would never go home.

My thoughts also turned to the fact that once recovered, I would never return to combat. I had done my time in service. I had been fortunate to live through it, and I would use my "impaired physical condition" to get me out for good. Someone else could take my place in that godawful war. I was going home.

I slept on and off for the several hours it took to reach Clark. When the engine pitch changed, I awoke. My ears began to pop, which meant we were changing altitude. The crewman came back and said we'd be on the ground in about ten minutes. He asked if I thought it would be best if he tightened up the head harness on the traction device again. I agreed and spent the remaining time in that uncomfortable stretched condition. The pilot put the aircraft down with three minor tire squeaks, which is unusual for carrier pilots, who are used to cutting power just over the deck, then letting the aircraft slam onto the deck to catch one of the arresting wires . . . known as a controlled crash landing.

I thanked the crewman and pilots, and was quickly unloaded into a waiting gray ambulance, then was taken to the Clark Air Force Base Hospital.

As we drove along, I thought about the events of the past twenty-four hours and suddenly realized that I did not even know the name of the aircraft carrier to which I had been taken by the rescue helicopter. It didn't really matter, but it would have been nice to have known.

John was dead! And that still hurt far more than my back. I was consumed with anger and sorrow. We had become very close comrades.

Chapter 16

Hospital Recovery

The other bed in my hospital room was behind closed draperies. I guessed someone was laying there, recovering from something.

This was the beginning of my six-week physical recovery from that free fall from the helicopter into the South China Sea. As I was being settled into the hospital bed by the orderlies and a nurse, I quickly developed feelings of safety and well-being. For so many months I had lived on life's knife edge. It was the absence of that way of life that made me superaware of the security I was finally enjoying.

I was greeted twenty minutes after my arrival by two young Air Force physicians, one an orthopedic surgeon, the other a general surgeon. They had reviewed my X rays, which I had carried with me from the aircraft carrier. They illustrated to me, using their hands, that two of the discs in my vertebrae appeared to be pinched and were slightly bulging, probably as a result of my fall into the water from the helo. They prescribed extended traction to see if this would solve the disc problem. My ribs had multiple small breaks and should heal quickly. But the Clark doctors, like the aircraft carrier doctors, expressed particular concern over the two broken transverse processes in the lumbar section of my back. They ordered more X rays to decide if the position of the bones endangered any of my nerve ganglions.

With perplexed looks on their faces, the surgeons asked me to recount the fall from the helo. I explained in great detail the event that took less than three seconds from the time the crewman hit me as he fell from the helo until I struck the water on my back. My rifle had been slung across my back, and was obviously the cause of the diagonal bruise that traversed my body from above my left hip to my right shoulder blade. This had caused or contributed to the broken ribs; however, it did not explain how my transverse processes were broken in a downward position while my ribs were broken inward, toward my lungs.

I tried to recall anything else that would aid the perplexed doctors in to understanding what had transpired. Once again, I mentally rolled back through several missions in which I had sustained various injuries until I finally recalled an incident several months earlier, in Soc Trang, where I had been working out on a makeshift chinning bar, doing chin-ups as part of my exercise regimen. The chinning bar, installed about eight feet above the concrete floor of the Quonset hut, had broken loose as I strained to finish the last chinup. For some reason I had brought my knees up against my chest as I strained in this last effort, and my foot hit the wall opposite the bar. When the bar broke loose from its moorings between the exposed rafters, I fell with my back hitting the concrete floor. The pain in my back was almost instantaneous, and I recalled feeling very foolish that something like that could have happened to me. I quietly groaned at every movement of my back for at least a month after this incident, and eventually, with the help of aspirin and some painkillers, I managed to cope with the pain. In fact, I had forgotten about it altogether. I told no one about the incident.

As I was transferred to a gurney and rolled down the hallways to the X-ray area I finally comprehended the serious comments of the doctors concerning the dangerous condition of my back. I feared that if I moved my torso in the wrong direction, even slightly, the lumbar processes might cut into the ganglions. Here I was, finally out of harm's way in Southeast Asia, no more bullets, no more claymore mines, no more enemy soldiers. But one wrong move and I might become instantly paralyzed, at least partially. The fear heightened when the two X-ray technicians moved over to the gurney and got ready to lift my six-foot-two-inch, 175-pound frame onto the

X-ray table. The same situation occurred as when I was on the aircraft carrier.

"No! No!" I shouted. The X-ray techs stood back in surprise at my warning shout. "You'll need four men to move me," I said. "If the two of you guys try to move me, you might cause further spinal injury. Get some other men in here and move me very carefully. NOW!" I ordered them with as much authority as I could muster.

Shortly, four techs were in place, and after some discussion between them as to how I was to be lifted, they moved me from the gurney onto the X-ray table, with the care of a treasured antique dresser. The X-ray table was ice cold on my bare skin, but frankly I was glad that I could even feel the cold. I tested the use of my legs and toes and was reassured to know I still had full sensitivity. My fear of further movement remained. This time only three X rays were taken, each requiring me to move painfully into a different position with the assistance of the technicians. When the X rays were developed a few minutes later, the radiologist was summoned to the X-ray room.

After further reviewing my X rays, the radiologist supervised the techs in placing my torso in two other positions for more X rays. I felt strong pain in my back. After being returned to my hospital bed, I demanded a shot of morphine to relieve the pain. A male nurse came in five minutes later and administered the much needed gift of painlessness. Shortly thereafter, the orderlies, supervised by a physician, set up my head-to-foot traction unit, leaving me relatively immobilized except for my arms. Then I slept for about two hours.

When I awoke I could hear a low mumbling of words from the direction of the adjacent bed. Constrained by the traction system, I rotated my eyeballs to the edges of their sockets in order to see if the draperies were still pulled around the other bed. I was curious about what was happening to the person in the adjacent bed. The male voice continued in muted words. I listened carefully. The words sounded like the incantations of a man praying softly. This was confirmed by an *Amen.*

A nurse entered to see about my level of pain and to check the traction system. I told her that the pain was under control but that they should be on standby for more morphine when I needed it. She replied that the doctors wanted to wean me from morphine and get me on Demerol again.

"No," I pleaded innocently. "I'm really enjoying this morphine; tell the doctors to wean me very slowly because I am addicted to the stuff."

The nurse chuckled quietly. I laughed aloud and experienced a sharp twinge of pain, which diminished shortly.

It was early evening. I began to fall asleep again. I slept intermittently. The traction gear was most uncomfortable, bordering on claustrophobic. Nurses would come in from time to time, peer at me in the dim light, and ask if I needed anything. An adorable blonde, blue-eyed Air Force nurse came in with my dinner and liquids. I instantly fell in love. She asked if I needed help eating. The sound of her voice melted me like butter in a hot skillet.

I said, "Honey, if you'll feed me, I'll give you a diamond ring!"

She laughed and said she'd feed me if I behaved myself. Her name was Sally, and this was to be her last day at the hospital. Her thirteen-month overseas tour was up, and she was headed home to her parents in Columbus, Ohio, in two days. I was heartbroken.

I watched the sunlight through the blinds as morning arrived. During the night I had heard the person in the bed next to me moan softly, twice. It concerned me. Nurses had checked him from time to time behind the drawn privacy curtains, but they never spoke. I guessed my roommate was out of it . . . maybe in a coma. I wondered about him, but for some reason I refrained from asking the nurses about my roommate. A doctor whom I had not seen before came in with a stethoscope around his neck, stepped inside the draperies, said nothing to my roommate, and left a few minutes later, nodding politely to me in the dimmed light as he passed by the foot of my bed.

About 7:30 A.M., as I lay there half-awake wondering when I had eaten last, a man in an Air Force uniform walked into the room. He acknowledged me with a slight smile and a nod, saying only, "Good morning, young man, how are you feeling?"

I grunted something in groggy reply. Then he parted the draperies beside the other bed. After about five minutes he stepped out from behind the draperies, closed them, walked to the side of my bed, and looked at me with a somber face. From the two embroidered gold crosses on the ends of the white scarf draped around his neck, I realized he was an Air Force chaplain.

"Hello," I said more cheerfully. "How's it going?" The chaplain walked over and stood beside my bed.

"I'm okay, fella. What is your story?" the chaplain asked kindly, moving to the foot of my bed where I could see him more easily.

"Well, I busted up my back in 'Nam and they're trying to patch me up here. Say, what's the story with my roommate over there? I keep seeing folks going in and out past the draperies. Can you pull the drapes and let us chat a while, or is he in rough shape?"

The chaplain replied in a very low tone, "I am afraid your roommate won't make it. She is in a coma and the doctors don't give her much of a chance. She has severe brain, liver, and kidney damage from gunshot wounds and a jeep accident in Vietnam, outside Long Binh."

The chaplain cleared his throat. "She is a young Army nurse. She had been over there only two weeks when a MASH convoy in which she was riding was hit by an enemy ambush. She was one of fourteen medical types hit."

I was dumbfounded and felt angry. I just couldn't fathom that an American *woman* had been hit by enemy gunfire. Women. What were they doing in harm's way? This wasn't some macho-chauvinist reaction of mine; I just felt as though women ought to be protected from bullets, mines, and bombs. At the same time I felt guilty. Here was a woman all shot up, probably going to die from complications, and here I was, on the road to healing. Tears came to my eyes as I stared at the chaplain. I heard her moan deeply. She seemed to be trying to cough. The chaplain pushed my call button and in a moment a nurse appeared. The next moan, more like a gurgle, was quite loud. Then there were several gurgling sounds. The nurse drew back the draperies and stood by her bedside. Because of my traction gear I was unable to turn my head and see what was happening. The chaplain joined the nurse by the woman's bed. Then it was quiet for a few minutes as the nurse stood there by her bed, not doing or saying anything. Then there came a gurgling sound, which came at intervals. Then quiet. I could not see the girl's face.

The nurse stepped back, removed her stethoscope, and slowly closed the draperies. She turned and looked solemnly at the chaplian, shaking her head, as if to say, "No. She's gone to be with God."

"I'm afraid she's gone, sir," she said with a bit of a catch in her throat as she spoke. "I'll notify her doctor."

I was speechless, and very sad.

"Why?" I shouted within. "What for?"

Death had come to my teammates and so many other men. It was always a wrenching emotional depression for me when I heard of or saw the death of a buddy or fellow American that I knew. In order to counter the remorseful feelings after such events, I had often consoled myself by thinking that while a life had just ended tragically, a new life was beginning for that person. It was beginning in a place far better than the one they had on earth. This, I reminded myself, is a transitory life; and while life is to be cherished, it is also a process that must be experienced in preparation for the life hereafter. Even with these thoughts, I was unsatisfied that a young nurse had died at the hands of the enemy—right next to me. I was angry. Very angry. And I had no way to vent that anger. To yell or throw things against the wall was, for the time being, beyond my capacity as I lay there in traction.

About 30 minutes passed when a nurse opened the door of my hospital room. There was a man dressed in a blue oxford shirt, open at the neck, standing in the doorway. With my limited eye mobility, I could not turn to see his face clearly. The nurse said a few words to the man as she stepped aside and let him pass by. As he approached the foot of my bed, I recognized Bill.

In a loud voice, ignoring the presence of the chaplain, Bill said, "Well, now, look at the old goldbricker, living the life of Riley in the hospital! When ya coming back to work, man? How are ya feeling, Big Guy? Hear you busted up your back a little."

The timing of Bill's visit could not have been worse. The chaplain excused himself and left the room as Bill approached and sat down on the wooden chair beside my bed.

"What do you want, Bill?" I mumbled with calculated, casual disinterest.

"Well, that's a fine greeting from the Great One! I just boondoggled my way all the way over here from 'Nam to see firsthand how you were doing, and you ask me what I want? Is it pretty rough going for you? . . . I mean the healing bit?"

I replied, "Look, Bill, I'm not in the mood for rah-rah stuff. If you are here to do a status report on me for the Company, just tell 'em I've got another two months of traction and rehab, then I'm out. Got that? *Out!*" I shouted, wincing in pain.

"Well, Big Guy, we need you back as soon as you are able," Bill said after a pause. "You did a helluva perfect job taking out that VC radio tower with ol' John. I was sorry to hear we lost him during the extraction . . . and we almost lost you too. I feel real bad about John. Great guy. Sure glad you made it. But I didn't come here to discuss when you'd be ready to come back and help us. We just want you to concentrate on getting better, then get yourself back into good physical shape, and we'll figure out what we are going to do with you when you are ready. Some great assignment will come up and you'll handle it the way you always have."

"Now, Bill, you look me straight in the eye and listen carefully to what I'm going to say. I want the truth. John is dead. Most of the others are dead. How many out of the original sixteen team members are alive? I want the truth, man!" I demanded with quiet ferocity.

After a lengthy pause, Bill said, "Well, we sent Robert Gomez on to Bethesda Naval Hospital some months ago. He's in pretty bad shape from a claymore mine. You remember that. He oughta be down in Miami with his parents in another month."

I growled, "You didn't answer my question, Bill. How many? *Answer* me!"

Soberly, Bill said, "Well, the answer is that you are the only one left over here. We've lost fourteen of the team over the last eighteen months or so. But Robert, as I said, is hospitalized and he's alive. Some of the others you already knew about. Others you may not know about because you've been working different operations. But you have your whole life ahead of you now, Big Guy, and there's a spot for you with us. You might really enjoy working in the covert section. . . . Great guys working in that area, and the pay is real good; much better than the average grad four or five years out of college.

Or you could come back to Saigon with me, and we'll work something out for you. You ought to expect to make about twenty thousand dollars a year to start. That's a helluva lot of dough!"

The door opened and a doctor came in, walked past my bed, and stepped between the drapes that surrounded the dead nurse's bed. Seconds later he reappeared, removing his stethoscope. He said nothing, and departed through the door.

I was quiet for a moment. Then, looking back at Bill, I said, "Look, I want you to hear me loud and clear on this. Years ago my dad would tell me, 'Every man has a basic obligation to his country. You do your time.' So I did my time. I get nothing out of this time except the knowledge that I did a job and did it damn well! My friends are dead, except Robert, who'll probably never walk or take a bowel movement by himself again. There is nothing to discuss between you and me, Bill. I'm out of this deal, and that is final."

The door to my room opened again and two orderlies with a gurney came in. They rolled the gurney around the far side of the dead nurse's bed, and I could hear the draperies being opened fully on that side, followed by the rustling of sheets.

"What's going on over there?" Bill asked in a hushed voice.

"Oh, that's just another victim of Vietnam. . . . A young female nurse . . . all shot up, dead, going home to Mom and Dad in a coffin with her name and address printed on the outside," I responded.

They rolled the nurse's body out, draped in a white sheet, probably heading to the morgue. Bill and I didn't speak for a couple of minutes. He paced back and forth, stroking his chin, deep in thought.

"Listen," said Bill, "you've been through a helluva lot. We know it. It's been tough. I'll do some things here in the Philippines for a few days, then get back here again and we'll visit for a while. Then I've got to get back to work. I hope you will have changed your mind about things. Okay? Think about it, Big Guy."

"No, Bill," I said. "I don't want you to come back. Just tell your people I'm washed up and want out on a medical discharge. I've done the job, and I refuse to go back to Vietnam or be a part of the Company anymore. I do not want a job with the CIA in any form. I'm through, and that's final. Finished. Find someone else to do your work. Nothing will make me change my mind. I want you to make arrangements for me to get discharged from this outfit; get my pay and my transportation back to Florida. I want your word that you will get this done before you leave here for Saigon. The only direction I am headed out of here is east!"

"Well," said Bill, "we'll have to go through the debriefing process at some point, make sure you know what you can talk about in public and what stays secret. But think about it. With your talent and experience you could make a whale of a lot of dough if you stay with the Company, earn a nice government retirement, live happily ever after. But if you are so foolish as to want to get out, then get out. We don't want any guys around who aren't Company men."

"Yeah," I said. "I was a team player. My team is dead. Sacrificed for the cause, whatever the 'cause' is. I don't even want to stand on the sidelines and call plays for the rest of the game now. I want out of the freakin' stadium. You make the arrangements now, Bill, and forget the debriefing crap. I ain't talking to nobody about nothing! Anyway, there's nothing I know that could benefit anyone if I did talk."

Bill came over to the bedside, extended his hand. I shook it.

He smiled at me and simply said, "Good luck, Big Guy," and left without further words.

It was a difficult parting for me. Bill and I had become friends over the last several months. But at that point in the hospital I was writing him off. It was a tough day for me.

Being in traction is miserable. In fact there is nothing in this world more boring than lying in a hospital bed, staring at the ceiling, watching lousy Filipino television, having to use urinals and bedpans, and with nurses checking in on you every forty-five minutes or so. I read a few books; however, my arms quickly became tired from holding the books up in my line of sight. The food . . . well, it was hospital food.

The new nurse who came in to feed me was not particularly attractive and, at age thirty-two, she was old in my opinion. I was twenty-four.

The orthopedic surgeon assigned to my case tried on several occasions to get me to talk about my experiences in Southeast Asia, but

I was unwilling to go into any detail. I just didn't care to relive my expeditions, triumphs, and failings. But when alone with my thoughts, particularly when asleep, my recollections were vivid with detail, sound, and color. Automatic weapon gunfire would roar in my ear; bombs from close air support would explode me awake; and wounded men would scream in agony in the darkness of my dreams. I would see the tension-filled faces of the enemy being shot or cut with my own weapons. A hundred times I felt the salt spray in my face as I fell from the helicopter. It was as if Satan himself was out to drive me mad. I thrashed and hollered aloud in my sleep, to the consternation of the nurses in the hospital. I often woke myself with self-inflicted pain from thrashing.

The confines of the traction gear around my head and neck often caused me to feel as though I was in the stranglehold of an unseen enemy. Because of my nighttime thrashing in bed, my doctor thought I should be protected from myself at night. He ordered arm, leg, and torso restraints. This caused me greater stress. The only test I failed in my early training was the metal box test for claustrophobia used at the Coronado Escape and Evasion School. To this day, nearly thirty years later, I cannot abide being tightly confined. Since leaving Southeast Asia, various foolish accidents have caused me to break my left kneecap, right tibia, and right wrist. In each case the orthopedic surgeons would read the X rays and prescribe a plaster cast to immobilize the limb. In each case, claustrophobia set in within a few hours and I went after the cast with a knife, cutting it off and freeing myself. Then I wrapped the limb in several elastic Ace bandages. The bandages effectively immobilized my limb; however, psychologically I knew I could free myself by removing the bandages, which seemed to assuage my claustrophobic reaction. Still now, my ever-present, deep-seated fear is that I would get into an accident requiring more plaster casts. I have told my wife in serious discussions many times that if I am ever put in a cast, I must be heavily sedated until the cast is removed. Being totally confined drives me toward insanity and is my true Achilles' heel.

In the hospital, after two nights of being more fully restrained, I refused to let the nurse tie me down. An orderly was brought in to do the deed, and I advised him that if he attempted to restrain me he would be in the O.R. (operating room) undergoing surgery for multiple compound fractures and torn flesh in the region of his private parts. He reached for my right wrist somewhat tentatively, and I quickly immobilized him, bringing him nearly to his knees with a shrill scream of pain as I grabbed a nerve pressure point on the top of his hand, and pressed it with all my strength, without mercy. The nurse helped the orderly to his feet and together they verbally threatened me, saying they would have the doctor in to authorize an injection that would slow me down. I wasn't afraid; I was angry.

When the duty doctor arrived thirty minutes later, he barged into the room with the nurse and the orderly. He shouted and lectured me that I had no right to act like a savage in the hospital, that I was being restrained for my own protection and healing. I listened to the berating for a few minutes and held up my hand in an appeal for silence. Asking the nurse and orderly to leave, using my kindest voice, I explained to the doctor my problem with claustrophobia. He listened and did not comment. They did not restrain me further. Another battle was won.

The following morning, a senior staff Air Force psychiatrist came in and sat down on a chair beside my bed. On his inquiry I explained my problem with claustrophobia in moderate tones, and added my complete understanding of the rationale behind their desire to restrain me.

I said, "Doctor, please try to understand. I cannot allow myself to be restrained, regardless of the probability that I may injure myself during my nightmares. I will do more physical and mental damage to myself if restrained than if not restrained." He probed further to learn why I had this problem, but I had no answers from my childhood experiences to satisfy his queries.

The psychiatrist was a cool fellow, and I had many long talks with him in the following weeks about my feelings and my patrols in Southeast Asia. I never had much faith or confidence in psychiatrists and psychologists. I felt that their's was an inexact science, and my father (a well-regarded surgeon) had frequently made scornful remarks about their profession. In retrospect, I sincerely believe that I suffered no post-traumatic stress syndrome, so common to other Vietnam veterans, in part because of the time this fine doctor spent with me.

He made me aware that I could only diminish myself by wallowing in past transgressions and fears. In times alone, I realized that in my more monstrous, ghastly, and lethal experiences of the war, there were no witnesses, no accusers, just the power of my own conscience to deal with. Gradually I began to talk openly with this doctor about the details of my experiences. This seemed to relieve a great deal of my inner stress. But the most influential relief came from one of the many simple techniques suggested to me by this doctor.

In one of our sessions he counseled that rather than trying to forget the past, I might try working toward developing the mind-set that the guy who went through those horrid encounters was someone else; someone whom my mind could visualize going through combat experiences; someone with whom I could relate, but was not related. That person carried out the orders of his superiors for the war cause, for the safety and preservation of friendly forces, and especially for his teammates.

Later in my life a friend, who is also a psychiatrist, suggested to me that the advice I had been given by the Air Force psychiatrist would not help most patients because it allowed the patient to avoid dealing directly with the problems of the past. I disagreed.

Because war is irrational, it frequently renders reason impotent, I concluded in my hospital bed. However, every attempt must be made to rationalize one's covert, murderous actions in war. If manipulating one's own mind, as suggested by the Air Force psychiatrist, helps in the rationalization process, then it should be pursued. It worked well for me. There is no way to amputate the past, but there are ways to deal with it in the future, and I found the best way for me.

Two weeks after Bill left my room, I received a thick package in the typical government manila envelope, delivered by courier. The contents were most interesting. First, there were multiple copies of U.S. Navy orders in which I was referenced with the U.S. Navy rank of "Lieutenant, junior grade." In essence, the orders stated that upon my release from the Clark Air Force Base hospital, I was to proceed, with priority boarding privilege, via government aircraft to Travis Air Force Base in California. I was to transfer via government surface transport to Treasure Island Naval Station, near San Francisco, and present my orders to the Treasure Island Officer of the Day in preparation for discharge from the U.S. Navy. I was authorized to receive the standard military National Defense Service Medal, which was given to any American who served in the Armed Forces. Then there was a U.S. government check for just more than $1,800 to cover my last month's pay. The final document in the envelope was my government authorization to fly coach via commercial airline, to my home in Florida.

Bill had obviously done what I had asked him to do. He had not returned for the debriefing, and I never heard from him again.

On the standard military form, DD 214, it was indicated that my last duty station was Sangley Point Naval Air Station, a small facility located across Manila Bay from the city of Manila in the Philippines. I was being detached as Top Secret Control Officer and as Mess Treasurer from the Naval Air Station. The dates of my service were indicated, but incorrectly. There was even a form signed by the commanding officer of the base containing an officer's evaluation and fitness report . . . which was excellent. The orders and forms looked legitimate and in order, as did the other forms included in the envelope . . . except that it was all fabricated. It was part of the reverse "sheep-dip," and I was briefly amused at the lengths to which the Company would go to cover my activities over the last eighteen months or so.

With the help of the psychiatrist, I held down any depression and quelled my anger by concentrating on the fact that I knew how much FRAM 16 had accomplished. I knew that our deeds often were carried out under the highest levels of risk to our lives, and we needed no medals to validate ourselves.

It was over now, and I was going to get on with the rest of my life. That guy who performed some incredible feats, cheated death from time to time, and saved many lives, could be proud within himself.

Chapter 17

The Return Home

On 24 January 1967, I boarded an Air Force C-135 at Clark Air Force Base for the first leg of my trip home. The doctors had indicated their satisfaction with the condition of my spinal discs, but admonished me to avoid lifting heavy objects for another twelve months, and to avoid strenuous or contact sports. I was given a written regimen of exercises to strengthen my back muscles. I have never since experienced any problems relating to my broken transverse processes.

Showing my orders to the boarding officer at the terminal desk, I was called to board the aircraft with very senior ranking officers.

The C-135, an equivalent to the commercial Boeing 707, modified for military use, was a four-engine jet aircraft, with a normal seating capacity of approximately two hundred. The rows of six seats, divided by a center aisle, faced aft. There were no windows in the passenger compartment. I sat in an aisle seat next to an Army general, while across the aisle sat a Navy admiral. Our seats were one-third of the way back from the entry door. Because of military rank, we would be first to disembark when we landed—except that officially I ranked as an O-2, near the bottom of the officer ranks.

I was dressed in standard camouflage fatigues, starched, creased, and rather snappy-looking, I thought. There were no unit recognition patches or rank insignia attached to my uniform. I was "traveling light," so to speak, carrying only a dop kit containing a toothbrush, soap, deodorant, shaving gear, and pain pills. These were the sum total of my earthly possessions, except about fifteen thousand dollar's worth of unused pay in my Florida savings account. That was a lot of money in those days.

We climbed into our aft-facing seats, fastened our seat belts, and waited for the engine start-ups. After settling in my seat, I noted a heavy webbed cargo net strung across the aft inside area of the aircraft. It was strung left to right and from the ceiling to the floor. Between the webbing I could see a stack from ceiling to floor of aluminum boxes with handles on the ends. There must have been fifteen or twenty boxes back there. Each had small black lettering stenciled on the end. It was difficult to see behind the webbing, and I could not discern what I was looking at. "Shit!" exclaimed the tall general sitting beside me.

I looked at him in surprise, since there was nothing readily apparent that would have caused him to use the expletive. He, too, was looking aft toward the cargo net and aluminum boxes.

"Those are coffins back there, and we have to sit here for the next twenty hours or so looking at those things filled with American lads killed in action!"

I momentarily felt sick to my stomach. There were probably more coffins in the cargo space below. A lump of sorrow grew in my throat as I looked at the seatback in front of me. The aisle was still filled with military personnel, stuffing small bags into the overhead racks, laughing among their friends. They were going back to the world aboard their "Freedom Bird." So was I. And so were those bodies of dead men and perhaps women, packed unceremoniously and cold in those metal boxes. Reaching into my chest pocket, I retrieved a Valium and a sleeping pill, swallowing them without the aid of liquid. I didn't think I could bear looking at the austere scenery and reminders of the past stacked in front of me. I preferred to check out for a while.

Before I could fall asleep, the general asked, "What branch of service are you in, young man?"

"I was attached to MACV Special Operations Group, sir," I mumbled back without looking at him, and keeping my eyes shut.

"Oh, do you work for the CIA? Were you flying for Air America?" he asked, obviously trying to start up a conversation.

"No, sir," I said. "I was in military ops and long-range recon, intelligence, that sort of thing."

"Well, I'll be damned. I wondered why you had no markings on your camos there. Then you were in the field for a while?"

He paused, waiting for me to reply. I was feeling the effects of the drugs.

"Yes, sir." I was rapidly slipping under a haze of sleep. "Sir," I said, slurring, "I just got out of the hospital at Clark and I'm . . ."

That's the last I remember saying until we slammed down on the tarmac in Guam.

My back was very sore when I woke up. I swallowed a Demerol for pain, one of four I had been issued at the hospital for the return trip, just in case I needed them. We had some time to kill while the aircraft was cleaned and refueled. By the time I reached the top of the ladder to disembark, I was approaching la-la land from the Demerol; I had an enormous sense of well-being, free of pain.

I easily understood why so many people became drug addicts. The absence of pain was one thing, but the other feelings were like none I had ever experienced before in my life. It was obvious to me why certain drugs could become addictive; but I never took up the habit.

After consuming two hamburgers with lettuce, tomato, mayo, catsup, and mustard (no onion), and a large vanilla milk shake, I found a seat in the Guam terminal and waited for the takeoff on the next leg of the trip. An hour later we were called for reboarding, and several waiting soldiers cheered and clapped their hands. This was the second leg to CONUS, and the soldiers were excited.

Taking my seat again, I put my mind on "ignore" as best I could and buried myself in a paperback novel for the long haul to Barbers Point Naval Air Station, Hawaii. This time I was seated next to an Army major who had exchanged seats with the general. The general probably preferred to sit next to someone nearer his rank, and someone who would talk to him—which I was not inclined to do. The major reeked of cheap, sweet-smelling shaving lotion. I could not ever recall an officer who wore shaving lotion while in uniform. I recognized the aroma of Old Spice from my school days, when I wore it during the summer because my girlfriend liked the smell.

The major was a talker. First he started a conversation with his seat-mate to his left about some colonel in Vietnam who had given him a rough time at the headquarters of some military group in Saigon. From the conversation I overheard, it was obvious he was a "REMF (rear echelon motherfucker)," which is what those of us engaged in combat called the officers and men who worked in supply, logistics, and other specialties far from combat.

Both men seemed to know the same colonel. I was not the least interested. An hour after takeoff the major turned his head toward me, and with breath that smelled of boiled hot dogs and two-day-old onions, said, "What's your story, fella?"

Not wanting to discuss my activities in Vietnam with this desk jockey who smelled like a barbershop delicatessen, I told him I was a newspaper reporter for the *Miami Herald.* I told him we were work-ing on a story concerning homosexuality and drug addiction un-dermining the readiness of our military forces in Vietnam. I fully an-ticipated that the major would pursue the conversation in order to learn what I had found through my investigation, and I was prepared to spin an awesome yarn.

Rather than pursue it, the major simply said "Oh." That was the last he spoke to me for the remainder of the flight to Hawaii. I chuck-led to myself and continued to read, eat, and sleep.

We landed at Barbers Point on the Hawaiian island of Oahu around 4:00 A.M. The night air was fresh; a light wind was blowing, carrying the wonderful smells of plumeria and carnations. It brought back memories of when my father was stationed in Hawaii and our family had lived there for eighteen months when I was ten and eleven years old.

Figuring about an eight-hour time difference between Hawaii and Florida, I dropped a coin in a pay telephone in the terminal and called home, collect. My call was picked up on the second ring and the operator cleared the reversed charges.

"Mom?" I said. "It's your wayward son, calling to let you know that I am in Hawaii now, heading shortly for San Francisco, and I'll be home in about five days after I muster out of this fraternity I joined."

Mom was conspicuously silent for a moment. "Is it true? Are you really coming home? Are you safe? I can't believe it!"

She began to cry a little and choked out, "Here, talk to Dad, I can't talk right now."

Dad got on the phone. "Hey, Big Shot! Kill any Communist gooks over there?!" he asked, laughing as if it were a joke.

That really bugged me. While I was in the hospital I had five conversations with my parents and had managed to write them three letters. Neither knew of the details of my military activities. But I was irked at my father's question. I was looking forward to going home for a while and then starting to job hunt. But when my father asked me that question, I suddenly withdrew into myself. I didn't want to talk about it. What I had been doing over there was no one's business but mine.

So I simply responded, "Might have hit a few, Dad. I don't want to discuss that stuff now, or ever. I'll be home in about five days. I'm at Barbers Point, near Honolulu. They're boarding my flight now for Travis. I'll call you in a couple of days and let you know my itinerary. Okay?"

"Okay," my father replied soberly. "We're really looking forward to seeing you. We'll have a big 'Welcome Home' party for you shortly after you get here, and we'll invite all your friends."

"*No*, Dad! I just want to come home, relax, go fishing, sit on the beach, take walks, and reenter civilization again very slowly. It's been rough, Dad. You know what I mean. I'm not going to be in the mood for a party or anything social for a while."

"What ever you say, Son. You take care of your back, and we'll listen for your call in a couple of days. We're proud of you and we love you. Come home."

"Okay," I said. "It'll be a few more days, and we'll be together. Good-bye, Dad." I hung up the telephone, feeling a bit upset by the call. Did my father think I'd been out for a walk in the park?

I was hungry then, and walked over to the terminal gee-dunk (small cafeteria) and ordered two half-pound hamburgers (all the way, hold the onions), a large order of French fries, and a large vanilla shake. I ate by myself, trying not to think about anything in particular and not wanting to engage in conversation, just enjoying good, fresh food; no C rations or hospital chow.

As the sun came up over the mountains of central Oahu, I walked outdoors to enjoy the morning, its peace and tranquility. We were very near Pearl Harbor, and I recalled the many film clips I had seen of the Japanese attack on our soldiers and sailors, moored ships, and parked aircraft. I was born six months after that fateful Sunday morning of 7 December 1941. Fleetingly I recalled the deaths of thousands of men and women by the weapons of the Japanese, the horror of fires from bomb explosions, of machine guns, and torpedo blasts. Trying to visualize that attack, I wondered why our government, which knew full well of the Japanese military buildup, could have allowed our armed forces to be so unprepared for that devastating attack. Where were the air patrols? Where was the command and control with the radar early warning system? We were caught napping!

At 8:00 A.M. we boarded the C-135 for the final leg to California. Because there were no passenger windows in the aircraft I could not see the beautiful view of Oahu from the air.

The flight lasted about five hours and we landed at Travis Air Force Base in the mid-afternoon (with the west to east time change). I retrieved my dop kit from beneath my seat and followed the senior officers to the head of the ladder. I felt the chilly blast of January air blowing through the open door of the plane. It was quite a change for me. Inside the terminal I asked for directions to the Treasure Island Naval Station and was directed to a Navy bus for the short trip.

After check-in at the Bachelor Officer's Quarters (BOQ), using my orders as ID, I reported to the duty officer for the base.

The duty officer looked over my orders carefully, then looked up and said, "I don't get it, Lieutenant. You are being detached from the Naval Air Station Sangley Point and you are going to muster out here? Why did they send you here? Why didn't you muster out in the Philippines at Sangley? We have no provision to hold a mustering-out ceremony here, except maybe once a month!"

"Well, sir," I said. "I don't know all the inner workings of these things. I sure don't need a ceremony to muster out! I'm just following my orders. I don't want to go through any ceremony, sir. I just want to get on back to my home in Florida."

"Okay," said the duty officer. "This is rather irregular, and I don't understand what's going on. I'll check this out with the base commander, and he'll probably tell me to call BUPERS (Bureau of Personnel) to confirm that we are to have you sign final papers and muster out here. I've never seen anything like this before. One more question, Lieutenant—why are you wearing camo fatigues with no rank or insignia? Let me see your Navy ID card."

Of course I had no ID card, no dog tags, no way of identifying who I was, except my orders. That was an interesting predicament, so I made up a story.

"Well, you see, sir, I was in an off-duty jeepney accident in Cavite City, outside Sangley Point in the Philippines, and was transported by medevac to Clark Air Force Base for treatment and recuperation. I was at Clark for two months, and while in the hospital, my military tour of duty obligation was completed. They whipped me up a set of detachment orders at Sangley and shipped them up to Clark. When I was released from the hospital, I hopped on the first plane for the States. In the accident, I lost my wallet containing my ID, and I left my Navy uniforms and dog tags behind at the BOQ at Sangley when I was flown to the hospital at Clark. But you have my detachment orders there in the envelope."

I was very proud of myself for coming up with this story for the duty officer so quickly. He seemed to buy it and suggested I get in touch with him around noon the next day. He wanted to discuss it with the commanding officer. He then called the BOQ and authorized a room for me.

Heading for the officer's club, I was looking forward to a nice cold beer, a huge steak, baked potato, fresh garden salad, and maybe a piece of cheesecake with black coffee. I walked into the small O-Club and over to the maître d's stand.

The civilian maître d' looked me up and down, and said, "Sir, you are not properly attired. In the evenings we require either the uniform of the day or a jacket and tie."

Frustration started to well up in me. But I decided there was no future in making an issue of the matter. I was hungry. I rationalized that the maitre d' was just doing his job and following O-Club regulations, so I said nothing, did an about-face, and walked out to the curb. Two sailors were walking by, and I asked directions to the enlisted men's club. They gave me directions, I found the building, no questions were asked, and I enjoyed the beer, steak, potato, salad, and apple pie (no cheesecake available), and probably paid about half what I would have paid at the O-Club. Then I walked back to the BOQ and caught a good night's sleep.

At 8:00 A.M., my phone rang. It was the new duty officer calling.

"Lieutenant, the base commander wants us to issue you a new ID card, and he wants you to go over to the PX and purchase or borrow a dress-blue officer's uniform. Then you are to join a small mustering-out ceremony day after tomorrow."

Remaining as calm as I could, I said, "Sir, I need to see the base commander immediately. There are some things he is not aware of, which I think will help clear up this matter and get me on my way."

"Well, Lieutenant, the captain is pretty tied up today; I'll see what I can do for you. Frankly, if you are mustering out of the Navy, I see no reason for you to spend the money to purchase a uniform, have it altered, shine your shoes, and . . . well, you see the point, I'm sure."

"Yes," I said. "And if the captain will see me, I think I can save that money and a lot of time."

Four hours later I was in the base commander's office. This time I decided to tell my story and not lie to the commanding officer about being in an jeepney accident. I briefly explained who I was, that I had been attached to MACV and was being detached from service by the CIA and the U.S. Navy.

There was one big hurdle here. I had no way of proving my identity. I carried orders, but I could have knocked off some Navy lieutenant and picked up his orders—and now was on a Navy base trying to get mustered out of the Navy so I could get a free trip home!

When I had completed my background story, the captain raised his bushy eyebrows, paused, and finally said, "Well, young man, you're the first of your kind I have run across. Why didn't you just tell the duty officer this yesterday? I'm not going to ask you any more questions—most of which I'm sure you wouldn't want to answer anyway. But I need to verify your story somehow. When that's done, I want you to get a military ID card. Then we'll get you vouchers for civilian air transportation back to your home. No need to buy a uniform now, but we probably ought to get you a silver bar insignia for lieutenant to wear on your collar points. Then you will at least look like a member of the U.S. armed forces. Now then, tell me how to verify you are who you say you are.”

“Well, sir,” I said, “as far as anyone is concerned I'm nobody, but I'm trying to reenter the ranks of real people, trying to become 'somebody.'”

I thought for a moment. I had never had personal contact with anyone who worked at CIA headquarters in Washington. I couldn't immediately recall the names of my instructors at Pensacola, nor could I expect them to still be there. I had no friends in California that I could recall. Moreover, I had no idea how to get in touch with Bill Dunn.

Suddenly I remembered something Bill had written in a short note attached to my orders.

“If you ever have any problems, call the CIA at Langley in Virginia and tell the operator you need to speak with the First Baseman for Vietnam.”

I suggested this to the base commander, who promptly had his administrative yeoman put through a call for him. I stood by the telephone extension next to the worn leather sofa in his office.

A few minutes later the yeoman knocked, entered, and said he had a CIA operator at Langley on the line. The base commander picked up the phone, and I simultaneously picked up the extension.

“Yes, I need to speak with the First Baseman for Vietnam,” I said nervously.

“Moment, please,” said the operator.

Seconds later, “First Baseman–Vietnam here,” said a nasal, baritone voice.

I gave him my full name, the FRAM 16 group to which I'd been attached in Vietnam, and quickly related to him my problem and what I was trying to accomplish. I also told him the Treasure Island commanding officer was on the line with me.

The First Baseman replied, “Hold a minute,” and put us on hold.

We waited for about five minutes and the First Baseman returned to the line.

“Okay. We can do one of two things. We can have them fingerprint you there, then send the figureprints to us for verification and clear your identity up from that. Or I can ask you some questions that probably only you would know the answers to. If you answer correctly, then the base commander can, if he wishes, have your ID card issued, get you the travel vouchers, and you can move on. Which would you prefer, Captain?" he asked the base commander.

"Well, if we do the fingerprint thing, it will take us several more days with the mail and all. I'd like to see this boy get home. Why don't you go ahead and ask him some of your questions."

"Okay. I'm getting this out of your file here," the First Baseman said to me.

"What college did you graduate from?"

I told him.

"What is your father's full name?"

I answered.

"What was the name of your CIA case officer in Vietnam?" I gave him Bill's full name.

"Okay, what does FRAM 16 stand for?"

I responded, "FRAM is not an acronym for anything, we were told. The '16' part perhaps refers to the original number of men on my team. We were divided up into two teams of five, one team of six."

He paused for a minute and I could hear him flipping pages.

"Okay, now what is the name of the man on your team who was killed in action when you were being extracted from your last mission, the one in which you were injured?

I was very surprised and wondered how such information could already be in my file. I surmised that Bill had filed a report on me and sent it in to the CIA. He probably mentioned John's name in that report.

I answered the question, "John Schneider."

"All right, Captain," the First Baseman said to the base commander. "I'm satisfied we have the right man, if that's enough for you."

"That's fine with me," he said. "We'll get the temporary ID card issued to this man and get him out of here as quickly as possible. Thank you for your assistance."

The captain hung up the telephone, smiled at me, and said, "Well, young man, let's get you moving. I'll have my yeoman escort you around and get you some J.G. bars for your collar, then get the picture ID card issued. We'll pull together your final discharge papers and not bother with any ceremony. Then we'll get the travel vouchers for you so you'll be set to fly commercial, and you can hit the road. Is there anything else we can do for you?"

I thanked the base commander and briefly apologized for the confusion. It was nearly 5:00 P.M. when we got the tasks completed. I opted to stay in the BOQ for one more night and have another meal at the enlisted men's club (since I still had an improper uniform for the O-club). The sight of round-eyed American girls accompanying the sailors at the club reminded me I had plenty to look forward to. On return to the BOQ, I called Eastern Airlines and made a plane reservation for the next morning.

Stretching out on my bed in the BOQ, I called home and alerted my father as to my time of arrival at Miami International Airport.

Fourteen and a half hours later, I left Treasure Island in a taxi for San Francisco Airport and the final leg home.

As I walked down the gangway of the Eastern Airlines plane, and as my feet touched Florida pavement, I had an urge to grandstand a bit by kneeling down and kissing the concrete. But I managed to summon my cool and avoided making such a symbolic scene. I had a growing feeling of elation as I walked into the terminal. I was safe now. I was home. I was twenty-four years old and had my life ahead of me.

I tried not to be emotional as my mother let out a shriek of joy and rushed past people toward me. She grabbed me in a bear hug, which caused me some pain in my back, but I said nothing about it. My father and sister were also there to greet me. We hugged, cried, and generally made a scene in the airport for a couple of minutes. Some people in the busy terminal stared at the reunion. Some smiled. Others looked bewildered.

My father finally took command of the situation, and said, "Okay, let's get out to the baggage claim, pick up your gear, and get this show on the road."

"Ah, Dad," I said. "I don't have any gear. Just my dop kit and my orders. That's it."

My father, always the jokester, said, "You mean you didn't get to bring home any souvenirs like a North Vietnamese flag, your K-bar knife, some photos . . . or how about a Vietcong ear?"

My mother was aghast at the suggestion that her wonderful son would bring home a body part from an enemy soldier. She quietly berated my father for this.

Refusing to take the comment seriously, I just laughed and said, "No, Dad, I'm sorry to disappoint you. The ear began to smell in the hospital at Clark. A nurse discovered it in my room by following her nose, and took it to the body-parts incinerator."

My father laughed heartily while my mother and sister just scowled at us as though we both were crazy.

I arrived home to champagne, a sirlon steak cooked medium-rare on the charcoal grill, my favorite mashed potatoes with green peas mixed in, and two pieces of homemade Key Lime pie. I was in bed by 9:30 P.M. that night, exhausted.

The next morning I was up at first light. While the rest of the family slept, I left a note in the kitchen, and I went for a walk on the nearby beach. I was alone with my thoughts, watching the sun seep over the horizon, safe from the enemy, and trying to deal with all my feelings.

As simple as it sounds, it was great to be alive. I walked along the beach, looked at the small waves from the Atlantic Ocean hitting the beach, and after a while sat down on the sand and talked to God— perhaps *really* for the first time.

I prayed and wept a little. I remembered my teammates. I saw each of their faces clearly, and I could hear their laughter and voices. I asked God to hold them close to him and to forgive them their sins and transgressions. I didn't know much about God. I really didn't know how to pray to Him. I asked for peace and comfort now that He had brought me home safely. I asked Him to forgive me for the mortal sins I had committed in the war, and I asked Him to show me what He wanted me to do from then on. I took the liberty of telling Him I didn't think I'd make a good preacher.

He responded over time by giving me a lovely wife, magnificent children, a good career in business, a fine home, money in the bank, and good health.

I am blessed indeed.

Epilogue

After convalescing for several weeks at Clark Air Force Base in the Philippines, I found little difficulty relaxing at my family's home in Florida. I was struck by the dichotomy of my life at the time: coming out of a searing and traumatic combat situation on the other side of the world into an idyllic setting among the Florida palm trees, my family, and Americans who gossiped about their social lives and their latest shopping sprees. But the transition back to "normal" life was not without problems for me. I dealt for a while with a mental turmoil that was debilitating for me. I retained considerable sadness over the loss of my friends in Southeast Asia, and there was likely some guilt sustaining my melancholy feelings. Why had I survived when the others had not? Did they risk more than I had risked? Had I held back? Were their lives any more on the line than mine? Should I have risked more? I should not feel ashamed that I survived, but the thought persists to a degree in my brain even to this day.

There was no one person then in whom I could comfortably confide my thoughts. I chose not to join any Vietnam veterans groups; however, I often thought about finding a priest, psychiatrist, or perhaps a friend who would listen to me ramble on, and ask questions. Instead I pushed these thoughts into remote compartments of my brain and refused to deal with them. This is why this writing has been somewhat of a catharsis for me. It aided me in dealing with feelings of guilt and regret, and to place them into a somewhat rational perspective. Also, the intensity of my sadness over friends lost has diminished with the passing of time, but will never be entirely eliminated. In 1974, and again in 1983, I tried to write about my experiences in Southeast Asia. On both occasions I found such writing to be too painful for me; hence, I threw my notes away, and stuffed my thoughts and feelings back into their compartments.

I experienced very few nightmares or flashbacks of my service. When these did occur, I was usually overtired from my day's activities. My strongest recollection of nightmares was the sound of automatic weapons fire close by as I lay asleep. I would awaken with great fear and panic. The first time this happened, I was at home in a dark bedroom. I recall three occasions when the sound of automatic fire erupted loudly in my dreams. Each time, I rolled out of my bed, lay on the floor, and listened for the source while thrashing about with my hands and arms trying to find my weapon. After the third occurrence, I determined I should sleep with a nightlight on to permit immediate orientation when I awoke from a nightmare. That helped.

On return from Vietnam, I married a fine lady, and we had a son who has been a great joy to me ever since. Unfortunately, we divorced after several years of marriage, and I remained single for three years before remarrying. My marvelous second wife has given us two children, of whom I am extremely proud, and who have given me great happiness and never-ending support. I am proud to be classified now as a "family man," because clearly my family is the most important thing in my life, above all else.

I have made my living as a consultant and financier in the real estate field, primarily with respect to the lodging industry. My experience in Southeast Asia has been of no benefit to my business life, and I cannot adequately define the impact, if any, it has had on me as a person and on my personal relationships. Simply stated, I have long reflected on my service as having been an important and difficult obligation in the course of an otherwise normal life. The Vietnam chapter of my life is long past, and I only look ahead to the new chapters being written. Unlike a few who have suffered varying degrees of post-traumatic stress syndrome from their combat experiences, I got on comfortably with my life in the civilian workforce immediately after my return home.

I have enjoyed my life, and tried to be a good husband, father, and provider. With the completion of this book, I feel that whatever wounds or damage the war did to me are healed.